# INNOVATION
# PASSION
# SUCCESS

## THE EMC STORY

> *Our staff was bright, energetic, persistent, and fearless. They believed anything was possible, that any obstacles were merely challenges, and that there were no limits to what EMC could accomplish.*

— Richard J. Egan

1936 – 2009

# INNOVATION
# PASSION
# SUCCESS

# THE EMC STORY

JEFFREY L. RODENGEN

Edited by Elizabeth Fernandez
Design and layout by Sandy Cruz

*Dedicated to the memory of EMC Co-founder Richard J. "Dick" Egan.*

## Richard J. Egan
1 9 3 6 – 2 0 0 9

Write Stuff Enterprises, LLC
1001 South Andrews Avenue
Fort Lauderdale, FL 33316
**1-800-900-Book** (1-800-900-2665)
(954) 462-6657
www.writestuffbooks.com

**WRITE STUFF**

The publisher has made every effort to identify and locate the source of the photographs included in this edition of *Innovation, Passion, Success: The EMC Story*. Grateful acknowledgement is made to those who have kindly granted permission for the use of their materials in this edition. If there are instances where proper credit was not given, the publisher will gladly make any necessary corrections in subsequent printings.

### Publisher's Cataloging in Publication
*(Prepared by The Donohue Group, Inc.)*

Rodengen, Jeffrey L.
    Innovation, passion, success : the EMC story / Jeffrey L. Rodengen ; edited by Elizabeth Fernandez ; design and layout by Sandy Cruz ; [foreword by Dick Egan].

    p. : ill. ; cm.

    Includes bibliographical references and index.
    ISBN: 978-1-932022-16-2

    1. EMC (Firm : Hopkinton, Mass.)—History. 2. Information storage and retrieval systems—Design. 3. Technology consultants—United States—History. 4. High technology industries—United States—History. I. Fernandez, Elizabeth. II. Cruz, Sandy. III. Egan, Dick. IV. Title. V. Title: EMC story

HD9696.8.U64 E43 2010
338.47/621392/0973        2010925070

Completely produced in the
United States of America
10  9  8  7  6  5  4  3  2  1

## Also by Jeffrey L. Rodengen

*The Legend of Chris-Craft*

*IRON FIST:*
*The Lives of Carl Kiekhaefer*

*Evinrude-Johnson and*
*The Legend of OMC*

*Serving the Silent Service:*
*The Legend of Electric Boat*

*The Legend of Dr Pepper/Seven-Up*

*The Legend of Honeywell*

*The Legend of Briggs & Stratton*

*The Legend of Ingersoll-Rand*

*The Legend of Stanley:*
*150 Years of The Stanley Works*

*The MicroAge Way*

*The Legend of Halliburton*

*The Legend of York International*

*The Legend of Nucor Corporation*

*The Legend of Goodyear:*
*The First 100 Years*

*The Legend of AMP*

*The Legend of Cessna*

*The Legend of VF Corporation*

*The Spirit of AMD*

*The Legend of Rowan*

*New Horizons:*
*The Story of Ashland Inc.*

*The History of American Standard*

*The Legend of Mercury Marine*

*The Legend of Federal-Mogul*

*Against the Odds:*
*Inter-Tel—The First 30 Years*

*The Legend of Pfizer*

*State of the Heart: The Practical Guide*
*to Your Heart and Heart Surgery*
with Larry W. Stephenson, M.D.

*The Legend of Worthington Industries*

*The Legend of IBP*

*The Legend of Trinity Industries, Inc.*

*The Legend of*
*Cornelius Vanderbilt Whitney*

*The Legend of Amdahl*

*The Legend of Litton Industries*

*The Legend of Gulfstream*

*The Legend of Bertram*
with David A. Patten

*The Legend of Ritchie Bros. Auctioneers*

*The Legend of ALLTEL*
with David A. Patten

*The Yes, you can of Invacare*
*Corporation*
with Anthony L. Wall

*The Ship in the Balloon:*
*The Story of Boston Scientific and the*
*Development of Less-Invasive Medicine*

*The Legend of Day & Zimmermann*

*The Legend of Noble Drilling*

*Fifty Years of Innovation:*
*Kulicke & Soffa*

*Biomet—From Warsaw to the World*
with Richard F. Hubbard

*NRA: An American Legend*

*The Heritage and Values of RPM, Inc.*

*The Marmon Group:*
*The First Fifty Years*

*The Legend of Grainger*

*The Legend of The Titan Corporation*
with Richard F. Hubbard

*The Legend of Discount Tire Co.*
with Richard F. Hubbard

*The Legend of Polaris*
with Richard F. Hubbard

*The Legend of La-Z-Boy*
with Richard F. Hubbard

*The Legend of McCarthy*
with Richard F. Hubbard

*Intervoice: Twenty Years of Innovation*
with Richard F. Hubbard

*Jefferson-Pilot Financial:*
*A Century of Excellence*
with Richard F. Hubbard

*The Legend of HCA*

*The Legend of Werner Enterprises*
with Richard F. Hubbard

*The History of J. F. Shea Co.*
with Richard F. Hubbard

*True to Our Vision: HNI Corporation*
with Richard F. Hubbard

*The Legend of Albert Trostel & Sons*
with Richard F. Hubbard

*The Legend of Sovereign Bancorp*
with Richard F. Hubbard

*Innovation is the Best Medicine:*
*The extraordinary story of Datascope*
with Richard F. Hubbard

*The Legend of Guardian Industries*

*The Legend of*
*Universal Forest Products*

*Changing the World: Polytechnic*
*University—The First 150 Years*

*Nothing is Impossible: The Legend*
*of Joe Hardy and 84 Lumber*

*In it for the Long Haul:*
*The Story of CRST*

*The Story of Parsons Corporation*

*Cerner: From Vision to Value*

*New Horizons:*
*The Story of Federated Investors*

*Office Depot: Taking Care of Business—*
*The First 20 Years*

*The Legend of General Parts:*
*Proudly Serving a World in Motion*

*Bard: Power of the Past,*
*Force of the Future*

*Innovation & Integrity:*
*The Story of Hub Group*

*Amica: A Century of Service*
*1907–2007*

*A Passion for Service:*
*The Story of ARAMARK*

*The Legend of Con-way:*
*A History of Service, Reliability,*
*Innovation, and Growth*

*Commanding the Waterways:*
*The Story of Sea Ray*

*Past, Present & Futures:*
*Chicago Mercantile Exchange*

*The Legend of Leggett & Platt*

*The Road Well Traveled:*
*The Story of Guy Bostick and*
*Comcar Industries*

*The Legend of Brink's*

*Kiewit: An Uncommon Company:*
*Celebrating the First 125 Years*

*The History of Embraer*

*Parker Hannifin Corporation:*
*A Winning Heritage*

*AECOM: 20 Years and Counting*

*A Symphony of Soloists:*
*The Story of Wakefern and ShopRite*

*JELD-WEN: Celebrating 50 Years*

# TABLE OF CONTENTS

# FOREWORD

## BY

## RICHARD J. "DICK" EGAN

EMC CO-FOUNDER and FORMER CHAIRMAN and CEO

*Written April 2009*

### Richard J. Egan
#### 1 9 3 6 – 2 0 0 9

I DON'T KNOW IF ANYBODY STARTS A company by defining its culture. I know we didn't. I don't even know if the term "culture" was in vogue at the time.

Roger Marino and I founded EMC in 1979 as manufacturers' representatives. We didn't have a business plan. We didn't even have venture capital, so one of the fundamentals of our early "culture," if you want to call it that, was taking a prudent approach to spending.

Our initial goals were practical. We needed to convince manufacturers to allow us to sell their products, and we needed to improve our cash flow. I vividly remember achieving this goal in six months, since it coincided with reaching our credit card limits. Fortunately, Roger is the best salesman I've ever met, and he enjoys teaching others this most underrated profession.

We had a tendency to hire young people right out of college, in part because we couldn't afford industry veterans. That decision would help define EMC. Our staff was bright, energetic, persistent, and fearless. They believed anything was possible, that any obstacles were merely challenges, and that there were no limits to what EMC could accomplish. It was that early mind-set that drove us to succeed.

Inspired by my work at Intel Corporation under Andy Grove, I instituted a policy of quarterly meetings right from the start. At the meetings, we always adhered to a practice of praising in public and critiquing in private, which led to increased collaboration between our sales and engineering departments. Everybody knew exactly what was expected of them.

Perhaps I'm giving away one of our secrets here, but we always tried to have our engineers meet our customers face-to-face. The customers would explain what their problems were, what their challenges were, which gave our engineers a unique opportunity to come up with innovative solutions. I've witnessed it over and over again—light bulbs going off in an engineer's head and in a customer's head at the same time. It was just magic watching these people communicate. Engineers are much like artists. They like to see their creation in action, actually accomplishing something. By collaborating with our customers, our engineers gain new insights that would not be possible otherwise.

I recall an example of this collaboration while working with Barclays in London during the 1990s.

Barclays had about a dozen very expensive ATMs that were always surrounded by long, frustrating lines of customers because the systems operated so slowly. We convinced Barclays to install our Symmetrix system and worked with our engineers to increase the speed of their ATMs. The new system worked so well that Barclays was able to cut the number of ATMs in half, while still providing its customers with quick and efficient service.

One of my own personal goals was to beat IBM, one way or the other. I'll always remember our sense of humor as we tried to keep IBM off balance, from our IBM boxer shorts to the infamous red-hot IBM poker. With the help of Mike Ruettgers, who initiated an extensive quality overhaul, for a brief period in the fall of 2000 our market capitalization exceeded that of IBM's.

As EMC celebrates its first 30 years in business, I can't help but look back with pride at EMC's outstanding technical achievements. However, I am just as proud that EMC has created thousands of good, stimulating, well-paying jobs in America and Ireland and beyond. Today, EMC employs approximately 40,000 people around the world. It is extremely gratifying to know that EMC products greatly improve the productivity of our customers. My successors, Mike Ruettgers and Joe Tucci, have continued to grow the company, while maintaining its unique culture and competitiveness. Thanks to their leadership, and the creativity of EMC's dedicated global team, the company Roger and I founded three decades ago will continue to expand and redefine technology in an increasingly complex digital world.

---

**B**OSTON NATIVE RICHARD J. "DICK" EGAN WAS among the tech industry's most innovative pioneers. He studied at the Massachusetts Institute of Technology (MIT), held an engineering degree from Northeastern University, and helped design the memory systems for the Apollo Guidance Computer that made it possible to land the first man on the moon.

In 1979, Mr. Egan co-founded EMC, alongside partner and longtime friend Roger Marino.

The company he started would go on to become the worldwide leader in information infrastructure technology and solutions.

Mr. Egan was well known for his charitable contributions to education and was a major donor to the Egan Research Center at Northeastern University. He also proudly served his country in the U.S. Marine Corps during the Korean War and served as U.S. ambassador to Ireland from 2001 to 2003.

# ACKNOWLEDGMENTS

MANY DEDICATED PEOPLE ASSISTED IN THE RE-search, preparation, and publication of *Innovation, Passion, Success: The EMC Story.* Research Assistant Ami Albernaz conducted the principal archival research for the book, while Executive Editor Elizabeth Fernandez managed the editorial content. Vice President/Creative Director Sandy Cruz brought the story to life.

Several key individuals associated with EMC provided their assistance in the development of the book from its outline to its finished product, including Peter Schwartz, senior director of strategic communications, and Mark Fredrickson, vice president of strategic marketing and communications. Special gratitude is owed to EMC co-founder Dick Egan, who contributed the book's foreword.

All of the people interviewed—EMC employees, retirees, and friends—were generous with their time and insights. Those who shared their memories and thoughts include: Laura Aubut, Bob Basiliere, Mary Bracoloni, Gary Breder, Jim Callahan, Dan Campbell, Steve Cerand, Maureen Clancy, Leo Colborne, Art Coviello, Mick Cunnane, Paul Dacier, Lennie Demarco, Doc D'Errico, Becky DiSorbo, David Donatelli, Steve Duplessie, Jack Egan, Howard Elias, Charles Fan, Steven Fitz, Brian Fitzgerald, Danny Fitzgerald, Bryan Fontaine, Mark Fredrickson, Brian Gallagher, Michael Gallant, David Gingell, Jeff Goldberg, Frank Hauck, Tom Heiser, Chuck Hollis, B. J. Jenkins, Monya Keane, Rick Lacroix, Steve Leonard, Chuck Loewy, Kathie Lyons, Nikolai Markovich, Sanjay Mirchandani, Erin Motameni, Tim Mulvihill, Rona Newmark, Paul Noble, Josh Onffroy, Tammy Osterman, Jude Pellegrini, Jim Pearson, Polly Pearson, Brian Powers, Gil Press, Mark Quigley, Malte Rademacher, Bill Raftery, Celeste Rippole, Barb Robidoux, Jim Rothnie, Mike Ruettgers, Diane Russell, Steve Savard, Bill Scannell, Mike Sgrosso, Irina Simmons, Peter Simmons, Ken Steinhardt, Tony Takazawa, Bill Teuber, Joe Tucci, Don Watson, Clarence Westfall, Moshe Yanai, and Stacey Yeoman.

Finally, special thanks are extended to the staff at Write Stuff Enterprises, LLC: Joseph Demma, senior editor; Elijah Meyer, graphic designer; Roy Adelman, on-press supervisor; Lynn C. Jones and Christine McIntire, proofreaders; Mary Aaron, transcriptionist; Donna M. Drialo, indexer; Amy Major, executive assistant to Jeffrey L. Rodengen; Marianne Roberts, executive vice president, publisher, and chief financial officer; and Stanislava Alexandrova, marketing manager.

When Richard J. "Dick" Egan (left) and Roger Marino (right) founded EMC in 1979, few could have imagined that the company they created would one day overtake the heavyweights of the computer industry in information storage and management.

CHAPTER ONE

# An Entrepreneurial Spirit

## 1979–1981

*When my partner Roger [Marino] and I founded EMC in 1979, we did not launch the company with a grand idea or innovation. We had no business plan, market, or capital equipment. In fact, if you exclude credit cards, we didn't have any capital at all!*

—Richard J. "Dick" Egan[1]

ON FEBRUARY 23, 1993, THE DATE of the first World Trade Center bombing, many businesses in New York City learned a hard lesson. When they tried to access the information they had backed up, including daily financial transactions and customer databases, it was days or even weeks old. Once this backed-up data was shipped back to their main data centers, it had to be reloaded onto their primary online computer systems. This proved a time-consuming task, made even more difficult by the fact that many of the systems were on the upper floors of the World Trade Center and therefore off-limits to personnel. In businesses where continuous access to information is money, any disruption to this access threatened their ability to serve their customers and maintain their revenue. In fact, the more time that passed without access to their information, the less likely these businesses would be able to ever recover.

Several financial services companies located in the World Trade Center turned to EMC to devise a sophisticated and automated backup solution—one that would automatically replicate their data to a remote location, where there would also be a second set of computers and applications. That way, in the event of a disaster as routine as a power outage or as devastating as an explosion, a company's operations could resume almost instantly from a remote site.

A little more than three years after the first World Trade Center bombing, on August 6, 1996, EMC filed patent number 5,544,347 for "Data Storage System Controlled Remote Data Mirroring with Respectively Maintained Data Indices." In plain English, EMC had invented a system that automatically provides and maintains an identical copy, known as a mirror, of data storage disks at geographic locations miles away from primary data storage devices. The ability to do this efficiently did not exist at the time of the 1993 World Trade Center bombing, but advances in fiber optics and the built-in computing capabilities of EMC's intelligent storage systems would soon make it possible for data to move at the speed of light between two systems located dozens of miles apart, all without slowing down the computer systems or impacting service. As EMC noted in its patent, previous approaches to protecting valuable information, in which archival data was kept within the same location as the primary storage location, proved simply unworkable in the event of any incidents that prevented or delayed physical access to the archives.

One of EMC's early insights was the centrality of information to business and life and the importance, therefore, of keeping information accessible around the clock.

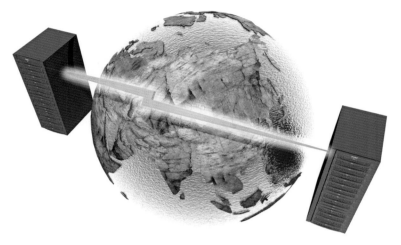

EMC's SRDF family of software was designed to enable continuous business operations through remote replication.

EMC's innovation was a software product called Symmetrix Remote Data Facility (SRDF). SRDF's main purpose was to ensure that a secondary set of updated data remained ready to go immediately should one of the systems or data centers go off-line. In a matter of years, SRDF became the most widely deployed set of high-end remote replication solutions in the world, installed in tens of thousands of demanding environments across the globe. As its popularity soared, customers found many more uses for replicating technology in addition to disaster readiness, including moving data centers, testing new applications, and shifting workloads during peak times.

And then, a little more than eight years after the first World Trade Center bombing, terrorists struck again, on September 11, 2001—a cataclysmic event that took nearly 3,000 lives. This time, there were no buildings to go back to. It was a disaster of such magnitude and horror that no company or city could have ever adequately prepared for it.

# FOUNDING VALUES

RIGHT FROM THE START, DICK EGAN AND CO-founder Roger Marino made certain to focus on the values that would become EMC's hallmarks. Values such as tenacity, dedication, and a ceaseless creative vision served as the reason behind the company's astounding success. In the beginning, the two men were driven by the constant fear of failure, but they still tirelessly searched for opportunities to grow their fledgling company.[1] No goal, however large, seemed out of reach. They were bold enough to bypass conventional thinking, astute enough to seize on promising ideas, and tenacious enough to see things through, no matter what the obstacles.

Early on, the company had a keen ability to listen to and be inspired by its customers and the people it wanted to attract as customers. Egan always remained determined to speak to customers. In fact, a simple sales call to a University of Rhode Island scientist inspired Egan and Marino to develop EMC's first computer product—a memory board compatible with Prime minicomputers. In the decades that followed, EMC would continue to transform customer needs into opportunities for development, using them as sources of inspiration and innovation. It marked the start of another constant in EMC's existence: competing head-to-head with larger and more established companies, from Prime Computer, Wang Laboratories, and Digital Equipment Corporation (DEC), to IBM and Hewlett-Packard.

In just one of many examples of how customer input has contributed to EMC's success, a vice president of what was then the Pillsbury Corporation, an EMC customer, mentioned in 1996 that he wanted a simple way to back up company data without shutting down production or buying an additional storage system. This inspired the development of EMC's TimeFinder software, released the following year. It would become one of EMC's most profitable products.[2]

However, on that tragic day, EMC's technology, developed in response to the first World Trade Center bombing, worked as designed for dozens of affected companies. As reported in the financial weekly *Barron's* two weeks after the attack:

*If any technology product emerged the hero from the recent disasters, it was an EMC product called SRDF. For systems that cannot afford to lose a single transaction record—as at a trading firm or stock exchange—the EMC product maintains a continuously updated copy on a disk array located far from harm's way. ... Most of EMC's customers in the Center had their critical data mirrored in uptown Manhattan, New Jersey, or as far away as Texas.*

As the morning of September 11 unfolded, EMC's customer service technicians on call at the company's 24-hour call center in Hopkinton, Massachusetts, watched helplessly as their online connection with storage system after storage system in the World Trade Center was lost. The color-coordinated system for showing a storage system's status turned from green to red, indicating these systems were off-line. The staggering human tragedy became clearer by the minute, and the disaster also threatened the national and global economy. Its location in the heart of New York's financial district meant that many of the companies in the complex's 13.4 million square feet of office space played a major role in world financial markets, with millions of people relying on the data they managed. The remote data centers where archival data had been kept suddenly became the primary ones.

EMC, which served two dozen customers in the World Trade Center, and on any given day employed dozens of people working in the complex, was very fortunate to not lose any of its employees during the attack. That said, many of EMC's customers, as well as friends and relatives of employees in the New

---

Egan credits Andy Grove, his boss at Intel, with instilling in him many of the management practices that would help keep EMC together and make every employee feel integral to the company. As EMC grew from a handful of employees, to hundreds, to thousands, Egan made a deliberate effort to stay in touch with every aspect of the company. This job included walking the floors to make all employees feel like their contributions mattered. Egan would also always write a short note (that included his phone number) to the author of any internal memo that passed through his office to send the message that he was personally engaged and available to help.

As a further incentive, Egan would occasionally bet the engineering teams that they would not accomplish particularly difficult feats by their target dates. "I used to lug around a suitcase with cash, sometimes $40,000," he recalled.

Just as Egan intended, the engineering teams most often succeeded, meaning the bet would pay off for both Egan and his employees.

EMC maintained its cohesion, even as the company expanded, through quarterly meetings, one of Grove's trademark practices. Department heads would share their quarterly goals and accomplishments (as well as their misses) with the rest of the organization, a tradition EMC has continued to follow since 1984.[3]

Although EMC faced very lean financial times during its early years, Egan and Marino never skimped on rewarding hard work. From the start, no chore was beneath them. Egan could be found cleaning the bathrooms on Saturday mornings. And when it came time to build EMC's famously aggressive sales force in the early and mid-1980s, Egan and Marino matched top-notch performance with top-notch commissions, a tradition that continues at EMC.

"If you're somebody who gets a big charge out of achieving something every day, of actually having a high bar to jump over and being accountable, then this is the type of place for you," said Mark Fredrickson, vice president of marketing strategy and communications, who joined EMC in 1995 from larger rival Digital Equipment Corporation.[4]

Fear of failure might have driven EMC in the beginning, but the very challenges that the company has faced are what have helped it to thrive.

Above: The February 23, 1993, World Trade Center bombing inspired EMC to create the Symmetrix Remote Data Facility (SRDF), an innovation that proved invaluable to businesses struggling to recover from the cataclysmic September 11, 2001, attacks.

Right: This note from EMC customer JPMorgan Chase & Co. underscored EMC employees' ability to help clients affected by the September 11, 2001, attacks.

York area, were not so fortunate. Focusing on where it could help, EMC's global services organization immediately began coordinating a response from an emergency command center at its headquarters in Hopkinton. With air travel halted and the nation in shock and mourning, employees in the field responded, with some providing around-the-clock support to impacted customers. One member of EMC's professional services organization single-handedly kept a New York City customer's data center online using temporary air conditioning units to cool the systems. No one was able to relieve him for days because the site was located within the off-limits secure zone just blocks away from the World Trade Center complex.

## JPMorganChase

William B. Harrison, Jr.
President and Chief Executive Officer

September 26, 2001

Mr. Michael C. Ruettgers
Executive Chairman
EMC Corporation
35 Parkwood
Hopkinton, MA  01748-9103

Dear Mike:

The tragic events of September 11th have left us all with indescribable sadness. We mourn with those who have lost family and loved ones. We have begun the enormous task of reconstructing our businesses and restoring stability to our lives.

Mike, I want to personally take a moment to thank you and your outstanding team of professionals for their immediate, unstinting and generous support in our recovery efforts. In particular, I want to acknowledge ████████████ and ████████████ for their technical support.

Inside our firm, we refer to EMC Corporation as our business partner. We saw the true meaning of partnership over the last 10 days, in your employees' every word and deed.

I believe adversity is a test of character. I am optimistic and confident that with your dedicated team, working alongside our J.P. Morgan Chase colleagues, we will meet the test.

Yours very truly,

William B. Harrison, Jr.

J.P. Morgan Chase & Co. • 270 Park Avenue, New York, NY 10017-2070

Today, EMC remains at the vanguard of a new perspective on the relationship between information and information technology. EMC's view is that, while information technologies may come and go, information itself persists and forms the permanent strategic core of an organization. Managed properly, this information can serve as the glue holding organizations together, the antidote to uncertainty and even unthinkable disaster, and the raw material from which new products and services can be developed.

EMC has always been deeply committed to its customers and has strived to see the world through their eyes, listen carefully to their individual needs, innovate with their future requirements in mind, and respond with everything it has when a customer's business or its IT infrastructure is in trouble. This customers-first attitude, this way of doing business, had its roots in the values and philosophy of EMC's two founders: Dick Egan and Roger Marino, two engineers who became masters at transforming customer concerns and needs into opportunities for development.

**The Computer Revolution**

Egan was no stranger to the computer industry when he decided to start EMC in 1979. Known as Dick, he grew up in the Boston neighborhood of Dorchester, in the fiercely proud Irish immigrant tradition. Suspecting early on that he wanted to be an engineer, he attended Boston Technical High School—part of what he fondly recalled as the city's "wonderful school system." After graduating, he served in the U.S. Marine Corps during the Korean War as a crew chief for rescue helicopters. By the time the GI Bill allowed him to begin his studies at Northeastern University in 1957, Egan had already learned the value of tenacity, leadership, and team spirit.

After earning an engineering degree in 1961, he began his career in Honeywell's Data Processing

Division, working as a design engineer focused on computer storage systems. In 1963, he began his graduate studies at the Massachusetts Institute of Technology (MIT), designing the memory systems for the Apollo Guidance Computer that would enable the first trip to the moon and back. "It was the heyday of the 'Let's beat Sputnik' era," Egan recalled, adding that his work on Apollo was his proudest achievement up to that point.

During the 1950s and 1960s, the space race between the United States and the Soviet Union—a contest Egan and countless other scientists and engineers happily participated in—helped spur innovation, leading the burgeoning computer industry to focus on improving speed and processing power. At first, computers were room-size behemoths that could only be

The Apollo Guidance Computer (inset), instrumental in helping Americans land on the moon, had a capacity of 256 bits. *(Right photo courtesy of NASA.)*

handled by experts and were used almost entirely for complex and time-consuming mathematical calculations.

As bulky mainframe computers came into wider use, International Business Machines Corporation (IBM) stood as the undisputed market leader. In fact, the computer market in the 1960s was sometimes likened to *Snow White and the Seven Dwarfs*, with IBM described as Snow White and its nearest rivals—Burroughs, Control Data Corporation, General Electric, Honeywell, NCR, Radio Corporation of America (RCA), and Sperry Rand—as the dwarfs. Because storage was still considered a mundane peripheral, no one questioned that only the computer vendors supplied the devices to accompany their own computer systems.

### The Promise of the Integrated Circuit

The development of semiconductor technology spawned a computer revolution and inspired many would-be entrepreneurs to get in on the action. Perhaps no place embodied this spirit more than Silicon Valley—the birthplace of the integrated circuit. Fairchild Semiconductor Corporation, founded in 1957 by eight engineers who had previously worked with transistor coinventor William Shockley, developed the integrated circuit.

The invention helped spawn a number of start-ups, including Intel in 1968, which developed a calculator chip that would later become the central processing unit (CPU), or "brain," of the personal computer.

Semiconductor technology was also a boon to minicomputers, making it possible to pack more power into smaller systems. Minicomputers began to gain popularity as silicon integrated chips and advances in transistor and core memory technology led to increased efficiency and computing power.

Companies and laboratories entered a heated and relentless race toward building ever faster and more reliable machines. By the 1970s, computers had become the lifeblood of many organizations of all types, storing vital information such as inventory, payroll, and personnel files.[2] As computer usage increased, so did the amount

These articles of organization marked the official founding of EMC Corporation in Newton, Massachusetts, on August 23, 1979.

of information they were required to store. Improvements in the functionality, capacity, and reliability of storage products, however, had lagged behind the performance of CPUs—a natural outcome of computer companies' R&D priorities, and a factor that eventually opened the door for independent storage companies. As the need for reliable storage took on greater urgency, a considerable performance gap evolved.

**The Birth of the Storage Market**

As the popularity of minicomputers began to grow, so did the number of manufacturers. And as had the manufacturers of the early mainframe computers, makers of minicomputers, including Digital Equipment Corporation (DEC) and Prime Computer, supplied the memory storage devices for their systems. Minicomputer pioneer DEC, Data General, Wang Laboratories, and Prime Computer began producing machines that were used primarily in research facilities. Although these computers were cheaper than mainframes, memory and storage products for them remained extremely expensive in this captive, proprietary model.

Much like their mainframe manufacturing counterparts, the companies that made minicomputers charged high prices. Spotting the outsized profit margins, a few shrewd industry insiders seized the opportunity to sell compatible devices more cheaply.

EMC initially focused on producing inexpensive memory boards for Prime computers. Equipment manufacturers included Storage Technology Corporation (later known as StorageTek), founded in Louisville, Colorado, in 1969 by four former IBM engineers, as well as Amdahl, founded in Sunnyvale, California, in 1970 by Gene Amdahl, another former IBM employee.

For a start-up to survive and thrive, especially in the volatile high-tech market, the keen ability to listen to customers' needs, along with the ability to spot or create new markets, would be crucial. In both of these areas, EMC quickly distinguished itself. The company expanded its early product line to encompass products compatible with manufacturers such as DEC, Wang, and, later, Hewlett-Packard and IBM.

EMC's versatility early on would become even more of an asset in later years, easing its expansion into disk storage—the arena that would ultimately propel the company from unknown start-up to leader of the pack. EMC, the nascent Massachusetts company Egan co-founded in 1979, would seize that opportunity and surpass all expectations. Through a fortuitous chain of events and an ability to see what none of its competitors saw, EMC would transform the value of storage technology to such a degree that customers really took notice.

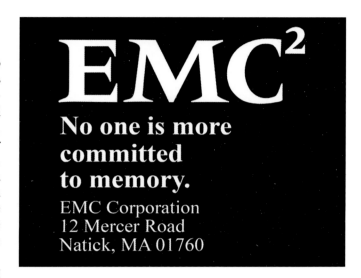

EMC's commitment to memory has consistently ensured its customers would have access to valuable information even in the midst of disaster.

**The Education of a Leader**

After his work on the Apollo Guidance Computer at MIT, Egan worked for three years at Lockheed Electronics Company, serving first as field sales manager in New England and then becoming marketing manager for the California-based Lockheed Aircraft division. Yet, an entrepreneurial spirit led him back East, where in 1968, he co-founded his first company—Cambridge Memories, Inc. The data storage company, now called Cambex, proved successful, but seven years later, Egan felt ready for a fresh challenge.

Robert Noyes, co-founder of the semiconductor manufacturer Intel, invited Egan to run Intel's commercial systems division. Egan was charged with turning around the floundering division. He worked directly under Andy Grove, the industry visionary who is today recognized as one of the world's most influential business leaders. "I learned so much from Andy Grove at Intel," Egan said. "Looking back, I would have paid him."[3]

The healthy paranoia that Grove has written about in his books—the sense that even when things are going well, one needs constantly to be looking over one's shoulder—rubbed off on Egan and would influence his management style years later at EMC.

Under Grove's mentorship, Egan took a failing division and transformed it into Intel's most profitable business.[4]

### A Business Is Born

Egan left Intel in the late 1970s, once again moving back to Massachusetts with his wife, Maureen, and their five children. He wanted his sons and daughters to take advantage of the top-notch Boston-area schools, just as he had. Rather than seek out a new place of employment, Egan decided to once again start his own company. He enlisted his best friend from Northeastern University, Roger Marino, who had gone on to work for RCA Memory Products and had established himself as a skilled salesman. The two men were not sure what direction their business would take, but they were convinced they could succeed if they hit upon an idea that did not require much capital for equipment.[5]

"We got together at my house and plotted this plan, and I persuaded Roger to leave his place of employment," Egan recalled.[6] For $85, Egan registered the name EMC—the initials representing Egan, Marino, and another former classmate. Egan thought he had persuaded his former classmate to leave his job, but "C" dropped out at the last moment. The identity of this third man has become something of a company mystery; both Egan and Marino have steadfastly refused to reveal his name in order to spare Mr. C the indignity of becoming the painful answer to a trivia question.

Egan did not want to spend another $85 to change the company's name, so on August 23, 1979, EMC was born in Egan's Newton, Massachusetts, home. To raise money for their future business, Egan and Marino began working as manufacturers' representatives, "one of the greatest, last bastions of independent entrepreneurship that you can start at a modest cost," Egan explained.[7]

A friend of Egan's who lived in California had approached the two men about selling a special desk in New England that was specifically designed for computer users. That desk, in a sense, became EMC's first product.

"I brought in another fellow who worked with me at Intel," Egan said. "So there was Roger, this other fellow who was an engineer, and myself, who was an engineer. I think between us, we had five engineering degrees, and here we were selling desks. It sounds crazy, but I think we made 40 percent on the stuff."[8]

Egan and Marino were not meant to stay out of the technology field for long, however. Selling desks served mainly as a way for them to raise enough capital to move on to their next endeavor. Through Egan's connections with his former employer, they began selling Intel's product line, including increasingly popular microprocessors. Thanks to their engineering backgrounds and prior experience in the computer industry, Egan and Marino knew that programming microprocessors required machines called microprocessor development systems, which cost roughly $30,000—a considerable amount of money in the early 1980s. As companies typically only needed to use these machines for very short amounts of time, many companies remained under-

Richard J. "Dick" Egan co-founded EMC in 1979.

standably hesitant to buy them. Spotting an opportunity, Egan and Marino decided to purchase the machines themselves and rent them out, which led them to greater profits than they expected.

"We made a fortune because, first of all, engineering projects always take longer than expected," Egan recalled.[9]

While representing Intel, the men also began selling memory for PDP-11s, a family of popular minicomputers sold by DEC. Soon after, EMC expanded its sales offerings to include products made by other companies as well. Through their contacts with minicomputer users, the men learned that some were frustrated at the monopoly the vendors seemed to have on memory products for their systems. One of these frustrated customers inspired Egan and Marino to find the niche that would lead to EMC's future success.

Egan contacted a researcher at the University of Rhode Island to try to sell him memory products for the PDP-11. The researcher was not interested, but told Egan that if he had any memory products compatible with Prime minicomputers, he would buy plenty of them.

"Prime users were also paying an arm and a leg for memory, and Prime Computer products benefited greatly from having larger memories," Egan recalled.[10]

Encouraged by a team of University of Rhode Island scientists, Egan and Marino began spending their weekends at one of the university's research labs, where they tinkered with their own lower-cost memory products. The duo's final product—a 64-kilobyte chip memory plug-in board for Prime's computers—cost half of Prime's $36,000 per megabyte.[11]

To market the plug-in board, Egan and Marino developed leaflets and sent them to 70 prospects they had obtained from a list, which they believed contained the names of the Boston Prime Users' Group. What they did not know was that among the names were Prime Computer employees. Prime wasted no time in suing EMC for industrial espionage, claiming that the list was "stolen proprietary information."[12]

When word of the lawsuit hit local television news, the negative publicity had a dramatic effect on EMC's fledgling reputation. However, never one to back down, Egan decided to fight. He took the entire EMC staff, totaling only six people, including family members, to Prime's annual users' convention in New Orleans. Not only would the EMC delegation prove to Prime that EMC refused to give in without a fight, it would also flaunt its product to Prime's own customers.

"We had this big booth, and we looked crisp, sharp, and professional, and people thought we were some big-deal company," Egan recalled in Sam Hill and Glenn Rifkin's book, *Radical Marketing: From Harvard to Harley, Lessons From Ten That Broke the Rules and Made It Big.* "Prime was blindsided."[13]

At the convention, Egan said, Prime's president refused to speak to him. However, the next day, they both happened to find themselves waiting at the airport together to catch the same plane back to Boston. Seizing the unexpected opportunity, Egan warned him that if Prime didn't drop its suit against EMC, Egan would countersue Prime for monopolistic behavior. Prime withdrew its suit the next day, and EMC's reputation recovered.[14]

Even during those early years, Paul Noble, hired by his uncle, Dick Egan, in 1981, recalled the drive and dedication that would guide the company on its path to success: "The ambience was one of constant motion and EMC's famous sense of urgency was already evident. We were on the job six days a week, ten hours a day minimum."

In the three decades since its founding, that drive, that urgency, have led EMC up the chain as the company eventually aimed to overtake IBM, the market leader in storage products for mainframes and other types of computers.

Paul Noble, hired by his uncle Dick Egan in 1981, rose to become executive vice president of Products and Offerings.

# EMC²

*EMC's new Corporate Headquarters in Hopkinton MA. capped a successful year of increased sales earnings and resource growth.*

EMC moved its headquarters to 171 South Street in Hopkinton, Massachusetts, in 1987 to accommodate its rapid growth.

### CHAPTER TWO

# INCREASING SUCCESS

## 1982–1987

*I think my partner, Roger Marino, said it best: "The harder we work, the luckier we get."*

—Dick Egan[1]

WITH THE SUCCESS OF EMC's Prime Computer memory boards, Dick Egan and Roger Marino had hit upon a winning formula: using new technology to enhance computers built on older technology.[2] By successfully adapting existing equipment to capitalize on market opportunities, EMC developed memory products featuring greater capacity and greater reliability at a lower cost than those offered by the original equipment manufacturers (OEMs).[3]

Egan and Marino were shrewd enough to realize that Prime Computer users were not the only ones who wanted an alternative to high-priced minicomputer products sold only through OEMs. In 1983, EMC began producing and selling solid state memory products for Digital Equipment Corporation's (DEC) VAX models 11/750 and 11/780, as well as Wang Laboratories' VS models 90 and 100.[4]

During the heyday of the minicomputer, advances in semiconductor technology quickly outstripped the useful lives of new computer models. As soon as a company invested in a particular system, a faster, more capable system would appear. As Moore's Law predicted, the number of transistors an integrated circuit can hold increased exponentially, doubling approximately every two years. The rapid evolution of the computer industry demanded that companies remain selective in upgrading their equipment. Businesses began to demand more choices, and EMC provided them, creating a niche that led the company toward increasing success. By the end of 1982, EMC's revenues rose to $3.3 million. The next year, they had doubled to nearly $6.7 million.[5]

Always looking for new markets to enter, EMC was the first independent manufacturer to offer complete memory conversion kits—pioneering the sale of memory conversion systems for DEC VAX computers.[6] The comprehensive kits included main storage enhancement boards, controllers through which peripheral devices such as printers and modems could be connected, a backplane, a power supply, and interface modules. The kits allowed businesses to replace entire computer storage subsystems with enhanced, flexible subsystems featuring increased upgrade capabilities.[7]

Before long, the company began selling auxiliary, or peripheral, storage products such as disk drives and disk subsystems compatible with manufacturers such as Prime Computer and Wang.[8]

---

Dick Egan guided EMC's successful forays into the Prime Computer, Digital Equipment Corporation (DEC), Wang, Hewlett-Packard, and IBM markets in the early to mid-1980s.

**"Hire Good People"**

Above: Dick Egan's son, Jack, avidly recruited recent college graduates to EMC's early sales force.

Left: EMC first found success in the technology market by producing memory boards compatible with Prime Computer products. By the mid-1980s, EMC began manufacturing memory for the entire family of Prime products.

In 1983, Egan and Marino moved their operation into a 20,500-square-foot office building in Natick, Massachusetts.[9] They turned to local colleges and universities such as Boston College, the University of Massachusetts, and Egan's alma mater, Northeastern University, to hire a corps of smart, talented engineers and a dedicated, hard-driving sales force.

Paul Noble, an EMC employee since 1981, recalled EMC's hiring standards:

> It was our tactic to hire people who had a 3.5 cumulative [grade point average] or better. They were involved in either some type of entrepreneurial activity or some type of sports, preferably captain of a sports team activity in college, and ... put them in an environment where they competed against each other so that the cream rose to the top.[10]

They started small, hiring just a handful of graduates recruited by Egan's oldest son, Jack, who had quit his job in computer services to join EMC. They hired ambitious, often single, employees willing to go anywhere on a moment's notice.

Marino, a formidable salesman in his own right, trained the recruits.

"We put them through boot camp," Dick Egan recalled. "Roger was not only a good salesman, but he was an incredible teacher of that underestimated profession."[11]

During the makeshift, six-month boot camp known as EMC University, the recruits attended seminars and talks by product managers. They watched videotapes and practiced selling techniques.[12] Out of those early training experiences emerged EMC's legendary tough and hardworking early sales force.[13]

Bill Scannell, executive vice president of Americas, joined EMC in February 1986. Reflecting on his experience at EMC soon after he joined he said:

> The hard work wasn't something that was new to me, but the culture was exciting at the time because everybody worked very hard. You wanted to try to outwork everybody else. So, in the training

*program, for example, everyone wanted to be the first person in and the last person to leave. I was getting in at 6:30 in the morning, and I was leaving at 9 o'clock at night. And then I was leaving there to go to bartend at night. It was interesting to see the competitiveness, and that was a culture instilled by Dick Egan and Roger Marino. Every time they walked through the building, they also were fighting to be one of the first in and the last out. So it wasn't as though the management was saying "do as I say and not as I do." I mean, they were doing it and leading from the front, and that culture is still alive and well today.*

According to Jack Egan:

*I think we identified a common goal. We were fortunate that all the folks who were in the company shared a common agenda, that the independent agendas that would dilute our efforts were few and far between, and the work ethic was terrific. There were Saturdays when you couldn't find a spot in the parking lot.*[14]

After their training, recruits were assigned to small satellite offices across the U.S. EMC's initial experiment worked so well that the company began

hiring increasingly larger groups of recent college graduates every few months.

Repeating the founders' practices from the early days, EMC turned to young college graduates for financial reasons. EMC simply could not afford experienced salespeople. However, willingness to work, eagerness, dedication, and ambition in its new hires benefited EMC more in the long run than having experience at another company would have. Years later, EMC's enduring hiring strategy could be distilled down to a few words.

"Hire good people," explained Tom Heiser, an EMC senior vice president who has held a number of sales and general management positions. "Hire people who want to work hard, who want to be with each other, who want to spend the time."[15]

Dick Egan and Roger Marino offered their young sales force a modest base salary with the opportunity to earn unlimited commissions.[16] For many of EMC's young recruits, like Heiser had been

Roger Marino (right), shown with Dick Egan (left), presided over EMC University. As Marino trained new recruits, he developed a set of rules that highlighted many of the employee practices that helped make the company a success.

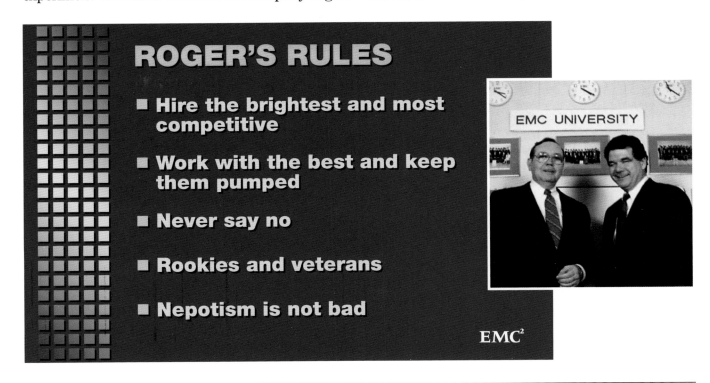

## ROGER'S RULES

- **Hire the brightest and most competitive**

- **Work with the best and keep them pumped**

- **Never say no**

- **Rookies and veterans**

- **Nepotism is not bad**

EMC²

EMC UNIVERSITY

in 1984, working independently and earning a salary that increased with each achievement sounded like the opportunity to build a dream career, one that posed formidable character-building challenges.

"After about four-and-a-half months [of telemarketing], Roger Marino said, 'Heiser, you're moving to New York,'" Heiser recalled. "I said, 'Okay.' He replied, 'You can open up EMC's first New York sales office.'"

Just 22 years old at the time, Heiser drove down to Long Island and opened a tiny office in Great Neck. Soon, he was joined by two other salesmen, and according to Heiser, the three spent their days "just hammering the phones."[17] His experience was mirrored by that of many other young recruits at the time. Much like the other recruits, Heiser believed anything and everything was possible, and he did not shy away from directly contacting the very top people within the companies he targeted for marketing.

"I would say we didn't know what we couldn't do," Heiser recalled. "Why not? Nobody ever told us we couldn't."[18]

Because EMC had a shoestring staff, the sales reps were often also responsible for installing

memory boards at customer sites. Some kept spare boards on hand and fielded customer issues from their homes.

That kind of dedication, the willingness to go above and beyond expectations, proved essential, since EMC was still an unknown entity. According to Brian Fitzgerald, vice president of marketing in EMC's RSA division and one of the company's first salespeople:

*The nature of the products was such [that] you could actually tell a customer, "Hey, we'll put it in for 30 days. If you don't like it, send it back. We won't charge you for it. If you like it, keep it. A demo test. No risk. Just give it a try."*[19]

That sort of persuasion, combined with an almost bullheaded perseverance, made the early EMC sales force something of a legend. One potential customer might receive as many as 50 phone calls. In the process of making what they called a "showcase account," EMC's sales staff would make steep discounts contingent upon company referrals and allowing repeated phone calls and site visits.[20]

"We started saying that the only difference between an EMC sales rep and a pit bull was that eventually the pit bull would let go," said the late Jeff Goldberg, a longtime vice president and former IBMer who helped build customer programs such as EMC's vaunted Executive Briefing Centers. "That was the tenacity of our DNA, and that was very important. People put a lot of attention to making sure employees had the right DNA."[21]

### Belief in the Product

During the 1980s, EMC remained a decidedly small player in a field of towering competitors, hoping to gain an edge in any way it could. No matter how knowledgeable and effective its sales staff was, the company always prided itself on the reliability of its products. That reliability was due to the work of the talented and generally young engineers that EMC hired. Unlike its much larger competitors such as Wang Laboratories or DEC, EMC offered its engineers

One of the earliest memory products EMC developed was for the DEC VAX 11/780.

# "It's the Products, Stupid."

the challenge of building products from the ground up. A great deal of responsibility rested on their shoulders.

Some of EMC's early engineers had come from fellow Massachusetts companies such as Wang and DEC. They relished EMC's smaller, more hands-on environment, which provided the challenge many of them had longed for.

Brian Gallagher, senior vice president of Symmetrix engineering, worked at Wang before coming to EMC in 1985 as a design engineer. Just before accepting the position, he had been considering proposals from both Prime Computer and DEC. When Dick Egan interviewed Gallagher, he made him a challenging offer that convinced the recent college graduate that EMC was the place for him. Gallagher recalled:

*Egan said, "You know, Gallagher, you can work up in your ivory towers over at Wang, and there are many people up there who will support you. They're going to do all the work for you. At EMC, you're going to have to do everything. You're going to have to design the product. You're going to have to design the test equipment. You're going to have to write the manufacturing procedures. You're*

Above: This sign, which once hung in Dick Egan's office, summed up one of the main reasons behind the success of EMC. According to Egan, "I liked having a sign that said 'It's the Products, Stupid,' just in case anybody thought it's about them."

Inset: By developing Prime-compatible memory products, EMC allowed its customers to upgrade their computers at a modest cost.

*going to have to support manufacturing. You're going to have to write the customer service installation manual. You're going to have to support customer service, and you're going to have to answer the phone at night."* [22]

Egan made it clear that at his company, there would be no one to hide behind. Gallagher accepted the challenge and joined a team of engineers who tested the compatibility of their memory boards by dismantling their competitors' machines. More than designing the products, Gallagher and his colleagues wanted to know their products from the inside out, to "think about what went through the minds of other engineers—what they were thinking, and why they would ever do things certain ways," he explained.[23] Like its sales team, EMC's engineers were driven to work long hours and constantly perform to the best of their abilities.

"Friday nights, for a while, we used to have a little social event at about seven o'clock," Gallagher recalled. "They'd bring in some sandwiches and some drinks, and Dick would always walk through the labs toward the end of the day. Especially on the weekends ... he would swing by, and I'd be out on the bench debugging the boards. He'd look at me, and he'd say, 'Well, Gallagher, I got all my work done for the week. So I can go home.' But that was kind of his message, that there's always work to do, and it's important work."[24]

### Valuing the Customer

Even with a tireless work ethic and a sales force that was becoming a big competitive weapon, Egan and Marino knew that the success of their company rested on the quality of their products. A sign reading "It's the Products, Stupid." hung in Egan's office as a testament to this central truth. Just as important was the necessity that customers both like and trust EMC's products. EMC's engineers were encouraged to think of ways to differentiate their technology by including distinguishing touches that customers would appreciate. Some boards, for instance, were designed with "indicators" of early trouble.

By 1985, more than 40 percent of EMC's personnel was in marketing and sales, which reflected Egan's concern with customer service.[25] This emphasis on customer service distinguished EMC from its competitors, recalled Celeste Rippole, who was hired as an administrator in 1986:

*The thing I remember most about the business was the service to the customers. The relationship with the customers was ... so much more personal. We prided ourselves on that. That's how we survived. We were just always the better company; it was because of our service.*[26]

An EMC tenet established early on was that marketing and product development departments would maintain close relationships. This allowed the company to remain porous. Ideas and challenges filtered in, allowing engineers to develop products based on those challenges.[27] According to Egan, by bringing customers and engineers together to exchange problems for solutions, EMC gained an incredible advantage in bringing products to market. As Egan explained in a 1986 Harvard Business School case study:

*Most of our competitors sell to the OEMs [original equipment manufacturers]. We sell to the end user. We need to know what they are thinking because we need to know the next generation of proprietary products. You can't just cast yourself as a "tech" guy ... you have to understand their whole world. So many computer users have love/hate relationships with their CPU vendor after the equipment has long been installed. ... It's amazing what an unsolicited call after a sale has taken place can do for you.*[28]

EMC also went to great lengths to guarantee the integrity of its products. A five-year warranty that EMC introduced in 1983 for memory upgrades became a lifetime warranty in 1984, the same year the company added 24-hour technical support.[29] Under the company's quick response service

In 1985, EMC introduced memory units for Hewlett-Packard's 3000 series computers, such as the one pictured at left.

programs, defective boards would be replaced within 24 hours. EMC also reimbursed any system maintenance costs that customers incurred from original manufacturers due to EMC products.[30]

**Reaching Milestones**

Faith in EMC's products created a growing customer base that produced tangible results. The company's revenues had nearly tripled between 1983 and 1984, and then doubled every year after until 1988. By 1985, EMC manufactured main and auxiliary storage products for the entire family of Prime Computer systems, along with main memory for DEC VAX and Wang Laboratories VS central processors.[31]

In the latter half of that year, EMC introduced a line of main storage units for the Hewlett-Packard 3000 series, as well as main storage units for the IBM System/38 series, including one-megabyte units for models 6, 8, and 18.[32] By expanding its product offerings, EMC could focus its efforts on overtaking IBM, the market leader.

Shortly after EMC entered the Hewlett-Packard and IBM markets, the company reached another major milestone. EMC went public and was listed on the NASDAQ on April 4, 1986, issuing 2.5 million shares of common stock at $16.25 per share. The initial public offering (IPO) raised $30 million that EMC used to acquire a new 205,000-square-foot headquarters in Hopkinton, Massachusetts, and a 76,000-square-foot manufacturing facility adjacent to it. The proceeds also boosted EMC's field sales and marketing operations in the United States and abroad.[33]

Still, Egan's decision to take the company public in early 1986 struck some observers as surprising, particularly in light of the ambivalence toward external financing options he had expressed prior to the IPO:

*I am under intense pressure from the investment banks to go public. They're blowing $200 million in my ear all the time and everyone knows a salesman is an easy sell. The Dow looks like it's going to break 1500 and lots of indicators are looking pretty attractive. But I'm just not sure. There are other things we could do. We've come this far by ourselves—maybe we should just wait.*[34]

PROSPECTUS

**2,500,000 Shares**

# EMC²

## EMC Corporation

### Common Stock

Of the 2,500,000 shares of Common Stock offered hereby, 2,150,000 shares will be sold by EMC Corporation and 350,000 shares will be sold by certain Selling Stockholders of the Company. The Company will not receive any of the proceeds from the sale of shares by the Selling Stockholders.

Prior to this offering, there has been no public market for the Common Stock of the Company. See "Underwriting" for information relating to the determination of the initial public offering price.

THESE SECURITIES HAVE NOT BEEN APPROVED OR DISAPPROVED BY THE SECURITIES AND EXCHANGE COMMISSION NOR HAS THE COMMISSION PASSED UPON THE ACCURACY OR ADEQUACY OF THIS PROSPECTUS. ANY REPRESENTATION TO THE CONTRARY IS A CRIMINAL OFFENSE.

| | Price to Public | Underwriting Discount | Proceeds to Company(1) | Proceeds to Selling Stockholders(1) |
|---|---|---|---|---|
| Per Share | $16.50 | $1.12 | $15.38 | $15.38 |
| Total(2) | $41,250,000 | $2,800,000 | $33,067,000 | $5,383,000 |

(1) Before deducting expenses estimated at $328,000 payable by the Company and $37,000 payable by the Selling Stockholders.
(2) The Company and the Selling Stockholders have granted to the Underwriters a 30-day option to purchase up to 375,000 additional shares of Common Stock to cover over-allotments, if any. If such option is exercised in full, the total Price to Public, total Underwriting Discount, total Proceeds to Company and total Proceeds to Selling Stockholders will be $47,437,500, $3,220,000, $33,836,000 and $10,381,500, respectively. See "Underwriting".

The shares of Common Stock are offered by the several Underwriters subject to prior sale, when, as and if delivered to and accepted by them, and subject to approval of certain legal matters by counsel and to certain other conditions. The Underwriters reserve the right to withdraw, cancel or modify such offer and to reject any order in whole or in part. It is expected that delivery of the shares of Common Stock will be made in New York, New York on or about April 11, 1986.

**Merrill Lynch Capital Markets** **Salomon Brothers Inc**

The date of this Prospectus is April 4, 1986.

**FOR INFORMATION PURPOSES ONLY**

EMC's initial public offering on April 4, 1986, raised $30 million. The company issued 2.5 million shares of common stock at $16.25 per share.

However, as Egan began setting his sights on cutting-edge technology products that could lead the market, rather than follow it, he realized external funding would help the company reach this aim. In addition, because Egan and Marino founded EMC using their own personal savings, without any external or venture capital, EMC's growth never allowed the company to accumulate substantial reserves. Because of his reservations, before Egan made the decision to take his company public, he considered various options for securing the company's financial future while continuing to capitalize on market opportunities. He did not consider venture capitalists a viable source of extra funds, since at the time, they were frequently skeptical of computer upgrade and enhancement companies such as EMC. Egan also refused to acquire any bank debt, fearing that

In early 1987, EMC moved into its new headquarters (below) at
171 South Street in Hopkinton, Massachusetts. The hall of
flags (above) within EMC's headquarters reflects the
increasingly international scope of the company's operations.

banks would unfairly abandon EMC if market conditions soured.[35]

Before EMC went public, the company had
already shipped more than 25,000 memory units to
more than 5,000 customers.[36] In early 1985, EMC
had opened assembly and testing plants in Hollis,
New Hampshire, as well as Canóvanas, Puerto Rico,
which operated under the company's subsidiary,

EMC Caribe, Inc. EMC had 15 sales and service
offices in the United States, and international locations in Toronto, London, and Munich.[37] As a sea-
soned entrepreneur, Egan knew the time to secure
funding was when a company was doing well, particularly in a market as fickle as the technology sector. There were never any guarantees that economic
conditions would remain favorable.[38]

His decision to take EMC public led the
company toward greater success. By
1987, fueled by proceeds from
the IPO, EMC grew to

## Revenue
### (in Millions)

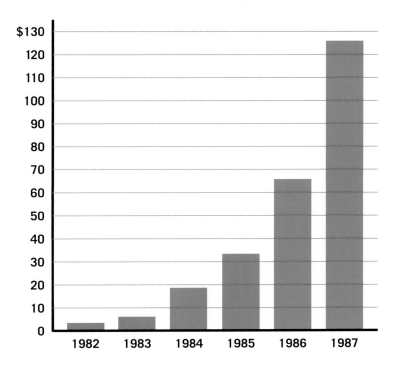

## Net Income
### (in Millions)

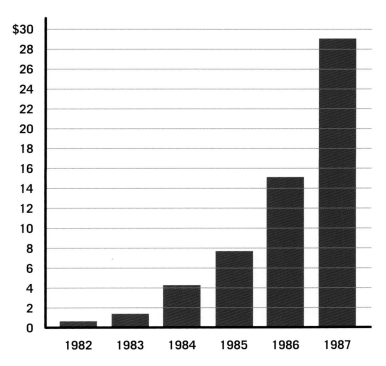

include 31 offices in North America and 10 European locations.[39]

EMC's staff also experienced considerable growth. In April 1986, the company had 192 employees—within a year, that number had doubled.[40] EMC's new headquarters at 171 South Street in Hopkinton could handle the rapid expansion.

Above: EMC experienced several years of rapid revenue and net income growth. Although revenue dropped slightly in 1988 due to multiple factors, the company would soon resume growth and profitability.

Right: EMC's ARCHEION optical disk subsystem allowed DEC VAX users to store and quickly access large amounts of archived data, solving a long-standing problem for VAX customers.

**Opening a New Market**

Entering the mainframe storage market opened new doors for EMC as it expanded into the burgeoning disk storage market. IBM peripheral storage, Egan realized, was expensive; he saw disk storage as a market with huge potential, just waiting for someone to tap it. Egan explained:

*Everybody had been segmenting the computer market into a pyramid shape according to memory size: High-speed memory for minicomputers formed the point of the pyramid; low-cost tape formed the base. We realized that if EMC "walked down the pyramid," it could reach a big but under-publicized market: disk storage. Storage turned the pyramid into a*

Above: EMC stock began trading on the NYSE on March 22, 1988. That day, the stock closed at $16 ⁴/₈ per share.

Right: Sandra Jaffee, then executive vice president of the New York Stock Exchange; Dick Egan; and New York Stock Exchange Specialist George Erdman of Bear, Stearns & Company, Inc., examine the specialist book during EMC's listing ceremony on the Exchange Trading Floor on March 22, 1988. *(Used with permission © 2010 NYSE Group, Inc.®)*

*diamond with a plump center reflecting a potentially huge demand.*[41]

The company began exploiting that demand with great success, beginning with the large-scale introduction of direct access storage devices (DASDs) in 1987. These devices relied on both new technologies, such as optical storage, and refined older ones, such as magnetic disk media.[42]

The challenges customers faced inspired the evolution of EMC's products. EMC's ARCHEION optical disk subsystem allowed DEC VAX users to store more than 150 million pages for immediate retrieval, solving their long-standing prob-

lems with storing, accessing, and retrieving large amounts of archived data.[43] Since auxiliary storage devices traditionally allowed slower access to information than main memory products, EMC integrated the latest technological advances in disk storage to give customers faster access to their data. EMC also expanded into the disk storage market for IBM computer systems, starting with its System/38 computers.[44]

The new market proved fruitful.[45] The company's momentum propelled it toward yet another milestone. On March 22, 1988, its shares began trading on the New York Stock Exchange, capping six years of successive growth from 1982 to 1987. By

Right: Jim Callahan, hired by EMC in 1984, fondly recalls EMC's early days as a time of exciting possibilities.

Below: Dan Fitzgerald, one of EMC's earliest employees, was hired by the company while still in college. He considered Dick Egan a personal mentor.

1987, EMC's sales increased 91 percent over the previous year, to $127 million, as net income grew 52 percent to $28 million. EMC—a hardware company serving a variety of computer markets—was the first of its kind listed on the exchange.[46] The next year, to accommodate EMC's growing European customer base, EMC opened a 40,000-square-foot manufacturing operation in Ballincollig, near Cork, Ireland, purchased from the Irish Development Authority. The plant would fulfill more than half of EMC's European demand.[47]

### EMC Culture

Now a larger company, EMC began solidifying its identity. Out of its founding values grew the company's culture—one that rewards hard work, values

communication, continuously strives for improvement, and always focuses on the ultimate satisfaction of its customers. Employees put in long hours but always knew their bosses were working alongside them. Egan and Marino could be seen making the rounds every day, sometimes attending to tasks not generally expected of senior executives. At EMC, managers were also doers.

A strong team spirit and a willingness to think outside of the traditional way of doing things characterized the growing company. Dan Fitzgerald, one of EMC's earliest employees, began working at the company as a Boston College math and computer science major in 1984. He recalled the atmosphere when he first joined EMC:

*I look back, and as much as people say, "Oh you're family," it's really just accountability. You have a win, they give you a little more, [and then] you have a win, and they give a little more, and then at some point in time, you don't even think about it. [You realize] what you need to do to get things done, and you agree to do it. … I think my mentors at EMC, especially Dick Egan, Jack Egan, W. Paul Fitzgerald, and Colin Patteson, taught me … integrity, accountability, and self-sufficiency.[48]*

# "YES, FOLKS, IT SNOWS IN NEW ENGLAND"

IN THE DAYS BEFORE E-MAIL, DICK EGAN'S HARD-copy memos acquired a legendary status among EMC employees. Those with the company in the late 1980s like to recall a particularly memorable memo he sent out following a February snowstorm. The commute that morning was treacherous, and though the workday started at 8:00 A.M., many employees arrived much later due to the inclement weather.

"Dick [Egan], who was usually formally dressed, was wearing very casual clothes. Almost like a hunting-type outfit—boots and kind of a wool overcoat and a hat," recalled David Donatelli, who joined EMC in 1987. "[He] did his lap around [the office] and noticed that people weren't there, which obviously led to Dick being pretty upset."[1]

The employees who had shown up began calling their absent coworkers, advising them to come to work immediately, but it was already too late. By the end of the day, a memo was distributed, titled "Yes, Folks, It Snows in New England."

"'Our customers live all over the world,'" Donatelli recalled the memo reading. "'They don't really know what the weather in Boston is, nor do

---

Because of the excitement and flexibility EMC offered, many employees describe their early days with the company as the happiest of their careers. Being part of an expanding business, where everyone's efforts had a direct and immediate impact on its success, contributed to the camaraderie and dedication of EMC's employees.

"It was just always good," said Jim Callahan, who was hired to debug and test boards in 1984. "Even when we were testing memory boards, it seemed like business was just constantly growing and getting bigger and bigger, and no matter how hard you worked, you couldn't keep up, and everything just ballooned and branched out. I loved this job when I came here. ... I said I could work every day of the week, 20 hours a day; it didn't matter."[49]

While team spirit would always remain one of EMC's strongest characteristics, individual efforts were always recognized, according to Maureen Clancy, retired director of executive development. Egan famously wrote notes on every status report and memo employees sent him, signaling his direct involvement in all of the company's operations.[50]

Originally hired as a product manager in 1986, Clancy recalled the deep connection between executives and employees:

*[Dick] would remember your name. He would know what you did, and he'd always make it very personal. Even someone on the manufacturing floor knew that Dick knew them, and it was a really nice feeling. Just a small company mentality. We felt a real connection to even higher management, and I still have tons of those memos saved.*[51]

EMC's culture also valued accountability, perhaps best demonstrated through the company's quarterly employee meetings. Egan, who had grown accustomed to quarterly meetings while working at Intel, implemented them at EMC early on. During the quarterly meetings, leaders from each department shared their goals from the previous quarter, noting what they had achieved and where they had fallen short. Triumphs and failures were laid bare before the entire company. "The public accountability was very, very important," explained Mark Fredrickson, vice president of marketing strategy

they particularly care. It's really our job to make sure that we support our customers no matter what the conditions are in the local Boston area.'"[2]

Because customers' reliance on EMC was not dependent on the weather, Egan explained in the memo, employees were expected to leave home as early as they needed to. Work started at 8:00 A.M. No exceptions. Should employees find that difficult to accept, Donatelli recalled, Egan recommended they "seek employment in a warmer climate like Florida."[3]

Maureen Clancy, retired director of executive development, was one of the employees who had arrived late. "I don't know if [the memo] was well received, but I think it just gives an example of the expectations of the company," she said. "It's a team effort."[4]

The memo worked; the morning of the next snowstorm, everyone showed up on time.[5]

Another of Egan's famous memos concerned communication. Many employees were regularly inundated with phone messages from the sales force, and they were sometimes slow to respond. "Dick wrote another very eloquent memo explaining to everybody that our sales force was our pipeline to our customers, and that if a salesperson was asking us a question, it's really the customer who is asking that question," Donatelli said. "It's our duty to make sure that we respond to that salesperson as fast as possible, so that we give an equally fast response to the customer who is asking the question."[6]

The memo ended with a typical Egan flourish that underscored both his wit and the gravity of his message. It read:

*If you ever find yourself so busy that you cannot take a call from the field, please forward your phones directly to me, and I will cover for you.*

*—Dick*[7]

and communications. His group still organizes "The Quarterly," though now for a global audience of thousands.[52]

Bonuses were tied to fulfillment of the objectives the department had laid out, and missing a goal meant less money earned. "Everybody understood that missing goals meant executives and their staffs would not get their full bonuses," Fredrickson said.[53]

### A-Level Talent

Due to its reputation for employee satisfaction, EMC developed into one of the most attractive technology companies available for college students weighing their career options. EMC became a top choice for recent college graduates due to its constant sense of urgency, something more established companies often lacked. That boundless energy, combined with the opportunity to earn a high salary based solely on skills and achievements, enabled EMC to hire the best and the brightest.

"They had a very interesting value proposition," recalled David Donatelli, one of four Boston College graduates hired by EMC in 1987. Out of his class of 550, Donatelli joked that about 546 had applied to work there.

"At least at that time, most companies, particularly the FORTUNE® 500s, paid about the same amount of money for a first-year grad," he explained. "Really, you took the job that was right for you, and you were going to make the same pretty much wherever you went. EMC paid double. ... Your base salary pretty much kept you on par with what everybody else was making, and with the incentives, you could make double what all of your friends were making."[54]

Of course, those who went to EMC would constantly have to prove themselves. They also bore witness to the often unpredictable reversals of fortune that frequently struck the technology industry. Today, along the Massachusetts high-tech highways of routes 128 and 495, the buildings that once housed now-defunct Prime Computer, Digital Equipment Corporation, and Wang Laboratories still stand.[55] Those companies, all giants in their day, have been outlasted by a small upstart that has proven its ability to repeatedly reinvent itself.

Mike Ruettgers (left), who joined EMC in 1988 and served as CEO from 1992 until January 2001, and Dick Egan (right) led EMC during the company's tumultuous difficulties in the late 1980s, and then to unprecedented new levels of success.

### CHAPTER THREE

# EMC's First Major Crisis

## 1988–1989

*We changed the whole way we look at design and manufacturing and customer service. … If it had kept going the way it was going, EMC would have gone out of business.*

—Chuck Loewy[1]

THE YEAR 1988 HELD GREAT PROMise for EMC. The company had successfully entered the IBM midrange and mainframe markets and seized upon the previously untapped peripheral storage market, which would propel the company toward phenomenal future growth.

In 1987, sales skyrocketed to 90 percent over 1986 totals, and EMC stock reached a high of $29 per share.[2] *BusinessWeek* magazine named the company to its list of top growth companies. The world, it seemed, had begun to take notice of the rising start-up. Then, in 1988, EMC unveiled the Guardian, the company's first disk subsystem. The Guardian garnered a great deal of buzz, and EMC was flooded with orders before the subsystem was even released.

"We had sales guys pumped up out of their minds selling these products as fast as they could," recalled Leo Colborne, former senior vice president of global customer services. "I think we had a $10 million backlog, which was big. We weren't even shipping the product yet, and we had a $10 million backlog."[3]

However, within the Guardian system lurked a danger nobody at EMC could have anticipated. Guardian's components included a 520-megabyte disk drive manufactured by a Japanese company, one of EMC's main suppliers. In response to EMC's skyrocketing demand for this drive, the manufacturer had hastily expanded its production volume by hiring less-experienced workers.[4] Although the process for manufacturing and assembling disk drives required a pristine "clean room" free from dust and air impurities, some employees wore facial powder to work. That slight breach of clean-room hygiene would eventually wreak havoc on EMC's Guardian line of products.[5]

Trapped particles from the facial makeup caused the disk drives to fail, sometimes within months or years, other times as soon as they were installed. One malfunctioning disk drive affected the entire array, which had no recovery capability.[6] Customers were forced to restore data from tape, which could mean days of lost productivity. Sometimes, as soon as one malfunctioning drive was repaired or replaced, another drive in the array would fail, resulting in even more days of lost productivity for EMC's customers.[7]

---

Facial powder worn by workers at a supplier that assembled disk drives for EMC caused one of EMC's first disk subsystem products to fail until the source of contamination was uncovered.

# EMC GOES GLOBAL

IN APRIL 1986, EMC WENT PUBLIC WITH 15 SALES AND service offices in the United States; sites in Toronto, London, and Munich; and aspirations to establish a stronger international presence. The company raised $30 million in its public offering to help achieve this goal. By the end of 1987, EMC had 10 offices in Europe and four in the Pacific Rim, all of which were staffed by direct sales representatives and support personnel who had graduated from EMC University, the company's sales training program.[1] The global expansion of the computer industry presented EMC with a world of market opportunities for its newly introduced Hewlett-Packard- and IBM-compatible systems and its direct access storage devices (DASD).

The countries where EMC opened offices in the late 1980s—Australia, France, Germany, Hong Kong, Ireland, and Italy among them—had the political and socioeconomic conditions that would allow the company to prosper. As these conditions took root in other countries around the world, an EMC presence often followed. The collapse of the Berlin Wall in 1989, for instance, opened a new and robust market for EMC's products, as the technological goods once prohibited for export to East Germany flooded in.

The company's international marketing specialists showed prescience in scouting out advantageous locations. One example was Belgium, which as the seat of the European Community was a magnet for foreign investment. This in turn helped bolster the market's receptivity to EMC's offerings in the country.

The 40,000-square-foot manufacturing facility that EMC opened in Cork, Ireland, in 1988 attested to burgeoning European demand. The plant supplied more than half of the continent's products and still remains EMC's largest international facility, with its activities supporting more than 40 percent of the company's worldwide revenues.[2] Having such a solid base abroad allowed EMC to tap opportunities it might not have been able to otherwise. A 1991 deal sealed by the company's United Kingdom office, for instance, allowed EMC to supply main memory and storage to the international sites of Credit Commercial de France, one of the world's largest banks.[3] By 1992, European sales made up nearly a quarter of EMC's revenues, with Asia Pacific/Japan business accounting for 5 percent.[4]

Today, as EMC continues its global expansion, successfully interlocking with oth-

The EMC customer service management team included (left to right) Ralph Eldridge, Bill Dacier, Leo Colborne, Dan Butler, Frank Hauck, and Gary Bastarache.

"We had a very strained technical support organization because the call volume just started going through the roof," Colborne said. "We had engineers in the field running around all over the place, replacing disk drives as fast as they could."

### A Test of Willpower

For the sales representatives, many of whom had no technical experience prior to joining EMC, the crisis proved a serious test of their willpower. Many found unique ways to convince customers to remain loyal despite EMC's manufacturing difficulties.

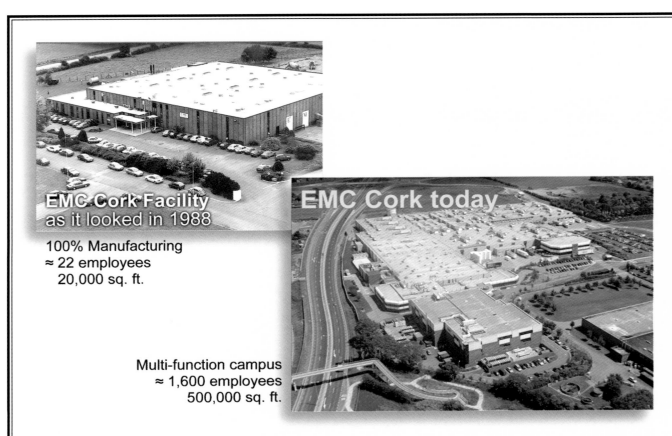

EMC Cork Facility as it looked in 1988

100% Manufacturing
≈ 22 employees
20,000 sq. ft.

EMC Cork today

Multi-function campus
≈ 1,600 employees
500,000 sq. ft.

er cultures remains an ongoing endeavor. The company has made integrating and learning from other cultures a priority through initiatives such as its "Living Inclusion" strategy, a partnership between EMC senior management and employees around the world aimed at strengthening diversity within individual organizations and throughout EMC as a whole.

Such efforts have served the company well as it looks to gain a toehold in newly emerging markets and extend existing inroads.

Clarence Westfall, who was hired by the company in 1986, recalled selling the first Guardian subsystem to "Terry Crawl at World's Finest Chocolate, which is the company that makes the charity chocolate bars that you buy for a dollar."

According to Westfall, he used EMC's association with World's Finest Chocolate to his distinct advantage:

*Everybody knows who they are because every company in the world sells them. Terry [Crawl] bought [the Guardian system], but then he left World's Finest Chocolate, and the people that followed him didn't want to install Guardian. However, we stood firm and said, "Hey, this is a solid deal, there's no reason not to [go through with it]."*

*Ultimately, throughout the entire faulty component debacle, World's Finest Chocolate never had a service outage, so they became our showcase account in Chicago. [Potential customers] would say, "These things don't work," and we would reply, "The first one sold is at World's Finest Chocolate. It's running great. You want to talk to them?" We just leveraged that to death. I just think that as things get good, or things get bad, you stick with it and you show some loyalty.*[8]

Some engineers, such as Tim Mulvihill, hired in 1987, relished the technical challenges that the

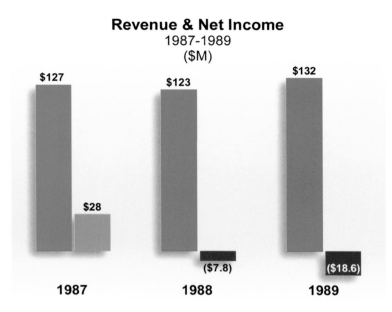

**Revenue & Net Income**
1987-1989
($M)

EMC faced declining earnings in the late 1980s. In 1988, the company posted its first loss.

disk drive crisis presented. "I never wanted to look at anything that worked," Mulvihill explained. "If it worked, it didn't need me. I wanted the stuff that didn't work, and not only did I want the stuff that didn't work, I wanted the stuff that didn't work that nobody else could figure out. That's what I wanted to work on."[9]

Employees during that time acknowledged that EMC lacked the quality controls that are integral to the company today.[10] However, employees also recognized that perhaps even the most thorough testing might not have uncovered the Japanese supplier's latent defects, since the Guardian system disk drives might function reasonably well for several months before crashing without warning.[11]

The episode served as a trial by fire for the young company. Since Guardian was EMC's first disk product, the company had invested a substantial amount of time and money just trying to determine whether the problems were caused by the disks themselves or the company's design and production methods.[12] The manufactured disks soon began to impose serious financial hardships on the company. In April 1988, EMC reported first

quarter earnings had sunk to just over $1 million, down from $5.75 million for the first quarter of the previous year.[13] By the end of 1988, EMC realized its first annual loss, with sales down 3 percent from 1987.[14]

**The Edge of Bankruptcy**

EMC's financial woes were compounded by an unexpected and dramatic increase in the price of dynamic random access memory (DRAM) chips, which the company depended on for its main memory products.[15] Even as the price of DRAM chips came down after peaking in 1988, disk drive problems continued to plague the company, hurting EMC's reputation and halting its financial growth. Earnings plunged during 1989 as EMC lost 78 cents per share, an even sharper decline than the 33 cents per share the company lost in 1988.[16]

Replacing failing disk subsystems and establishing better testing and analysis systems cost EMC $55 million of the $60 million combined proceeds the company had raised during its initial public offering in 1986 and a secondary offering the following year.[17] By 1989, short on funds and facing plummeting stock prices, EMC was on the verge of filing Chapter 11 bankruptcy.[18]

Among their many challenges, EMC founders Dick Egan and Roger Marino had to contend with anxious investors, some of whom felt they had been kept in the dark about the disk drive problems.[19] At the annual shareholders' meeting on May 10, 1989, the pair promised to go without pay until the company returned to profitability. "Those of you who know me know I don't make bets I can lose," Egan said immediately after making the vow.[20]

The disk drive crisis simultaneously brought the company together while bringing it to its knees. Egan and Marino personally joined the sales team in visiting customer sites to replace failing systems, while, at the same time, frantically searching for another disk drive supplier.

"I felt terrible for our customers," Egan recalled in the book *Radical Marketing: From Harvard to Harley, Lessons From Ten That Broke the Rules and Made It Big*. "These guys had put their jobs on the line for us and trusted us to move away from IBM."[21]

### RAID Reliance

EMC had dared to take on IBM, but the technology giant was not about to cede its market domination without a fight. IBM, also known as "Big Blue," had long controlled mainframe storage by offering products with the highest speed and greatest density available, taking the lead in creating the standards other technology companies soon learned to follow.[22] Since IBM stood as the dominant manufacturer of mainframes, its competitors were forced to make their storage systems "plug-compatible," fully capable of integrating with customers' existing IBM systems.[23]

By the late 1980s, competitors had begun to challenge IBM's supremacy by producing systems that broke the IBM mold. In March 1988, Storage-Tek began developing its Iceberg mainframe disk storage system, which, instead of holding data in complete blocks on designated drives as in IBM mainframes, stored data wherever there was room, scattering it among all the disk drives in a system.[24] Although an appealing concept, designing Iceberg proved a lengthy and arduous process.

EMC, meanwhile, challenged IBM's supremacy by offering storage systems based on redundant arrays of independent disks (RAID) technology. The concept, which had been described in a paper written in 1987 at the University of California, Berkeley, involved stringing together relatively inexpensive 5¼-inch disk drives to hold portions of data instead of relying on one centralized storage device with larger, slower disks.

As the popularity of personal computers increased, 5¼-inch drives underwent significant improvement.[25] Connecting them seemed a viable response to resolving the discrepancy between processor speed and disk spindle speed, which had previously limited the performance of mainframe systems. Prevailing storage methods had sacrificed one for the other, but disk arrays offered improved mainframe performance by supporting a greater number of input-output operations than traditional

Customer service has remained a key area of emphasis for EMC since the company's inception.

# A FOCUS ON QUALITY

**Corporate Quality Policy**

EMC Corporation is committed to being a world class supplier of computer storage products and services, with focus on meeting our customers' requirements.

EMC employees at all levels are responsible to ensure all products, processes, and services are developed, provided, and executed in a controlled, and cooperative work environment founded on the principles of continuous improvement, with commitment to meeting our internal and external customers' expectations.

*Michael Ruettgers*
COO and President

*Richard J. Egan*
CEO and Chairman of the Board

**EMC²**

DURING THE LATE 1980s AND EARLY 1990s, Mike Ruettgers instituted a company-wide focus on quality in every aspect of EMC's work. He helped implement a number of quality initiatives known collectively as Conway's Continuous Improvement program—the first of a number of advances intended to increase EMC's design and manufacturing prowess. The Continuous Improvement program focused on improving all work processes by identifying and eliminating waste.

As part of its implementation of the Continuous Improvement program, EMC identified possible inefficiencies and wasteful gaps in the process, such as excess freight costs or under-utilized facilities. EMC then shifted its priorities as needed, deciding which specific projects to work on and setting up support, monitoring, and feedback systems to carry out those projects successfully.

EMC's adoption of the Continuous Improvement program coincided with, and paved the way for, a number of other similar measures. In 1988,

EMC established a quality assurance program to examine products from the design phase through the verification, manufacturing, testing, shipping, and support stages.[1] The company also launched the Material Requirements Planning (MRP) program, aimed at controlling inventory and preventing excess. All employees underwent extensive training and testing to become certified to comply with the new procedures.[2]

"[The program] was designed to help ... plan orders [and] customer expectations," explained Maureen Clancy, who was assigned to head the program in 1990.[3]

Since 2002, EMC has adopted the Six Sigma quality control system. Invented by Motorola and used by such diverse companies as Bank of America, Raytheon, and General Electric, Six Sigma focuses on producing better products and services faster and at a lower cost. EMC has continued to pursue Lean Six Sigma to make itself more efficient and to advance toward its goal of providing the best total customer experience in the industry.

systems of the same storage capacity.[26] The drawback of a system that used many commodity disks, however, was an increased risk of disk failure.[27]

EMC's RAID-based subsystems for IBM midrange computers had seemed an attractive alternative to IBM's expensive proprietary systems. This led EMC to develop its ill-fated Guardian system, designed to work in conjunction with IBM's minicomputer System/38 and AS/400 systems.

### Keeping Customers

Despite the widespread failure of its Guardian systems' disk drives, EMC did not lose its customer base in the midst of the crisis. This might have been, in part, because crashes were not uncommon, even among IBM customers.[28] However, the incredible solidarity EMC shared with its customers proved just as important. Replacing the defective drives became an all-hands-on-deck effort; sales offices around the country kept replacement drives stocked while the founders remained active in trying to rectify the problem. Every EMC employee pulled out all the stops in trying to solve the dilemma, an effort that went a long way toward retaining customer loyalty.

"It was probably the most terrible time, waking up every morning knowing you were going to be going to the office and having to talk to customers," Egan recalled. "We actually wound up buying IBM disk drives to replace our own to hold on to our customers."[29]

EMC's response to the catastrophe illustrated the company's core philosophy of serving its customers in the best way possible. "I remember Dick [Egan] back in the early days," recalled Steven Fitz, who started working at EMC in 1986 and would later run the Asia Pacific/Japan region. "He'd be on a sales call with a customer, and he'd write his home number on the back of the [business] card. [He was] just so passionate about the customers and the way we dealt with them. If a customer had a problem with their system, a delivery, an issue, we just harnessed and focused around it—very good crisis management."

Even as the company fought to retain its customers' loyalty, investors and analysts began to question whether EMC should even continue to compete in the disk storage market. Egan recalled

a Merrill Lynch analyst advising him to go back to solid-state memory:

*When we first stumbled in 1988, I remember her saying, "You know, it's going to take you six or eight quarters to resume growth and profitability."*

*After eight years of doubling each year and achieving 20 percent net profitability, we at EMC could not imagine such a lengthy recovery. Well, those estimates were pretty much on the mark.[30]*

Even facing a long recovery, Egan was determined to keep EMC in the storage business for the long run. Egan had realized that the money spent on mainframe storage far exceeded comparable figures for the minicomputer market. And he had a few new ideas that would take the technology world by storm.

"Storage would launch us, give us added respectability, and carry us past a shaky stock market," Egan explained. "We remained intent on 'moving up the food chain' to the IBM mainframe."[31]

### Turning Things Around

Even during EMC's most tumultuous times, Egan continued planning dramatic changes for the company behind the scenes. As part of his plans, Egan hired Mike Ruettgers in July 1988 to head up

Mike Ruettgers, a Harvard Business School graduate and former manager at Raytheon, was charged with improving quality at EMC when he joined the company in 1988.

operations and customer service. They had met six years earlier when Egan served on the board of Technical Financial Services, a Boston-based technology publishing and research firm where Ruettgers worked as chief operating officer. Egan noticed that Ruettgers was responsible for most of the company's earnings, and when Ruettgers decided he wanted to leave Technical Financial Services to run Datapoint Corporation, an electronics company in Austin, Texas, Egan made his move.[32] It took some convincing, but in the end, Egan found support from within Ruettgers' own family. "My trump card was that I knew Mike's wife, Maureen, didn't want to leave Massachusetts," Egan recalled in *BusinessWeek* magazine in 1999.[33]

Ruettgers' unique management style helped shake things up right from the start. Even before the full magnitude of the disk drive problem was known, Ruettgers had already begun searching for ways to improve the quality of EMC's products. In one of his first weeks on the job, Ruettgers called a meeting and placed airline airsickness bags all around the conference table. His arms folded in front of him, he announced: "The quality of our products makes me want to puke."[34]

Early EMC employees recalled how the company's short-staffed, highly charged environment had previously led to a decreased attention to detail in its products. The new focus on quality proved a welcome change. "We went through tough times, but 99.9 percent of it was our own fault," admitted

Above: Ruettgers instituted a company-wide focus on quality.

Left: EMC's product line in 1988 included storage subsystems and main memory upgrades.

Chuck Loewy, vice president and general manager of EMC's Interactive Systems Group.[35]

Ruettgers, an Oklahoma native and the oldest son of an Air Force officer, proved the perfect choice to instill a sense of discipline and a strict devotion to quality development within the company. Ruettgers grew up in five countries, packing up for a new place each time his father was given a different assignment. This may have instilled in him the cool, pragmatic detachment that allowed him to unsentimentally break with established ways of doing things and forge new paths—qualities that would prove instrumental to EMC's future success.[36]

Long before Ruettgers became a success in the business world, however, he underwent his own personal transformation. His first stint in college, as an engineering student on a Navy scholarship at the University of California, Los Angeles, ended in failure. He dropped out after spending more time playing bridge and pursuing girls than studying. "I had to come out the other side to develop some judgment and focus," he explained.[37]

Ruettgers brushed himself off, moved to Lacey, Washington, and enrolled at Saint Martin's University, then an all-male school known as Saint Martin's College. His grades distinctly improved, and he later transferred to Idaho State University. During those formative years, he read the *Wall Street Journal* religiously, promising himself he would one day be a CEO. His determination paid off, and he eventually earned an MBA from Harvard Business School. After graduation, he went to work at Raytheon Company, where he worked on the Patriot Missile program. After 10 years with the company, he rose through the ranks to become general manager. However, he left Raytheon after being told he would never become CEO without an engineering degree. Ruettgers then spent some time working at Keane, Inc., a business and information technology consulting firm, before becoming chief operating officer of Technical Financial Services.

Early on in his tenure at EMC, Ruettgers implemented a continuous improvement program developed by consultants at Conway Quality, Inc., aimed at eliminating waste, reducing costs, and improving quality throughout the company. He hired an outside continuous improvement consultant and ensured that all employees received training in Conway Quality Management techniques. Meanwhile, the newly established quality assurance organization standards ensured consistency throughout all stages of production, including the design, manufacturing, testing, shipping, and support stages.[38]

Ruettgers' organized approach proved to be just what the company needed. While drive, innovation, and dedication had helped EMC rise to prominence, an extra level of attention to quality and detail would be necessary to take the company to the next level. "We were bringing innovation into the company, [but] we had a [lack] of quality due to not hav-

ing a quality execution plan," explained veteran employee John Walton.[39]

Streamlining its efforts would help EMC earn original equipment manufacturer (OEM) contracts and better position the company to take on IBM, a goal that Ruettgers staunchly supported. Since leaving Harvard, Ruettgers had worked with many customers who relied on IBM mainframes. He and his management team soon realized that most of IBM's customers used only approximately 20 percent of their stored data on a daily basis; allowing customers to access that high-priority data faster would eventually prove a gold mine for EMC.[40]

**Gunning for the Market Leader**

EMC stepped up its efforts to expand into the IBM mainframe storage market in 1988, providing upgrades and a range of disk products compatible with IBM's popular 3090 systems. Intended to capture a sizable chunk of the storage market, the move was one of EMC's most expensive and extensive efforts at the time.[41] Orion, released in 1988, became one of EMC's most successful mainframe storage products. EMC designed Orion to resolve a long-standing frustration among computer users. Although dramatic strides had been made in pro-

The EMC OEM team gathers around a conference table in this 1989 photo. In front: Tom Knight. From left to right: Bob D'Errico, Tom Moore, Warner Hersey, Bonnie Bryce, Don O'Bryant, and Dave Guy.

cessing speed and data storage capacity, the ability of central processing units (CPUs) to access stored data had improved only slightly. The extra time necessary for mechanical components such as the heads that hover over rotating magnetic disks to find, read, and write data in traditional storage devices accounted for the discrepancy. EMC's disk subsystem designs included significantly expanded cache memory aimed at eliminating information bottlenecks. The design offered the capacity customers needed to safeguard their critical files, while allowing them the flexibility they needed to reassign system resources for enhanced performance.[42]

In June 1989, EMC signed a $100 million deal with StorageTek, a vendor of IBM-compatible tape storage systems, to serve as the exclusive distributor

The Orion solid state disk subsystem, introduced in 1988, stands at the Symmetrix museum at EMC's Hopkinton, Massachusetts, headquarters. The Orion was a precursor to the company's Symmetrix disk array storage systems.

of a special version of Orion featuring the industry's first four-megabyte RAM chip technology.[43] The four-megabyte chip stood in sharp contrast to the industry's standard one-megabyte chips, which EMC had also originally incorporated into its memory products before its competitors.[44]

Soon afterward, EMC improved on its standing as the only plug-compatible alternative to IBM's direct access storage devices by unveiling its SL935 and SL932 products. Not only were they fully compatible with IBM systems, they also included extra features such as self-diagnostics and automatic error threshold detection.[45]

The SL935 and SL932 were introduced to attach to IBM's S/38 and AS/400 midrange computers. As part of EMC's strategy, the company offered to trade new EMC systems for older IBM equipment, which was then brokered into the refurbished or used equipment market to cover EMC's costs and turn a profit. This swap strategy enabled EMC to go into an existing customer site and create a sales opportunity, even if that customer had no budget for memory or disk storage. It also allowed the company to build up an installation and reference base and gain credibility with customers that largely used IBM equipment. Both the SL935 and the SL932 products benefited from the stringent quality improvement measures Ruettgers pioneered.

EMC knew that being a significant contender to IBM required both price advantages and superior quality. The late Don Watson, former vice president of supply base engineering and longtime employee from 1989 to 2006, recalled in a 2004 interview:

*In those days, we were competing principally with IBM and we were trying to persuade the customers to buy our products, and it was a high-risk proposition. We offered affordable pricing, but if our gear didn't work, the buyer could actually be fired. So Dick [Egan]'s view was that we have to be better than IBM both on price and quality. It was strategically important for the company to develop our abilities in this space, and a lot of money was invested in doing that.[46]*

Carving a niche in IBM's mainframe market would take more than just a commitment to quality and innovative technology, however.

Above: The late Don Watson served as vice president of supply base engineering.

Right: Harold P. "Bob" Ano served as senior vice president of marketing during the 1990s.

In the face of reticent potential IBM customers, EMC pressed on with advances in its other markets. Its Allegro disk subsystem was similar to Orion but designed for the Prime Computer market. EMC also rolled out its MAXPORT disk subsystems for Digital Equipment Corporation's (DEC) VAX machines, allowing EMC to offer both main memory and disk storage systems in all of its markets.[49] The company also expanded its IBM midrange product line and introduced the SL/Series disk subsystems, featuring significantly enhanced price performance over EMC's first System/38-compatible disk subsystem.

### The Project in the Basement

Beating IBM, the market leader since the beginning of the computer age, required much more than marketing talent. While marketing would always play an important role at EMC, defeating Big Blue would require innovative ideas and a unique corps of engineers to execute them. Egan had already realized this by 1987, when he began recruiting talented engineers from around the globe to design EMC's IBM-compatible products. In the mid-1980s, one of

"We had a slight credibility problem," recalled Bob Ano, hired by Egan in 1990 to lead EMC's marketing efforts. "We had no track record on the mainframe disk drive side of the business, we were coming in with a radically different product to the most conservative guys in the world ... and we were trying to replace IBM."[47]

To tackle the image issue, Ano arranged focus groups of IT managers to explain how EMC's ideas could benefit their companies. Older executives, long-entrenched in IBM products, remained skeptical, while the younger ones, despite believing EMC's concepts held promise, were not ready to buy.[48] Ano recalled feeling like a child who announces he wants to be president, and is met with encouragement and condescension: "The attitude was, 'It's all very interesting, but no one will buy this.'"

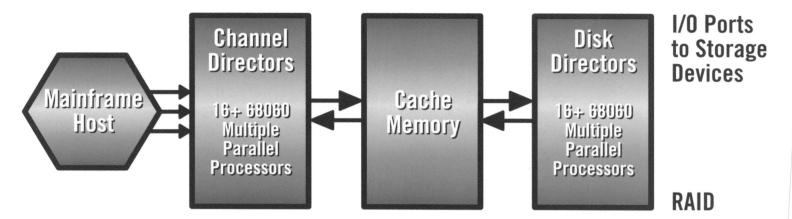

the largest suppliers of IBM-compatible products was a German-based company called Nixdorf, whose design engineers worked out of a small unit in Israel. After Nixdorf moved its Israeli operations unit to Burlington, Massachusetts, Egan wasted no time in persuading many of the engineers to relocate once again—to EMC.[50]

Each time Egan interviewed a potential recruit, he heard the name Moshe Yanai. Egan, curious about the engineer who had made such a dramatic impression on his recruits, decided he had to meet him. At the time, Yanai had been considering starting his own technology company. However, during their first meeting, Egan worked hard to convince Yanai to join EMC instead. "I was impressed by Dick and also by the spirit, the sales spirit, that I witnessed at EMC," Yanai said.[51]

Egan offered Yanai a position leading a team dedicated to developing a novel system of IBM-compatible direct access storage devices (DASD).[52] Yanai, a former tank division commander in the Israeli army, found the idea intriguing and joined EMC in August 1987 as an engineering manager. Egan gave the talented developer carte blanche in

planning the project, a trust that Yanai recalled with gratitude, "He supported me 100 percent—more than 100 percent."

Yanai assembled a team that included several engineers from Israel, longtime friends he felt comfortable working with. Together, Yanai and his team developed a new product based on the disk arrays characteristic of RAID technology. In this new system, which they called Integrated Cached Disk Arrays (ICDA), the disk arrays maintained an exceedingly large cache of available read/write high-speed memory, generally only used by computers to process instructions or hold temporary data. In traditional memory storage systems, data was written directly onto slower disk drives, only utilizing rapid access cache storage systems on a temporary basis while actively accessing and manipulating data. The ICDA system, on the other hand,

Above: In the late 1980s, EMC engineers began building Integrated Cached Disk Arrays (ICDAs), a novel architecture through which arrays of disk drives would provide a large amount of cache memory, significantly increasing computer performance.

Right: Moshe Yanai, a former tank division commander in the Israeli army, helped design a solid-state disk system that would be compatible with IBM.

benefited from powerful microprocessors, multiple drives, and newly developed algorithms, effectively allowing the entire array to act as one enormous memory cache, producing impressive gains in both speed and efficiency.

This platform made mass storage, for the first time, an equal partner with the CPU in overall system performance. And the ICDA platform was based on EMC's MOSAIC:2000 architecture, a framework into which improvements in basic technologies essential to creating storage products can be easily incorporated. The end result would be called Symmetrix, a storage system significantly faster than anything the competition had to offer, yet small enough to free up 40 percent more space over previous systems. The brilliance of the Symmetrix system was that it did all this while making use of technology that was already freely available. Instead of starting from scratch, Yanai and his development team combined relatively inexpensive components into an innovative product that would take the world by storm.[53]

Egan realized very early on in the project that Yanai and his team were on to something big, and he granted Yanai free rein.[54] As Steve Cerand, an engineer hired in 1989, explained, "Dick would essentially let Moshe do whatever he wanted. He would knock down as many roadblocks as possible."

However, even as Yanai and his team were working hard to develop the product that would make EMC an industry juggernaut, the rest of the company still struggled with the backlash from its malfunctioning disk drives. As David Donatelli recalled:

*So we're losing money. All this bad stuff is going on. And I run into Dick Egan in the bathroom one day. ... He looked at me, and he said, "Donatelli, I'm sick of you walking around with a frown on your face. Come to my office."*

*In his office, he said, "Hey, do you know what Moshe is working on in the basement? Symmetrix."*

*He pulled out a Gartner Group report that said ... no one else is going to have RAID technology until 1994. He told me we were going to get there ahead of everyone else—that we were going to sell a ton of these things, and we were all going to be rich."[55]*

EMC's emphasis on quality earned it certification for the prestigious ISO 9001 international quality standard. Its Cork, Ireland, facility was certified in 1991, and its Hopkinton, Massachusetts, facility the following year. The certification signified that EMC's quality and consistent reliability met the world's top standards. Shown here, Mike Ruettgers speaks at the awards ceremony.

### CHAPTER FOUR

# RETURN TO PROFITABILITY

## 1990–1994

*We're back to Brie and Chablis!*

—Roger Marino[1]

Aᴛ ᴛʜᴇ sᴛᴀʀᴛ ᴏғ ᴛʜᴇ ɴᴇᴡ ᴅᴇᴄᴀᴅᴇ, the groundwork that EMC had laid during the tumultuous late 1980s began to pay off. The company emerged from its crisis transformed into a leaner, smarter machine—driven, in great part, by Mike Ruettgers' commitment to drastically improving quality and implementing strict process standards throughout all aspects of the company. Even the company dress code changed, as certain departments distinguished themselves by wearing specific colors—green for the engineers and maroon for customer service employees.[2]

Ruettgers was promoted to president in 1990, with Egan continuing to serve as CEO. In his commitment to taking on IBM directly, Ruettgers also began wiping out product lines, especially those concentrating on the minicomputer market, a segment that had generated half of EMC's revenues up to that point but which depended on a declining industry segment.[3] Not everyone agreed with his decision, but Ruettgers firmly believed that to take the company in a new direction, he would have to go all the way, disconnecting EMC in some ways from its past.

Much of Ruettgers' zeal for sweeping changes had to do with the project in the basement—cabinet-size boxes of disk arrays that Moshe Yanai and his team of engineers spent their days and nights perfecting. As Ruettgers had hoped, the groundbreaking storage system known as Symmetrix would become the golden ticket to EMC's skyrocketing success in the next few years. At first, EMC's own employees did not understand the impact Symmetrix could have on the storage market.

"Nobody really, at least not myself, [had] any idea how big it was going to be," recalled Steve Cerand, who joined EMC in 1989.[4]

### Symmetrix

Although Ruettgers had done away with a sizable chunk of EMC's product line and implemented numerous changes, the philosophy that had served the company in its earlier days remained intact: Build products that are compatible with the major computing platforms, and offer superior performance at a lower price.

Yanai and his team followed that philosophy, while demonstrating the vision and innovation that would help take EMC to the next level. Anticipating the explosive growth in information that companies

---

The first generation Symmetrix 4200 and 4400 were introduced in 1990. They had a total drive capacity up to 24 gigabytes.

worldwide would soon face, the team designed a storage system capable of accessing data 200 times faster than the existing systems of the time.[5]

In September 1990, EMC unveiled the fruit of its years of labor—the Symmetrix ICDA storage system, so named for its symmetrical design. The 4200 and 4400 models, the first available, featured a capacity of 24 gigabytes, impressive for its time, and took up only 20 percent of the floor space that competing products required.[6]

Despite the impressive gains Symmetrix offered customers, the immediate reaction to its debut was less than favorable. When the product was launched in New York, only six analysts and no reporters showed up.[7] Symmetrix seemed so different at the outset from all of the preceding mainframe storage technology that EMC's competitors did not take it seriously. The idea of linking together inexpensive personal computer drives to provide viable mainframe storage seemed too absurd for any other provider to feel threatened. One StorageTek executive recalled:

*It looked like they were building a toy, not a system that anyone would want to hook up to their mainframes and rely upon for the storage of mission-critical information.*[8]

To attract customers at the beginning, EMC offered businesses free installation of Symmetrix systems on a trial basis.[9] After these companies realized the benefits Symmetrix could provide for them, they were hooked. One insurance company, for instance, used its free trial to process its year-end data, a task that normally took two weeks. With Symmetrix, the company completed it in three days.[10]

Since Symmetrix enabled users to access and organize data with greater ease and speed than other

This EMC Sales Club 101 meeting took place in Bermuda in 1990.

mainframe storage systems, banks and airlines, both of which store massive amounts of data, flocked to EMC's new product. Within a year of the debut of EMC's Symmetrix system, Delta Airlines and Security Pacific Bank would be counted among the many Symmetrix converts.[11]

According to Yanai, Symmetrix succeeded because he and his team focused on the real needs of EMC customers, eschewing marketing surveys that focused on what customers wanted in favor of his own investigation and instincts for what was truly essential in a storage product. Those instincts proved spot on. He explained:

*I knew what customers needed. It's not that they need cheap storage and protection. They need all of the features that really make storage work for*

*you, instead of you working for storage. They needed reliability, serviceability, performance, function, and many, many other features. There is a difference between what the customer wants and what the customer needs. ... Marketing and analyst statements, of course, focus on what the customer wants but the important thing is to determine what the customer needs.*

In September 1991, EMC introduced its Symmetrix ICDA platform for Unisys computers, extending the company's reach into yet another market segment. The product proved so popular that within six months, EMC and Unisys signed a $44 million agreement. Under the terms of the contract, Unisys sold Symmetrix systems directly to users of high-end Unisys 1100/2200 systems.[12]

By the end of 1991, financial analysts began betting on EMC to become the next hot stock. In its "Year Ahead" report, Merrill Lynch predicted that EMC "will have a complete family of disk arrays at a time when other companies will be first entering this expanding market."[13]

The success of Symmetrix was reflected in the company's bottom line: Its 1991 revenues reached more than $232 million, up 36 percent from 1990.[14]

**New Ways of Operating**

If the subsequent success of Symmetrix blindsided high-tech industry observers, it also came

Above: The engineers who brought enterprise storage to the world pose with their creation in 1990. (Left to right) Bruno Alterescu, Hana Moreshet, Danny Castel, Moshe Yanai, and Natan Vishlitzky.

Right: After it was released, Symmetrix ramped up quickly in terms of capability. The 4800 series offered a greater storage capacity than the original 4200 and 4400 systems.

# INVESTING IN RESEARCH AND DEVELOPMENT

UNVEILED IN 1990, SYMMETRIX WAS THE CULmination of EMC's new emphasis on research and development (R&D). That year, the company invested millions in an integrated product design and simulation system that allowed engineers to determine possible flaws in the Symmetrix design even before the prototype was manufactured. In the years since, research and development has remained a critical part of EMC's operations. The company's investment in research has only increased as EMC has grown into the world's leading developer of information infrastructure solutions.

In the early 1990s, EMC devoted its steadily increasing R&D expenditures to hiring and training its technical staff and purchasing state-of-the-art computer-aided design tools. The opening of its R&D facility in Israel in 1993, the rollout of its Harmonix line for AS/400 systems, and the establishment of an Open Systems Storage Division also took up a large portion of EMC's R&D budget. In 1992, 1993, and 1994, R&D expenditures represented 8.7 percent, 7.5 percent, and 8.6 percent of revenue respectively—meaning that as the company's revenues jumped from year to year, so did the amount it spent on R&D.[1]

As the 1990s progressed, R&D served as the foundation of the company's meteoric success. The network-attached storage and enterprise storage systems it would unveil later in the decade—along with its forays into software—could all be directly attributed to EMC's rigorous design and testing procedures, as well as a staff representing some of the most talented, storage-focused engineers in the world. As the decade came to a close, EMC's already large investment in R&D as a percentage of revenue increased. For 1998, 1999, and 2000, the num-

as a surprise to many of EMC's own employees as well. Paul Noble, former executive vice president of products and offerings, recalled that it took some time for the new reality to set in. He explained:

*Back then, I don't think anybody could have known that EMC was going to be what it is now; as a matter of fact, we weren't even in the business we're in now. ... You could tell we had great leadership, and I already knew that anything Dick Egan touched turned to gold. So I was happy to be there. I don't think it was until Mike Ruettgers had been there for a couple of years that we really thought that EMC had the possibility of being not just big, and not just "doing well," but of becoming an important company.[15]*

Symmetrix was the culmination of many changes that had taken place behind the scenes at EMC in the years leading up to its release, including the intensified focus that came from Ruettgers' decision to decrease the number of products EMC offered. Symmetrix also represented a significant increase in research and development investment at EMC, an emphasis that would continue to serve the company well in the future.

"Back then, we had a lot of different things going on—we were trying out many different things and seeing what would succeed," recalled Mike Sgrosso, who joined EMC's engineering team in 1987. "When we have one thing that we're allowed to work on, such as Symmetrix, everyone is focused, which is an advantage."[16]

Ruettgers implemented a program known as Materials Resource Planning (MRP) to tighten operations and help the company eliminate wasteful overstock. According to Maureen Clancy, who was chosen to head MRP planning in 1990, the program allowed "EMC to forecast more upfront,

### Technology's Top R&D Spenders
#### 2007

| Rank | Company | Spending |
|---|---|---|
| 1 | Microsoft | $ 7,420,000,000 |
| 2 | IBM | $ 6,153,000,000 |
| 3 | Intel | $ 5,755,000,000 |
| 4 | Cisco | $ 4,730,000,000 |
| 5 | Hewlett-Packard | $ 3,632,000,000 |
| 6 | Oracle | $ 2,496,000,000 |
| 7 | SAP | $ 2,296,330,000 |
| 8 | Google | $ 2,120,000,000 |
| 9 | Sun Microsystems | $ 1,937,000,000 |
| 10 | Advanced Micro Devices | $ 1,847,000,000 |
| 11 | EMC | $ 1,526,928,000 |
| 12 | Yahoo | $ 1,084,000,000 |
| 13 | Seagate | $ 939,000,000 |
| 14 | Symantec | $ 890,000,000 |
| 15 | Apple | $ 844,000,000 |

Source: CIO Zone

As a technology company, EMC's philosophy has been: "In good times and bad, in sickness and in health … spend on R&D."

bers were 9 percent, 9.6 percent, and 9.8 percent, respectively.[2]

When the company fell on hard times during the dot-com crash at the beginning of the millennium, new CEO Joe Tucci wisely refused to pull back the company's R&D spending. In fact, Tucci has maintained, and in some cases enhanced, EMC's R&D funding to help the company extend its product technology edge. In 2006, that figure topped 10 percent of revenues as the company added to its global development centers in the United States, France, Belgium, Israel, India, and China.[3]

EMC consistently opens its new development centers in places with large pools of engineering talent, designed to foster collaboration. According to Rona Newmark, senior vice president of global sourcing and development:

*The global development centers are some of the few locations at EMC where engineering teams from multiple product lines work side by side, share laboratory space, and share office space.[4]*

In 2007, EMC opened a development center in St. Petersburg, Russia, the site of one of the world's fastest-growing information technology markets.[5] By 2008, nearly 12 percent of revenue was spent on R&D—$1.7 billion.

to plan orders, and to know what the customer expectations were."[17]

Ruettgers selected nearly 700 people to receive special certification training for the program—the majority of EMC employees at the time. EMC also purchased design and simulation software that would allow engineers to eliminate production flaws before they became an issue and reduce the transition time between the planning and manufacturing stages. Thanks in part to the strict new quality controls Ruettgers helped establish, EMC received ISO certification from the International Organization for Standardization for both its Cork, Ireland, and Hopkinton, Massachusetts, facilities—the first American storage company to reach such a milestone.[18]

EMC's new tightly controlled methodology also influenced its external relationships. Around the time EMC released its first Symmetrix system, it began establishing micronetworks, close ties with suppliers that enabled EMC to better control its manufacturing costs and the quality of its finished products. In an example of a micronetwork arrangement, EMC engineers worked hand in hand with its Symmetrix disk drive supplier, California-based Seagate Technology, Inc., to help avoid any future manufacturing problems.[19]

Precis Metals, Inc., the Maine-based company that supplied the cabinets for Symmetrix, also worked very closely with EMC. According to Chuck Caron, Precis Metals' president and director of operations, his employees "lived at EMC before any metal was cut or shaped."[20]

The close-knit mutual cooperation even allowed suppliers to negotiate lead times for the components needed to build products for EMC.[21] Because EMC's products were manufactured within its own micronetworks, and the implementation of standardized procedures helped the company avoid waste, EMC was able to reduce the number of its facilities and avoid faltering under the weight of excessive manufacturing costs.

Yet, as Michael Schoonover, EMC's senior vice president of operations at the time, noted in *Electronic Business Buyer*, the close working relationships proved too challenging for some suppliers:

> *We go through a period where potential suppliers just don't get it, where it does not compute. There are some shops that never do get it—where they are too traditional and we can't work with them. Other suppliers, meanwhile, regarded the arrangements as beneficial; in exchange for disclosing financial data, inventory levels, and information on their suppliers to EMC, they gained a steady and reliable stream of business.[22]*

### "The Storage Architects"

By early 1992, EMC had set itself squarely on its new path. Ruettgers, having served as president since 1990, was offered a promotion to CEO—a title he "earned in so many ways," Dick Egan said.[23] Egan

realized that Ruettgers' more formal and structured management style was exactly what the new, larger EMC needed. And if there were some who had at first remained skeptical of the company's transformation under Ruettgers, all of EMC had by now rallied behind him. As Maureen Clancy recalled:

> *He was very well respected, cool, and calm. Never showed any type of stress. Good to his people. Treated everyone fairly. Just extremely well respected, the best leader I've ever had the opportunity to work for.[24]*

Although EMC continued supplying main memory upgrades for IBM's AS/400 and System/38 computers, the company now focused more on its Symmetrix systems and its Champion Integrated Cached Tape Arrays, designed to improve backup functions and reduce backup times. Along with the new focus came a new tagline: "EMC—The Storage Architects."

In April 1992, EMC expanded on its success with Symmetrix with the introduction of the Harmonix Integrated Cached Disk Array for the midrange IBM AS/400 market. Harmonix, which was released at around the same time that competitors began unveiling similar products, immediately garnered accolades from industry analysts. That October, the *Computerworld* Buyers' Scorecard placed Harmonix above all of its competitors, noting the product's overall performance and reliability, as well as the responsiveness of EMC's customer service.[25]

Above right: Members of the EMC Boston-based sales team. From left to right: John Hand, Larry Murray, Chip Aldondi, Bob Scordino, and Bill Scannell.

Below: Members of the Symmetrix engineering team. Standing (left to right): Roman Shulman, Phil Rosegay, Tim Mulvihill, John Fitzgerald, Danny Castel, Shai Hass, Haim Koplovitz, Haim Avni, and Bruno Alterescu. Seated (left to right): Natan Vishlitzky, Simcha Ran, Bill Therrien, and Greg Vanderpoel.

EMC also began to receive recognition beyond industry circles, gaining broader attention from the general public. In early 1992, John Markoff, a technology reporter at the *New York Times*, wrote:

> *EMC provides a striking example of how a small American company, with careful strategic planning and attention to manufacturing detail, can succeed by finding profitable, high-technological niches with huge growth potential.*[26]

And in June of that year, the *Boston Globe* named EMC to its list of the top 10 fastest-growing companies in Massachusetts, noting in particular Ruettgers' bold gamble in shifting the company's direction.[27]

The company's success was also reflected in its revenue growth. Revenues for 1992 rose to

Above and below: By 1991, EMC's revolutionary storage structure inspired a new company tagline: "EMC—The Storage Architects."

# EMC$^2$
# THE STORAGE ARCHITECTS

$385 million, up 50 percent from 1991. By 1993, revenues had increased an astonishing 103 percent over the previous year.[28] Even in the midst of a worldwide recession, analysts' recommendations and brisk sales enabled the company to significantly expand its international presence. In addition to its North American and European direct sales sites, EMC forged distribution agreements in Europe, Asia, South America, Africa, and the Middle East.[29] In June 1993, EMC opened a research and development facility in Israel, joining high-tech giants Intel, IBM, Microsoft, and Motorola.[30] From

around 1,500 employees at the end of 1992, the company increased its worldwide head count to 2,300 during 1993. The company's continued emphasis on compensating hard work and innovation yielded impressive productivity gains—more than $400,000 in revenue per employee that year.[31]

### A Sense of Urgency

For all its newfound success, the company inevitably experienced some growing pains. For one, there was a shift in mentality. "Obviously I think the big thing is the transformation from a very small, entrepreneurial, very flexible company to more of a traditional corporation where you have a lot of process," explained Peter Simmons, who was hired as a manufacturing technician in 1987.[32] "It seems more of that corporate stereotype ... where before [EMC] was much more fluid. Things would get done much quicker. It was kind of that young, start-up attitude."

Longtime employee Jude Pellegrini described the camaraderie at EMC: "Everybody mingled; everybody used everybody's first names. No one went out of their way to say, 'I'm the president, I'm the vice president.' It didn't really matter."

The bonds that longtime employees felt in the earlier days stretched thinner, according to Lennie Demarco, who started with EMC in 1984:

*I think up until we became a public company, it was like a family, and everybody knew everybody else. Because we grew so rapidly, after we became public, [we] came up with a lot of new products, [and] I think*

Top: Longtime employee Jude Pellegrini has always enjoyed the camaraderie at EMC.

Bottom: Laura Aubut (formerly Perkins) started at EMC in 1984. She appreciated Egan's personal touch as he led the company he co-founded.

*we started to see that we could not be in the same buildings anymore, and Dick [Egan] couldn't speak to everybody all at once. And I know Dick always wanted to have people together, [but] it got to a point where we could not be together. ... That total understanding of the business kind of went away, because now you had groups that were located in other towns.[33]*

At the same time, even with the greater emphasis on process in the company, there remained a degree of freedom to chart one's own path—to contribute what one could do best. Technology, including internal Web sites and a heavier reliance on electronic communication, would serve as a strong glue for the company, keeping disparate units aware of what others were doing and helping to cement the company culture.

Meanwhile, Egan, now chairman of the board, strove to provide the same level of motivation that had propelled the company out of its infancy, even with employees based in separate sites. According to Laura Aubut, who started at EMC in 1984, "Dick [Egan] always sort of made you feel like, no matter what you do, you're very important to this company. He knew everyone by name, and he had something funny to say about someone all the time. ... I think he gave a lot of encouragement to people."

That encouragement helped employees see projects through when they stretched late into the night. "I think we just believed in Egan, we believed in Ruettgers, and everyone just banded together," Senior Vice President Bill Raftery explained. "We had a great time together."

Josh Onffroy, an engineer who arrived at EMC in 1993 after graduating from Worcester Polytechnic Institute, recalled Egan walking the manufacturing floors with a cash-filled briefcase, betting engineers that they could not accomplish particularly difficult feats, or meet aggressive

# THE RISE OF THE INFORMATION ENTERPRISE

URING THE MID-1990s, THE BUSINESS WORLD experienced a profound shift in priorities. Tangible goods and services, long considered key to business success, began losing ground to a different sort of commodity—information. In this new market reality, the best companies were no longer the biggest, but the fastest: those that could rapidly develop and deliver new products, fulfill orders as fast and efficiently as possible, and provide the speediest, most comprehensive customer service.[1]

Businesses also realized that the workday could no longer be contained between the hours of 9 A.M. and 5 P.M. In an increasingly connected global marketplace, survival often depended on the ability to offer round-the-clock information availability. On-demand access to constantly updated information developed into a top priority for businesses, including airlines in need of up-to-the-minute travel notifications, banks requiring instant retrieval of all transaction histories, and transportation companies tracking deliveries. Tracking data and streamlining information processes now took on overriding importance.

EMC anticipated these needs before any other company and focused its resources on helping companies make the most of their information. In addition to continually improving its existing mainframe storage products, EMC offered customers new ways to connect information housed on disparate servers running variants of UNIX and network operating systems, allowing customers to link together data regardless of whether it resided on mainframes or open systems platforms. Open, intelligent, flexible information storage served as the foundation for the new marketplace, and EMC stood at the vanguard of the information revolution.

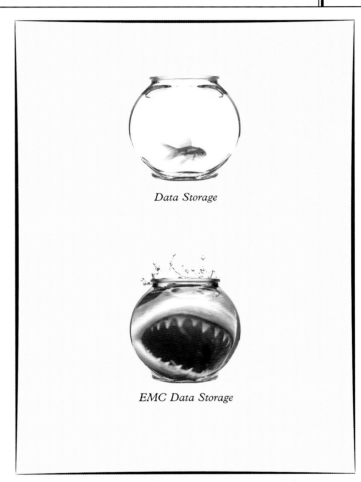

*Data Storage*

*EMC Data Storage*

*While ordinary storage just sits, EMC storage thinks, moves and distributes your data. Quickly devouring your competitors.*

**EMC²**
THE STORAGE ARCHITECTS

EMC's Harmonix for IBM AS/400 systems was released to industry acclaim in April 1992.

deadlines, in an effort to inspire them to push themselves harder:

*He would call out your name and you'd walk up and shake his hand. If you were actually working on the product, in development, you could bet him and he'd pay you 10 to one. You could win more than a thousand dollars. ... We would be here until eleven o'clock at night two or three days a week for weeks and weeks and weeks.*[34]

That attitude remained true even as EMC spread across the globe. Malte Rademacher, former marketing manager for EMC Germany and a DEC veteran, served as one of the first employees in EMC's German office in 1993. "We had from the beginning very strong technical people who could create confidence on the customer side, create the confidence that the product was working, and the customer service people coming in and fixing any problems," he said.[35]

By this time, EMC had begun making considerable gains on IBM. In 1993, EMC became the lead-

ing independent supplier of disk array technology within the computer industry, as well as the leading independent supplier of disk storage for IBM midrange systems.[36]

In the summer of 1993, EMC acquired Magna Computer Corporation, which specialized in tape storage technology for IBM AS/400 systems. The acquisition complemented EMC's Harmonix disk system, as well as its memory upgrade products, allowing EMC to offer even more robust storage options for AS/400 users. Around the same time, client/server computing had come into vogue as corporations began moving away from centralized repositories for storing information and focusing instead on computing and storing information within individual departments. To help broaden its ability to follow the changing trends in computer technology, in July 1993, EMC acquired Epoch Systems, based in Westborough, Massachusetts. Epoch developed storage management software for client/server systems. After the acquisition, EMC established a Client/Server Division to apply ICDA technology to this emerging paradigm.

Along with increased success came greater responsibility, particularly on the customer service front. As Yanai explained, customers needed their systems to work continuously. According to Yanai, this required employees to remain constantly ready to resolve problems, "even in the middle of the night, even if you're [on] vacation."[37]

"Engineers and machines were fallible," he added, "and what mattered was that systems could be back up and running again quickly after experiencing a problem."

Even as EMC grew so rapidly, the company did not have time to stop and congratulate itself. Egan had used the healthy paranoia about the competition instilled in him while working with Andy Grove at Intel to motivate employees to continuously top themselves since EMC's early days. The staff of the new and improved EMC continued that tradition, realizing that they could not afford to rest on their laurels, regardless of the company's success. Many employees speak of a sense of urgency, a feeling that there is always much to be done, which, instead of making them panic, constantly keeps them productive.

### Keeping in Touch

As EMC expanded into a truly global company, responding to customer requests had become considerably more complicated compared to the early days, when a phone conversation with a University of Rhode Island scientist inspired Egan to build EMC's first computer product. To ensure that EMC could effectively capture and channel customer requirements, the company called its first Customer Council in 1993. The first meeting drew 25 customers and allowed EMC to assess its product features and better understand how its products fulfilled customer needs.[38] In subsequent years, the company would hold four or five such meetings annually in the United States, Europe, and Asia, each meeting bringing in as many as 80 EMC customers, with participants ranging from people launching Internet start-ups to executives at leading banks.[39]

"Nondisruptive upgrades—the ability to upgrade microcode or software without having to bring the storage frame down, was the No. 1 item at Customer Council for three years running," said

### Quarterly Report Card for Q1 1994

| Department | Results | Comments |
| --- | --- | --- |
| Finance | 5/5 | Year end audit |
| Marketing | 4/5 | Field support contract |
| U.S. Sales | 5/5 | Bookings |
| European Sales | 5/5 | Bookings |
| PacRim Sales | 5/5 | Tokyo office |
| OEM Sales | 4/6 | Bookings |
| Quality Assurance | 5/5 | Re-engineering studies |
| Operations | 3/5 | 0-90 day reliability |
| Customer Service | 5/5 | International Plug & Play rates |
| MIS | 4/5 | |
| Human Resources | 3/4 | Open requisition backlog |
| *Subtotal* | *48/55* | |
| Mainframe LOB | 4/5 | ESCON betas |
| Midrange LOB | 5/6 | EMC Direct |
| Client Server LOB | 3/5 | Industrial design |
| Epoch LOB | 5/6 | Revenue |
| *Subtotal* | *17/22* | |
| *Total* | *65/77 = .884* | |
| Prior Q4 | 69/88 = .784 | |
| Prior Q3 | 60/67 = .896 | |
| Prior Q2 | 55/71 = .775 | |

Above: From the beginning, EMC held people and departments accountable for quarterly goals and reported on this performance to all employees at quarterly review meetings.

Below: Throughout the 1990s, EMC experienced rapid growth as the necessity to safeguard expanding volumes of critical information became increasingly important to businesses worldwide. In 1993, EMC was named to the FORTUNE® 500 list of companies with the biggest sales increases and best investment opportunities. EMC scored third in both categories.

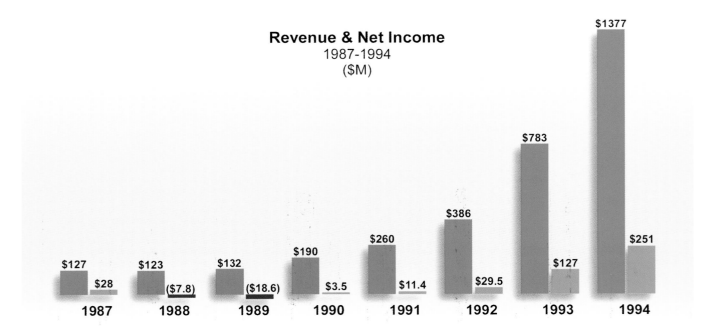

**Revenue & Net Income**
1987-1994
($M)

1987: $127 / $28
1988: $123 / ($7.8)
1989: $132 / ($18.6)
1990: $190 / $3.5
1991: $260 / $11.4
1992: $386 / $29.5
1993: $783 / $127
1994: $1377 / $251

# SURVEYING THE STORAGE LANDSCAPE OF THE 1990s

IN THE EARLY 1990s, EMC COMPETED WITH MANY storage providers, including Hitachi, Amdahl, StorageTek, and, of course, IBM. While each company differed in its approach to handling information storage, they all offered devices compatible with the IBM systems that dominated the mainframe and midrange computer marketplace.

IBM, as the CPU provider, had an inherent advantage in producing compatible storage devices. Because it designed the entire system, IBM could begin planning for a computer's storage needs long before it ever came to market. This resulted in market share dominance that was, for a long time, unsurpassed; in 1990, IBM controlled 76 percent of the mainframe disk subsystem market.[1]

IBM's competitors fervently devised data storage solutions that followed the storage standards set by IBM, while altering the mechanisms enough to differentiate themselves from the computer giant. StorageTek, for instance, spent much of the late 1980s and early 1990s focusing on its Iceberg system, which aimed to improve data management by storing information wherever there was room on disks, instead of keeping it in complete blocks on designated drives, as was the norm for IBM.[2]

Symmetrix, on the other hand, represented a completely different approach to storage, one that would set the standard for the field in the years following its release and in fact create a new industry for truly independent storage. Although EMC's competitors at first doubted the suitability of a string of 5¼-inch disks as a mainframe storage system, they soon began trying to design similar products.

Even Big Blue bowed down to the storage prowess of EMC's Symmetrix system. In September 1992, IBM released a version of its 9340 drive based on the smaller disk set up.[3] As the storage race progressed, other companies such as Compaq Computer Corporation, Data General, Sun Microsystems, and Digital attempted to hold on to their own customer base during the first half of the 1990s by offering more competitive disk arrays.[4] Data General and DEC began offering storage that could attach to other server types, seeing the same potential EMC did.

Meanwhile, the tension between centralizing and decentralizing data started shaping the storage market in new ways. Data began to move away from centralized repositories and toward departmental UNIX servers and personal computers in an attempt to more effectively manage departmental information and meet deadlines.[5] Yet, by the early 1990s, decentralization had already become an unwieldy proposition, as the data scattered on departmental servers often suffered from a lack of uniform protection from outages and data loss.[6]

A new storage market serving open systems was born. EMC led the pack with its Symmetrix 3000 family for open systems, released in June 1995.

Although having two separate types of systems for mainframe storage and open storage made sense at the time, heterogenous enterprise storage would emerge—EMC's next revolutionary approach to storage capable of supporting mainframe and open systems data on a single platform.

For one of EMC's most important product launches ever, Ruettgers and his team went to San Francisco, breaking a long-held tradition of making major company announcements to financial analysts and major customers in New York. The logic was twofold. First, EMC's initial attempt at an open storage disk array, the November 1994 launch of Centriplex in New York, had created a lot of attention but the product was slow to be embraced by customers. EMC's meteoric stock price appreciation had stalled in the first half of 1995, as investors worried whether the company could expand its available market beyond the slow-growth mainframe market. Unbeknownst to the public, EMC had an internal competitor to Centriplex in Moshe Yanai's labs in Hopkinton. The company needed "Open Sym," as the Symmetrix 3000 series was dubbed, to make a big splash and get some early momentum in the open systems marketplace.

Second, Silicon Valley was the home of most players who would be both competitors and partners for EMC in open storage. Public support from the major independent database software providers would be a big credibility boost, since EMC was largely unknown among this new potential base of customers. To underscore the game-changing potential of Symmetrix 3000, EMC invited executives from Oracle, Informix, and Sybase—themselves bitter rivals—to appear onstage at the launch and endorse this new approach to storing and protecting large data warehouses. Each database company initially balked at appearing onstage, not because of EMC, but because they normally never appeared alongside each other. But the power of EMC's

potential value to their own ambitions for terabyte-scale databases overwhelmed those concerns; none of them wanted to see their rivals gain an upper hand in the minds of customers for partnering with EMC. Industry observers suggested it was the first time Oracle, Informix, and Sybase all appeared on a stage together to agree on anything.

As word of EMC's Open Symmetrix launch reached Wall Street from the West Coast, the verdict was swift. EMC shares closed at an all-time high that day. The newswire photo of Ruettgers at the podium in San Francisco appeared in full color on the front page of the *Boston Globe* business section the next day. It was another indication that EMC had arrived. Mark Fredrickson, hired from Digital in January 1995 to run public relations, recalled the plane ride home from San Francisco. "Mike opened *Computerworld* and pointed to a full page ad from Sun Microsystems," said Fredrickson. "The ad boasted of the data warehouses reaching a few hundred gigabytes. We had just told the world, with the top database software providers there to support us, that terabyte-size data warehouses would emerge and EMC would be the only provider that could handle them. Mike smiled in a way that told you he knew something the rest of the market didn't."

EMC's Symmetrix product line offers customers near-instantaneous access to their important data. Thanks to the company's innovative solutions, EMC continually gained an increasingly larger share of the mainframe direct access storage device market, ultimately surpassing its rival IBM.

William "B. J." Jenkins, senior vice president and, at the time, head of global marketing. "It became part of our road map out of that."

These meetings have guided EMC as it has expanded its focus outside of products and into solutions. And, especially in more recent years, as EMC has made more acquisitions, the meetings have helped inspire new ways to integrate acquired companies.

EMC had also begun to attract a committed group of investors. They came from highly varied walks of life, and some showed surprising devotion to the company. "They were loyal, passionate people," said Polly Pearson, vice president of global investor relations at the time. She added:

The license plate belonging to EMC investor Mark Mendlen demonstrated shareholders' devotion to the company.

*These people were just grassroots spokespeople and advocates. We had one set of guys down in New Jersey who had a shrine in their house with photographs of Mike Ruettgers and Dick Egan, and they'd light candles. Their license plates were EMC. They had the EMC boat. They'd drive up to our annual meetings like it was the Second Coming with their Mercedes with the EMC plates on it. They'd sit in the front row. They gave quotes to newspapers. They sent us cakes at product launches—custom cakes.*[40]

### Open Systems Storage

Having taken its first steps into client/server environments, EMC deepened its focus on storage for open systems. With the decentralization of company-wide information and the promise of less expensive computing environments, UNIX servers manufactured by Digital, Hewlett-Packard, Sun Microsystems, IBM, and others began to house data with individual departmental "servers."[41] While these separate servers offered a certain degree of freedom within companies, they were ill-suited to handle the ever-increasing amounts of information storage required of modern businesses. These server manufacturers had their own storage systems, one disk array for each server, which were outmatched by the growing volumes of data and the rising importance of the applications to the business. These small arrays were actually known as JBOD, for "just a bunch of disks," because they lacked the intelligence

and software functionality that was becoming standard in mainframe environments. Systems often crashed, and data would be lost. Stable, large-scale storage systems were needed. This requirement presented yet another opportunity for EMC.[42]

A meeting between Ruettgers and an IT manager at John Deere inspired EMC's first steps into open systems storage. Enraged that his warnings to his colleagues about the perils of decentralized computing were being ignored, the John Deere IT manager had been further infuriated when they came crawling back and asked him to help them switch back to a centralized data center.[43] In the man's frustration, Ruettgers saw opportunity. EMC soon began developing a system that could store data simultaneously from different servers running UNIX and network operating systems.

The company established a separate open systems division in the nearby town of Milford, Massachusetts, in September 1993. Neal Waddington, formerly a senior vice president at Tandem Computers, was hired to lead the division; Waddington, in turn, hired computer industry veterans to fill the engineering and marketing departments. In November 1994, the division unveiled Centriplex, the industry's first open storage system designed to centrally manage data from disparate UNIX-based platforms.[44]

Under pressure from investors to enter new markets, Ruettgers made a bold prediction at the Centriplex launch: EMC's goal was $200 million in revenues from open systems storage in 1995. Little did they know that his plan called for more than just Centriplex to capture such lofty first-year success.

Back in Hopkinton, engineers began working on a line of Symmetrix systems for the open storage market.[45] Once again, Ruettgers' unique vision paid off. EMC's open systems storage products would rake in $200 million in 1995. Sales reached an astonishing $800 million by 1996.[46]

Creating a viable open systems product meant ensuring it would work with different products, a challenge that EMC engineers embraced. As Doc D'Errico, vice president and general manager of infrastructure software, explained:

*Interoperability is really about driving through the standards that are out there to define interoperability and taking them really to the next level, defining how they really work.*

*Not just if things work ... but do they work, and how do they work? What happens? We try to stress these environments. We define envelopes for how things work. We define limits for scalability, complexity, heterogeneity, and we just push the limits until they break, and then we look at what our customers do and ask "is this good enough?"*

*To us, "good enough" just isn't the same level. It means that we have to be beyond what the customers want to do. If the customer wants to run 10 thousand devices on his system, we're going to run 15 thousand to 20 thousand devices on that system and stay ahead of that. If the customer wants to put 500 systems in a network, we're going to put 700 to 1,000 systems in a network and make sure that we can create the best possible environment for the customer to run their systems on.[47]*

Although separate storage for mainframes and open systems was the only approach in the early 1990s, on the

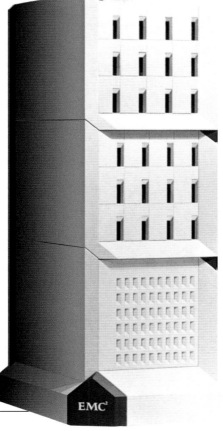

horizon, a new trend in storage promised to blend the best of both worlds, offering reliable data management, regardless of whether that data resided on a mainframe or an open system. EMC called this "enterprise storage," and it would once again set the company apart from its competitors as the decade wore on.

### Saving Data

While the industry around it was known as the computer industry, EMC had long ago recognized the true importance of storage and had staked its future on protecting and providing access to the valuable data that allows businesses and organizations to thrive in the new digital economy. The company also recognized the importance of backing up data, so that in the event of an outage or malfunction, irreplaceable data would not be lost and access to it would be as timely as needed by the customer.

Yanai and his engineers developed a system that prevented bottlenecks and allowed for the replication of large amounts of data in real time, while correctly maintaining the data sequences at high performance standards. "It was all about optimizing system resources and taking into consideration all the things that a storage system needs to make remote mirroring happen in the right way," Yanai explained.[48]

After Symmetrix Remote Data Facility (SRDF) debuted in October 1994, customers around the world quickly embraced the system. Even people far from the site of the World Trade Center bombing in 1993 understood the implications in an increasingly digital world. Being able to retrieve vital digital information in the midst of a disaster, or even just

In 1994, EMC released Centriplex, the world's first open storage system designed to manage data across multiple UNIX-based platforms. The product never took off, but its existence sparked the internal competition that led to "Open Symmetrix."

during an unplanned outage, would prove invaluable to businesses and organizations of all kinds.

SRDF soon became a staple of financial institutions across the globe, and EMC would continue to improve on the product in the years that followed. When disaster struck the World Trade Center again in 2001, this time on a more devastating scale, the critical information of EMC's customers would be safe and accessible.

### Scaling New Heights

EMC had gained tremendous ground at the outset of the decade, and by 1994, everyone in the industry knew the company's name. Far from the fledgling start-up it had once been, EMC received its first FORTUNE® 500 ranking in April 1994, entering the list at 412. Boston's two most widely read newspapers, the *Boston Globe* and the *Boston Herald*, gave the company top billing in their lists of the best Massachusetts businesses.

"Today [EMC] pulls off something akin to an Academy Awards sweep," *Boston Globe* business reporter Aaron Zitner wrote in a May 17, 1994, article describing the achievements that had earned EMC its ranking.

Besides being named the state's best-performing publicly traded company, EMC topped the paper's list of Massachusetts' 50 fastest-growing companies, as measured by profit and sales increases, and was the state's top stock market gainer on account of its soaring share price.[49]

EMC followed up these accolades by providing increasingly advanced storage offerings. Its

Massachusetts Governor William Weld, flanked by then EMC Chairman Dick Egan (left) and then EMC President and CEO Mike Ruettgers (right), attends the ribbon-cutting ceremony marking the opening of EMC's facility in Milford, Massachusetts, in 1994.

Symmetrix 5500-9, known as the "terabyte box" and released in May 1994, boasted the largest mainframe storage capacity in the industry at the time, allowing customers to store an unprecedented 1 trillion bytes of data in a single system. With each new release, Symmetrix sales multiplied, netting more and more customers across a variety of industries.

In 1994, Symmetrix sales to telecommunications companies jumped 500 percent over the previous year, with customers including AT&T, MCI, and British Telecom.[50] For its Harmonix system, meanwhile, EMC was named the leading independent AS/400 storage provider by the market research firm International Data Corporation. *Computerworld* called Harmonix the No. 1 AS/400 storage device in 1994, as it had two years earlier.

In 1994, EMC reached another impressive milestone, with revenues topping $1 billion for the first time. It seemed that things couldn't be better.

The introduction of EMC's Enterprise Storage line of products in 1995 also inaugurated a strategic new shift in identity.

### CHAPTER FIVE

# THE FAST-PACED LIFE OF A NEW MARKET LEADER

## 1995–1997

*I compare my job to sitting on a wild horse. It's a combination of fun and panic. You know where you're heading and why you want to get there, but you also know there'll be moments to test your skill, determination, and flexibility.*

—Mike Ruettgers[1]

THE YEAR 1995 PROVED PIVOTAL FOR EMC. Throughout the previous five years, EMC had experienced tremendous gains in both top- and bottom-line growth. However, EMC's greatest feat that year would have seemed unimaginable during the company's early days. In 1995, EMC finally overtook longtime leader IBM in the mainframe storage market.

When EMC sold its first Symmetrix system in 1990, the company only reached 0.2 percent of the mainframe disk subsystem market in terms of terabytes shipped, compared with IBM's 76 percent share. In only five years, EMC's market share catapulted to 38.2 percent, compared with IBM's 35.2 percent.[2] Mainframe storage was a small part of IBM's total business, but EMC's dramatic rise had huge symbolic importance and provided tremendous motivation to EMC employees.

By 1995, EMC's revenues reached $1.92 billion, a 10-fold increase over the $189 million it pulled in for 1990, representing a compound annual growth rate of 58.87 percent.[3] The company's $327 million in net income for 1995, compared with its 1990 figure of $3.5 million, represented an astonishing compound annual growth rate of 147.4 percent.[4]

Right around the time EMC and IBM swapped places, Dick Egan had begun engaging in some not entirely good-natured jousting with James Vanderslice, who had recently been appointed to revive IBM's floundering storage division. A sign of the division's struggles was the delayed release, due to engineering glitches, of its RAMAC 2 disk array—the product meant to help IBM regain ground it had lost to EMC.[5] Perhaps to boost the morale of his team, Vanderslice sent out an internal memo stating that IBM, nicknamed Big Blue, would soon "stick EMC in the eye with a hot poker."

The incendiary correspondence found its way to EMC and into Egan's hands.[6] Egan wasted no time in sending a brass fireplace poker to Vanderslice via Federal Express, with his own note attached:

*I understand you've implored your troops to stick EMC in the eye with a hot poker. Enclosed is a fireplace poker. Rest assured we'll supply the heat.*[7]

Egan also found other creative ways of antagonizing his chief rival—via its customers. He would send those who refused to consider another vendor blue underwear with "IBM" stenciled on the bottom. Although some recipients didn't appreciate the message, many found the joke humorous and eventually

---

CEO Mike Ruettgers led EMC through a period of remarkable growth during the late 1990s.

gave EMC a chance to make a sales pitch.[8] Always relishing a good gag, Egan even sent a pair of boxer shorts to IBM CEO Louis Gerstner.[9] This sort of taunting earned EMC a reputation among IBM employees, who worked for a company with a very different corporate culture.

According to Stacey Yeoman, who worked at IBM for 20 years beginning in the 1980s and joined EMC in 2005, "IBM would sometimes move slowly, but EMC is very quick if you really want to get something done. I think that is probably the most dramatic difference."

### A New Industry Is Born

Surpassing IBM heralded many more changes to come for EMC. Storage, which had long been an afterthought, had become exceedingly important to companies—a strategic technology in its own right. In the past, customers had only expected storage systems to serve as peripheral containers. Older systems had been fraught with reliability and information availability problems. However, as companies handled ever-growing amounts of increasingly complex data, they needed a scalable storage infrastructure capable of accommodating any unforeseen rise in their information needs. EMC was the first company to recognize these new market realities.

According to Gil Press, a marketing manager in EMC's early network-attached storage phase and then director of corporate information in the late 1990s:

Right: Gil Press, director of corporate information in the late 1990s, was part of the effort to make EMC synonymous with storage.

Below left: In 1995, EMC surpassed IBM to become the leader of the mainframe storage market—a watershed event for the once-fledgling upstart.

*We defined storage as an industry. It wasn't before the early 1990s. Mostly it was an add-on to a server sale. So the server companies—IBM, Hewlett-Packard (HP), and Digital Equipment Corporation (DEC), at that time—focused on the server, and the server came with storage because you had to put the information somewhere.*

*EMC was the first to do two things. First, disconnect the storage from the server, sell it separately, and convince people that, for a variety of technological and business reasons, it's a much better way to treat storage as an independent buying decision, and [that] they can even consider buying it from an independent vendor. That's the second thing we did. ... We focused completely just on that, and didn't try to do everything like IBM. That was a dramatic changing of the landscape of the IT industry, and we did it almost single-handedly. Then, of course, other companies jumped in, including the server providers themselves.[10]*

As a result, an increasing number of customers counted on EMC's high performance, robust reliability, and low ownership costs. In the coming years, EMC would stay one step ahead of its competitors by continuing to operate in symbiosis with its customers. Inspired by a meeting between CEO Mike Ruettgers and a frustrated IT manager from John Deere, EMC released the Symmetrix 3000 family for open systems storage in June 1995 to a market full of skeptics. That sort of keen ability to listen to prospective customers' needs, along with the capacity for the bold conceptualization of products and solutions and the ability to attract top talent, would enable EMC to further revolutionize the storage marketplace.

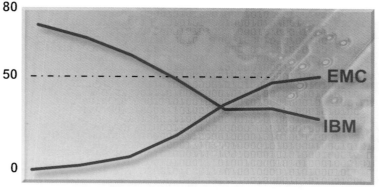

## Mainframe Storage Market
### Market Share of Terabytes Shipped

EMC

IBM

1991  1992  1993  1994  1995  1996  1997

SOURCE: META GROUP

## Shoring Up a Worldwide Presence

During the mid-1990s, EMC extended its reach even further across the globe. In 1996, EMC added to its presence in Ireland by opening an international customer support center. The following year, the company announced plans to more than double manufacturing capacity in the United States and Europe.[11] Perhaps the company's most impressive moves, however, were in the form of its new geographic footholds. In 1995, the company established EMC Computer Systems South Africa, its first direct sales presence in that country. That same year, with the opening of EMC Nordic, the company began direct sales operations in Sweden, Denmark, Norway, and Finland.[12] EMC also captured the leading share in the largest Latin American markets through distributors.[13] Direct selling in Latin America began in February 1997 with the opening of EMC Brazil, headquartered in São Paulo and supported by a satellite office in Rio de Janeiro.[14] The company had maintained local third-party distribution partnerships in Brazil since 1992, and Symmetrix systems were already installed throughout many of Brazil's largest companies and major government agencies.[15]

In 1997, Ray Fortune, then senior vice president of international sales, said:

*By establishing a direct presence in Brazil, we will expand our enterprise storage customer base in a market that is growing close to 20 percent annually in total IT spending, according to IDC [International Data Corporation], and continue to build on our growing involvement in Latin America.[16]*

The increase in international direct sales characterized EMC's ability to spot places around the world where information technology use had already begun to blossom—an ability that has continued to benefit the company.

---

In 1996, EMC opened an international customer support center adding to its presence in Cork, Ireland.

Raymond Fortune, an industry veteran and British native, EMC's senior vice president of international sales during the mid-1990s, oversaw EMC's growing global expansion, including the company's first direct sales presence in Latin America.

### Competitive Solutions

During the mid-1990s, EMC reaped the benefits of Ruettgers' decision to enter the open systems storage market. In 1995, EMC became the top independent storage supplier in the open systems market, and by 1997, its open systems storage sales surpassed its mainframe systems storage sales. The growing popularity of Windows NT and the concern many IT managers felt toward managing the growing volume of information stored on NT systems helped fuel EMC's rise to the top of the open storage market.

After EMC succeeded in making storage relevant as a category, the company needed to establish itself as the premier provider of that storage. Rick Lacroix, director of public relations for EMC's storage business, saw the publicity benefits of aligning EMC with popular brands well-known within the computer industry. To that end, EMC struck deals with leading original equipment manufacturers (OEMs), cultivating important alliances with HP and NCR Corporation, both major UNIX

server vendors that agreed to market and sell Symmetrix 3000 systems. Meanwhile, Oracle, Informix, and Sybase—the three leading independent database software vendors—agreed to use Symmetrix 3000 systems in conjunction with their own proprietary software in data warehousing and large database applications.

As they led their company to the top of the open systems storage market, EMC engineers kept fit for battle by competing against each other. While EMC's Hopkinton, Massachusetts, engineers were working on Symmetrix 3000, the engineers in the designated open storage facility in Milford, Massachusetts, were building the midrange Centriplex open storage system from the ground up.

Nikolai Markovich, an engineer who began working on EMC's midrange systems in 1993, recalled a degree of ongoing rivalry between the mainframe and midrange teams:

> *Back then, there was ... a rallying around the midrange products against the mainframe products. My memory gets a little blurry, but around the popular notion that Symmetrix was the first to come up with the open storage model, if you asked some of the midrange people, they would tell a different story. Bill Conway, back in the 1994 timeframe, was working on hooking up [Sun Microsystems servers] to [EMC's] systems as well. ... I think [competitiveness] probably helps to foster some aggressiveness, and you need to have that sort of an edge to be successful, since it's certainly tougher outside the four walls of EMC. So I think that it's a good thing.*

Along with the competition between the engineering groups, EMC needed to get its sales force to sell into the open systems market and not remain focused strictly on mainframe accounts.

When EMC had a poor initial quarter with Centriplex sales, Ruettgers had the unsold units installed directly into the offices of the executives responsible for this product to make a statement about the need to sell into the open systems market.

Such a competitive corporate culture led to increased camaraderie among employees. According to Monya Keane, manager of employee communications, "You join the club, or you quit the club. So I joined the club. I embodied that sense of urgency, and I started with the other new employees, trying to encourage them to get things done promptly and efficiently and accurately, and really, the company as an entity somehow raised my bar as to what I felt was acceptable in terms of work performance."

EMC had already matched its employees' competitive drive to innovate in 1993 by creating the Customer Council, which proved invaluable in allowing EMC to anticipate emerging trends through the experiences of its best customers. Consumer input, which had spurred innovation at EMC since the company's inception, helped propel the company toward its next plateau—enterprise storage.

As coined by EMC, an enterprise storage system stores and retrieves data from all major computing platforms, including mainframe and open systems environments. It acts as a shared central repository for information, providing common management, protection, and information-sharing capabilities. Customer Council members had voiced their eager-

ness to share information among mainframe and UNIX systems, and EMC's research highlighted a clear shift in commercial storage environments as customers dealt with what had swiftly become a crisis in information management.

Several major annual surveys of hundreds of senior IT executives conducted during the mid-1990s by the research firm FIND/SVP found that a very large majority of the executives had been given the mandate to close the "information gap" in their companies created by the wide variety of IT systems used to get all of the digital information that they needed to do their jobs.

EMC's enterprise storage strategy includes a shared central repository for information that provides common management, protection, and information-sharing capabilities compatible with all major computing platforms, including mainframe and open systems environments.

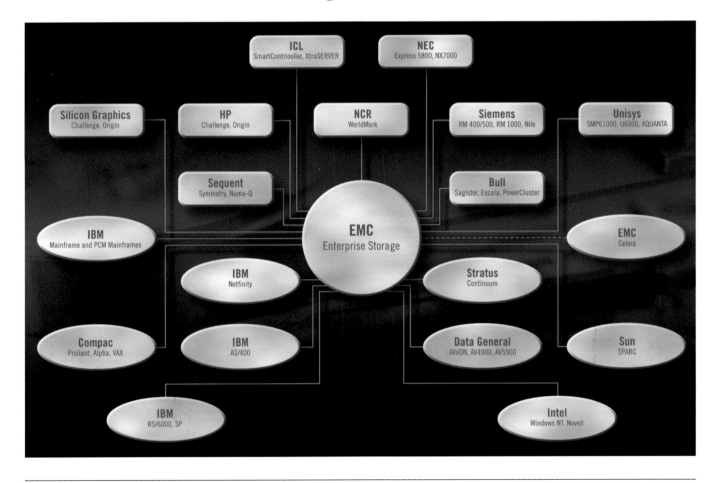

Above: With offerings such as Symmetrix Manager and Symmetrix Manager for Open Systems, EMC continued its ascent as a software company.

Left: Contributors to EMC's open storage success included, from left to right, John Fitzgerald, Thai Dang, Eyal Zimran, Todd Donaldson, John Madden, John Copely, Jeff Lasker, Erez Ofer, Robert Mayer, Tim McCain, Ken Chilton, Phil Tamer, and Bob Cicone.

To compete effectively, however, these companies needed the ability to provide information to those who need it, when they need it, regardless of the computing platform used to create that information.

EMC's November 1995 introduction of the Symmetrix Enterprise Storage Platform (ESP) marked the industry's first successful attempt to rectify that situation. Symmetrix ESP was the first system to provide simultaneous storage of mainframe and open systems information on the same system.

In another example of EMC successfully creating a whole new storage industry, Symmetrix ESP earned the praise of countless customers. "They're the corporation of the 1990s!" exclaimed Customer Council member John Lindeman, director of storage solutions for the Pennsylvania-based SunGard Recovery Services, Inc.[17]

By 1997, the market for enterprise storage was valued at $10 billion, and according to Gartner Dataquest, EMC remained the largest and the fastest-growing company in the industry, with a worldwide market share of around 27 percent.[18] Many of the world's major server vendors came to recognize the value of EMC Enterprise Storage. HP, Silicon Graphics, NCR, and Unisys, among others, soon began supplying Symmetrix ESP as their preferred storage solution through reseller agreements with EMC.[19]

In developing the EMC Enterprise Storage Platform software, EMC engineers utilized the existing Symmetrix 5000 architecture, including firmware, hardware, disk drives, and cache, in a whole new way. Enterprise Storage integrated multiple interfaces with brand new software, providing connections to both mainframes and open systems servers simultaneously, allowing for seamless parallel I/O operations. The idea proved so successful that, in an effort to bolster its enterprise storage offerings, EMC began to invest even more heavily in software development.

Following EMC's release of Symmetrix Remote Data Facility in 1994, the pace of the company's software releases escalated rapidly. Between 1994 and 1997, EMC generated $177 million in software sales, making it one of the world's fastest growing major software companies.[20] EMC also prepared for its next step in networked data storage by acquiring McDATA Corporation, a leading ESCON director vendor, in late 1995.

In October 1996, EMC announced its Symmetrix Multihost Transfer Facility (SMTF), later renamed InfoMover, and Symmetrix Network File Storage (SNFS), later renamed Celerra. SMTF enabled high-speed transfers of large files between mainframe and UNIX servers, speeding up network traffic and reducing CPU use. SNFS provided high-capacity, high-availability file service by linking Symmetrix directly to the network.[21] The new EMC Data Manager (EDM) system backed up the large volume of information carried in enterprise storage networks, while EMC's pivotal TimeFinder software, released in 1997, offered companies the ability to conduct application testing, data warehousing, updates, and other data-based administration tasks without taking systems offline, saving time and increasing productivity.

EMC's multipronged approach solidified its reputation and helped make its name synonymous with storage. In February 1996, EMC announced it had shipped one petabyte, or one quadrillion bytes, of mainframe storage capacity via its Symmetrix systems.[22] As the *Boston Globe* reported, "EMC wants to be to computer storage systems what Intel is to computer chips and Kleenex is to facial tissue."[23]

EMC continuously forged new categories of storage. Its Extended-Online Storage systems, introduced in 1996, allowed customers to store vast amounts of historical data on disk, rather than utilizing slower offline, tape-based systems.

Revenues continued to reflect EMC's increasing dominance. In 1996, it broke the $2 billion mark, and the following year, it approached $3 billion.

### Capable Networks

EMC renamed its SNFS system Celerra Clustered Network Server (CNS), and in 1998, the system evolved into the first-generation Celerra Network-Attached Storage (NAS) family of products, opening up a whole new segment in the data storage industry. Specially engineered NAS heads

worked in unison with storage systems, allowing server applications to run separately from file sharing, freeing up bandwidth and enabling greater speed and improved performance.

Celerra advanced the push to access and analyze large amounts of corporate data spread over different systems. It also helped to close the "information gap" that resulted from disparate computer systems creating isolated pockets of data. Even as technological advances helped close the gap between CPU speeds and storage I/O performance, severe lags remained within networks as information slowly transferred between computers.[24] Celerra NAS systems not only helped resolve this problem, but they also used IP connectivity to network storage, making it easy to add and upgrade capacity, attractive qualities for companies with already overburdened IT departments.

EMC's purchase of McDATA Corp., which was becoming an expert in Fibre Channel enterprise directors, helped pave the way for the company's increased networked storage offerings.[25] Fibre Channel, a high-speed data interface technology for connecting mainframes, workstations, and storage devices, had begun to replace the copper Small Computer Systems Interface (SCSI) as the connectivity standard at the time. By late 1997, EMC was incorporating Fibre Channel connectivity into its Symmetrix Enterprise Storage systems, enabling customers to expand their data centers' walls even further. The connectivity allowed for much greater bandwidth and much greater distances between storage systems and servers, enabling customers to consolidate information from hundreds of heterogeneous distributed servers onto a single Enterprise Storage System. In a Babson College case study, one EMC executive called Fibre Channel "as significant a switch as the PC was to the word processor."[26]

Fibre Channel would lay the groundwork for EMC's foray into another variation of networked storage—Storage Area Networks (SANs). Within two years, EMC would roll out its Connectrix Enterprise

EMC introduced its Celerra Network-Attached Storage (NAS) family of products (formerly called SNFS) in October 1996, opening up a whole new segment in the data storage industry.

# Broadening Value Proposition

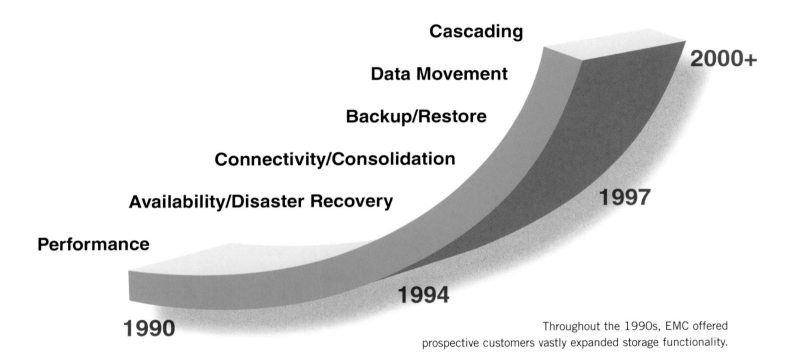

Cascading

Data Movement

Backup/Restore

Connectivity/Consolidation

Availability/Disaster Recovery

Performance

2000+

1997

1994

1990

Throughout the 1990s, EMC offered prospective customers vastly expanded storage functionality.

Storage Network system, which it proclaimed the "world's first integrated, large-scale, enterprise-class SAN solution."[27] While SANs share some of the key features of NAS systems, such as the ability to access data across different platforms, they differ in terms of network connection technology.[28] In a SAN, disk arrays or tape systems connect to one or more servers via a direct Fibre Channel interface. Like NAS, SANs consolidate data from multiple platforms, making it easier to share data across multiple servers.[29]

**No Rest for the Weary**

By 1997, EMC's customers included the Chicago Board Options Exchange (CBOE); Toys "R" Us, Inc.; and United Parcel Service, Inc. (UPS), as well as international heavyweights Bertelsmann, General Telephone and Electronics (GTE), and the Swiss Bank Corporation.[30] In March of that year, EMC ranked No. 16 on the Standard & Poor's index of the top 50 corporate performers.[31] Yet, even given EMC's many accomplishments, employees recognized that they could not afford to rest on their laurels.

EMC employees realized that many onetime giants of the computer industry had already crumbled after just a few decades. If they stopped to take pride in the company's accomplishments, they quickly reminded themselves of the need to stay on task. According to Barbara Robidoux, vice president of storage product marketing, in the auditorium of EMC's Milford facility, which at one time was owned by the now-defunct Prime Computer, "We intentionally, behind the big screen that came down, left the Prime logo up there as a reminder to ourselves of what could happen if we slowed down."[32]

Meanwhile, Dick Egan, from his seat as chairman of the board, continued to take an active role in the company, striving to make customers

# CREATING NEW STORAGE SOLUTIONS

EVEN AS EMC MADE HEADWAY IN THE MAINFRAME storage market in the late 1980s and early 1990s, information storage had already begun to move out of corporate data centers and onto UNIX- and Windows-based servers in individual departments. Such decentralized client-server architectures often allowed businesses greater autonomy, but also frequently led to lost data and added frustration as users often underestimated the difficulty in managing multiple disparate computer networks.[1] During the first half of the 1990s, the decentralization trend came full circle, as centralized storage once again came into favor as the best way to protect information.

Within this trend, EMC saw opportunity. Engineers began working on a system capable of managing data storage within multiple UNIX-based platforms. In November 1994, EMC's open systems division released Centriplex, a midrange product designed with the added flexibility businesses required.[2] The Symmetrix 3000 system, released half a year later, also filled that role, and eventually supplanted Centriplex. EMC had not only seized an opportunity, it had created a new category of storage.

From there, EMC moved quickly to take advantage of the situation. Why stop at connecting data from UNIX-based platforms when it could

feel just as important to EMC as he had in the company's early days.

Egan also never stopped scouting for the best talent, recognizing that staying ahead required constant motion from everybody in the company. When Northeastern University awarded Egan an honorary degree in 1997, he took advantage of a break in the graduation ceremony to recruit engineering graduates. As the legendary Fidelity Magellan Fund manager Peter Lynch recalled, Egan interviewed four of the graduates and hired at least one.[33]

### Alliance Programs

As EMC's sales rose, the company reinforced its partnerships with customers to help them derive the most value from EMC's offerings.[34] As the pioneer of open storage, EMC also directed a lot of energy toward promoting and evaluating the adoption of industry standards. These standards make life easier for customers and expand EMC's market opportunities.

In early 1999, EMC led the establishment of the FibreAlliance to help customers easily implement

enterprise-class storage networks built from components supplied by a variety of vendors. The 11 original members included providers of Fibre Channel hubs, switches, routers, servers, and management software. Working together, EMC and FibreAlliance drafted engineering specifications designed to become industry standards.[35]

In the 21st century, EMC would extend its Alliance Programs into universities, sponsoring open storage technology curriculums aimed at helping to educate a pool of highly skilled storage managers and professionals.[36] EMC also chaired a number of business alliance programs in schools, bringing together businesses, communities, and school leaders in public-private partnerships.[37]

### The Coming Information Boom

Around 1996, EMC began anticipating the impact the Internet explosion would soon have on data storage needs. The escalating volume of e-mail correspondence, company intranets, online transactions, and online multimedia applications required massive amounts of storage capacity.

also work toward a system that would store data from both mainframe *and* open storage systems? Just six months after the release of Symmetrix 3000, EMC unveiled its Symmetrix Enterprise Storage Platform in 1995, which for the first time provided support for both mainframe and open systems data on the same system.

Enterprise storage would fuel EMC's growth over the next few years, providing a long-awaited solution for companies struggling to rein in burgeoning amounts of data. The culmination of this endeavor would come in 1999 with the unveiling of the Enterprise Storage Network, which expanded on the enterprise storage structure and allowed companies to connect hundreds of servers with dozens of storage systems. EMC's expanded storage network solutions came at just the right time, as the Internet boom had begun to create an explosive volume of data for companies to contend with.

EMC's advances in storage had been driven by paying close attention to the needs of its customers.

"We talk to customers at the business and technical level so we can steer products in the direction they need," CEO Mike Ruettgers told *IndustryWeek* magazine in 1996. "Our customers can see their ideas in our products within 18 months."[3]

EMC executives rightly anticipated the enormous impact these trends would have on how companies managed information as they planned the company's future growth strategies.

As information management transcended simple storage capabilities, it became increasingly apparent to executives that their companies needed an information infrastructure that would allow them to even more efficiently and effectively satisfy their customers. EMC touted its Enterprise Storage Network as essential to keeping businesses and organizations competitive by allowing them to effectively bring together and share their data, no matter where it resided. By targeting and expanding their software offerings, EMC expanded on its identity as *the* comprehensive information management solutions provider. The coming Internet explosion would allow EMC to further build on that reputation, leading the company to skyrocketing profits through the end of the millennium.

From left to right: Polly Pearson, EMC's former vice president of investor relations; former New York Stock Exchange (NYSE) Chairman Dick Grasso; and then EMC CEO Mike Ruettgers with his wife, Maureen Ruettgers, and two of their three children at the floor of the New York Stock Exchange after EMC was named the best-performing stock of the 1990s.

### CHAPTER SIX

# THE EMC EFFECT

## 1998–2000

*The Internet may be a big part of the company's future, but EMC's rise largely predated the rise of the World Wide Web. Simply put, the company recognized the importance of storage before the rest of the world and used that edge to beat the pants off its competition.*

—*The Boston Globe*, 1999[1]

AFTER HAVING GROWN STEADILY THROUGHout the decade, the Internet experienced explosive growth near the end of the 20th century. According to the Online Computer Library Center, the number of Web sites skyrocketed, from 2.85 million sites in 1998, to 7.4 million by the year 2000.[2]

Alongside such growth came vast increases in business storage needs. In addition to e-mail, intranets, and Web pages, there were online transactions and multimedia applications to contend with, as well as the increased expectations of 24-hour capabilities.[3] Traditional brick-and-mortar businesses vied for an online presence while competing with a new breed, "dotcoms," that had begun to spread like wildfire—companies relying solely on the Internet. Many of these companies had few employees and little revenue, yet found themselves in urgent need of extensive information infrastructure to remain competitive.[4] A stronger online presence often meant a stronger company, school, or organization, and building that online presence required extensive storage capabilities.

EMC remained well positioned to respond to—and capitalize on—these developments. Its Enterprise Storage Platform would soon evolve to the next stage: the Enterprise Storage Network, which allowed hundreds of servers to connect with dozens of storage systems across the globe.

With the Enterprise Storage Network, equipped with software such as Symmetrix Remote Data Facility (SRDF) and TimeFinder, companies would not only be able to pull together information from disparate systems, but also be able to ensure business continuity in disaster situations, while hastening product development and the consistent release of e-commerce applications.[5] As *FORTUNE®* magazine noted in 1999:

> *A company called EMC has tapped into one of the central truths of the computer age: Every time you hit "send," buy a stock online, or click on an ad, you generate data that has to be put somewhere for safekeeping. Finding that space —creating that space—is crucial to the InfoTech revolution.*[6]

### New Sales Order

As businesses and organizations faced increased pressure to expand their Internet presence, a distinct market opportunity developed that EMC's

---

EMC's stock shot up 80,575 percent during the 1990s, as commemorated in this award given to the company at the end of the decade.

# DIFFERENT NEEDS, ONE SOURCE

BY THE LATE 1990s, EMC'S CUSTOMER BASE INcluded 90 percent of the world's major airlines, the world's 20 largest phone carriers, and many of the world's leading banks—each of which depended on rapid access to vast amounts of data and 24-hour, seven-day-a-week availability.

EMC met these challenges with its trademark versatility and dedication to customer service. By 1999, the top 25 U.S. banks were all EMC customers. The nation's top five banks—Citibank, Chase Manhattan, NationsBank, Bank of America, and First Union—spent a combined $8 billion on information technology each year.[1]

International giants such as Deutsche Bank relied on EMC Symmetrix in their trading floor operations because its versatile scalability supported fast-moving, high-volume transactions.[2] When Deutsche Bank acquired U.S.-based Bankers Trust, also an EMC customer, EMC systems allowed the two operations to share information seamlessly, facilitating uninterrupted operations for clients during the transition.[3]

Airlines relied on EMC Enterprise Storage to ensure the stability of their reservation systems, as well as for transport, cargo, and customer service operations. Japan Airlines, for example, utilized EMC systems to store passenger meal and seat preferences, allowing customer requests to generate future offerings.[4] When the airline rebuilt its information systems to meet the increased demands of the 21st century, Symmetrix served as a central part of the project, allowing for faster information access while ensuring continuous system availability.[5]

During the mid-1990s, the use of Symmetrix systems rose fivefold among the world's leading telecommunications companies, including AT&T and British Telecom.[6] As the field advanced to support the convergence of cell phones and aggressive sales force quickly capitalized on. As CEO Mike Ruettgers said at the time:

> Internet companies quickly go from nonexisting to 30 terabytes in 12 to 18 months. This puts them in the top 10 percent of customers. Most of these people understand that they are selling information, and they need as bulletproof an infrastructure as the old mainframe guys. EMC has created new sales districts that just chase after these companies.

Once again, EMC's prescience paid off, netting such heavyweights as Amazon.com and FedEx as clients, as well as online brokerage firms including E*TRADE Financial and The Charles Schwab

## STORAGE FIRST

"The foundation of my company's IT infastructure is ..."

Servers 12%
Other 3%
Networks 20%
Applications 25%
Information/ Storage 40%

SOURCE: SURVEY OF SENIOR IT EXECUTIVES CONDUCTED BY FIND/SVP IN 1999.

Information Storage remains the most important priority for IT departments in companies around the world.

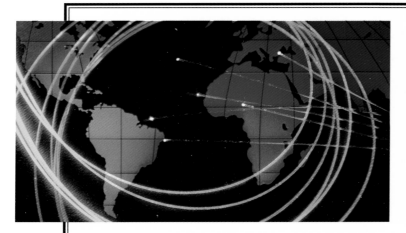

the Internet, allowing phones to send and receive e-mail, check stock quotes, and browse the Internet, providers such as the innovative NTT DoCoMo of Japan relied on EMC as the backbone of its IT infrastructure. NTT DoCoMo's technological foundation was built on EMC's Enterprise Storage products, in conjunction with UNIX servers and Oracle databases.[7] EMC Enterprise Storage helped NTT DoCoMo deliver the speed and continuity that customers needed.

As the year 2000 approached, Internet companies would form a growing portion of EMC's customer base. The popular search company Excite, Inc., for example, turned to EMC products to store e-mail, Web pages, and customers' online purchases.[8] As speedy information access and Web transactions became the established and expected standard, a growing number of e-businesses turned to EMC. As John Hnanicek, then chief information officer for eToys.com, explained:

> *EMC plays a huge role in ensuring that our customers receive prompt response time—and that our company can accommodate the dramatic business growth and range of services that uniquely position eToys to be the leader in a booming global market.*[9]

Even among online businesses, EMC maintained a global reach. Brazil-based Universo Online (UOL), Latin America's largest Internet service provider, also based its infrastructure on EMC Enterprise Storage, using its added flexibility to allow the provider to handle a rapidly expanding user base and increasingly varied, multilingual content while ensuring high availability and speed.[10]

Corporation.[7] The strategic targeting of prospective customers proved indicative of a much larger change in EMC's approach to sales. The company had become more thoughtful since its early days. Steve Savard, who started with the sales force in 1985, described the transition:

> *Before, it was more just "spin that dial," a phrase that we had, if you want to make money, and that's why we contacted so many people. So it was kind of hit-or-miss, and now it's more strategic ... and [includes] positioning and finding the right fit between our products and what the requirements of the customers are.*[8]

As part of that evolution, EMC University, once the institution from which the company's aggressive sales force emerged, took on a more mature identity—one that reflected the large and diverse organization EMC had become. EMC University became a training ground for developing the company's top

Tom Clancy (far left corner), vice president of global education and productivity, and Brian Powers (in front of Tom), director of EMC University, with members of the EMC Education Services and EMC University teams. EMC ranked second on *Training* magazine's list of the world's companies with the best workforce training and development.

executive talent. Brian Powers, hired in 2002 to head EMC University, explained:

*EMC University is focused on learning and development, which is our traditional business. We offer talent management services identifying the talent gap in organizations—who are our high potentials and our future leaders. ... It's an extreme focus on what our top executives need to continue to grow, but also to continue to execute our transformational, evolutionary strategy.*[9]

As EMC boosted its worldwide presence and secured a growing number of high-level accounts,

# REMEMBERING JEFF GOLDBERG

ON JANUARY 13, 2008, JEFF GOLDBERG, ONE OF the patriarchs of EMC's sales organization, died at the age of 60 after a battle with cancer. During a career spanning two decades with the company, Goldberg's unmatched ability to crystallize EMC's message and convey it to customers helped transform the little-known upstart focused on memory products into one of the world's leading storage solutions providers.

"If you asked me for the two or three top people who are responsible for the success of the company, Jeff is one of them," co-founder Dick Egan said in a 2004 interview. "This guy walks on water in my eyes."[1]

Goldberg joined EMC in 1988 and served as a mentor to many in the early sales force. He instilled in his young charges an emphasis on customer service and an approach to sales that centered less on the technical specifics of the company's products than on what, in simple terms, the products could do for potential customers. "Jeff taught us all how to boil down a proposition or message to its bare essentials," recalled Chuck Hollis, vice president, global marketing chief technology officer. "Whatever we came up with as a team, Jeff could do one better."

As the company expanded, Goldberg developed marketing programs across the globe. He

later served as vice president of customer programs and spearheaded the 1994 creation of the Executive Briefing Center in Hopkinton, Massachusetts. Goldberg aimed to bring customers and partners together with EMC executives and engineers, facilitating the face-to-face interactions that he considered most important. In 1995, he began the EMC Fire Walk Experience, in which new sales hires walk across a bed of hot coals as a way of overcoming fear and expanding comfort zones. The program proved very successful and has remained popular ever since. Part of the inspiration for the program was one of Goldberg's many well-known mantras at EMC: "The penalty you pay for holding onto fear is much greater than the fear itself."

Goldberg also possessed an effortless sense of humor, endearing him to customers and colleagues alike. Yet it was his perfect grasp of customer sales relationships that that he will be best remembered for at EMC. For Goldberg, thinking like potential customers was in his nature, whether they be IT specialists or CEOs of FORTUNE® 500 companies, explained Bob Basiliere, vice president of customer programs and one of Goldberg's many protégés. "In this place, there was never anybody better," Basiliere added.

## EMC is #1 in Overall Customer Satisfaction
### On a Scale of 1-5, with 5 = Most Satisfied

| Vendor | Leadership | Performance | Function | Reliability | Price | Overall |
|---|---|---|---|---|---|---|
| EMC | 4.4 | 4.2 | 4.3 | 4.2 | 2.5 | 4.0 |
| Hitachi | 3.2 | 3.8 | 3.5 | 3.9 | 3.5 | 3.3 |
| IBM | 3.1 | 3.1 | 3.2 | 3.8 | 2.9 | 3.0 |
| StorageTek | 2.5 | 3.0 | 2.8 | 3.4 | 2.7 | 2.7 |
| Data General | 2.3 | 2.6 | 2.6 | 2.6 | 3.1 | 2.5 |
| Amdahl | 2.0 | 2.8 | 2.5 | 2.9 | 3.0 | 2.2 |

SOURCE: SOUNDVIEW/GARTNER GROUP SURVEY JULY 1998

Above: EMC was rated No. 1 in overall customer satisfaction in 1998.

Below right: In 1998, EMC's revenues rose 35 percent over 1997 to $3.97 billion and its stock price rose more than 210 percent, lifting the company's market value by $29 billion to a year-end market capitalization of nearly $43 billion.

the company began opening additional Executive Briefing Centers across the globe. The briefing program started in Hopkinton, Massachusetts, in 1994 and later expanded to include locations in Tokyo, Japan; Cork, Ireland; and Santa Clara, California.[10] According to Bob Basiliere, hired to run the worldwide program in 2000, potential customers were invited to two-day briefings at the centers, giving them a chance to learn firsthand about how EMC's products could best suit their company's needs, as well as "why they should put their trust in EMC versus someone else and what they will get for that trust."[11] The number of briefings held correlated with the company's revenue. During the 1990s, the two grew in almost direct proportion.[12]

EMC's approach to sales clearly worked. By 1998, the company's clients included 90 percent of the world's major airlines, the world's 20 largest phone carriers, and the top five Internet service providers.[13] Surveys revealed EMC's customer satisfaction rating at a steady 98 percent, and its customer retention rate at an astounding 99 percent.[14]

As Carl Howe, research director of Forrester Research, told *Forbes* magazine:

*EMC has the highest ratings we've ever seen—in any customer survey, for any company, ever.*[15]

### Information Specialists

EMC's growth during this period paralleled that of the Internet. Its 1998 revenues approached $4 billion, and its stock price finished more than 210 percent higher than in 1997.[16] Yet the company had already begun to look beyond storage, positioning

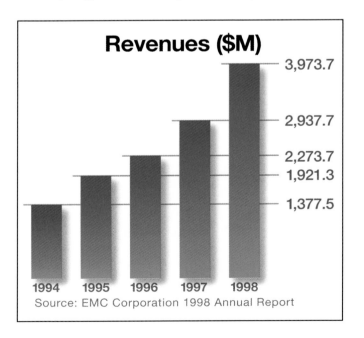

Revenues ($M)

| Year | Revenue |
|---|---|
| 1994 | 1,377.5 |
| 1995 | 1,921.3 |
| 1996 | 2,273.7 |
| 1997 | 2,937.7 |
| 1998 | 3,973.7 |

Source: EMC Corporation 1998 Annual Report

# DISK TECHNOLOGY IN THE NOBEL SPOTLIGHT

HARD DISK DRIVES, THE MINUSCULE DEVICES capable of storing reams of data, owe their existence to the efforts of physicists around the globe. In 2007, the Nobel Prize in Physics went to the creators of one advance that helped usher in iPods, advanced EMC Symmetrix storage systems, shrinking laptops, and other digital devices that can store massive amounts of data in a tightly compressed space.

Giant magnetoresistance (GMR), an effect in which very weak changes in magnetism generate larger changes in electrical resistance, allows for extremely sensitive detection of magnetically stored information that is then converted into electrical signals that computers can read. Discovered independently in 1988 by French physicist Albert Fert of the Université Paris-Sud in Orsay and German physicist Peter Grünberg of the Jülich Research Center, GMR helped lead to smaller storage devices, because fainter magnetic signals on smaller disks could now be detected.

All digitized information, including music and video, is stored on hard disks in the form of ferro-magnetic electrons. A small head scans the magnetic direction of these electrons and converts it back to electrical signals. This process, and the principle that magnetic fields can affect electrical resistance, have long been known. As early as the 19th century, physicist William Thomson, better known as Lord Kelvin, described the process.[1]

Advances during the 1970s allowed the production of layers of material only a few atoms thick, and Fert and Grünberg took advantage of the scientific breakthrough in their experiments. To their surprise, they found that these super-thin layers showed heightened magnetic sensitivity—giant magnetoresistance. The effect is caused by an unusual property displayed by materials at this level of thinness, concerning electrons' "spin." Electrons' actions, either moving freely or getting stuck within the layers, depend on the direction in which the magnetic fields are pointing. Extremely thin layers amplify the effect, causing more dramatic changes in resistance.[2]

Considered one of the first applications of nanotechnology, GMR offered scientists a potential solution to the problem of storing ever-larger volumes of information in increasingly smaller spaces. Shortly after GMR was discovered, scientists began developing read-out heads based on the effect. The first such device was unveiled in 1997, and the technology has since become the standard.[3] Such technology has today advanced to the point where even the smallest laptops currently contain at least 100 gigabytes of storage—enough information to occupy a kilometer-long bookshelf.[4]

GMR, the Nobel committee noted, is an example of a scientific discovery that would yield unexpected results. Though iPods and Symmetrix systems capable of storing massive amounts of data may have seemed like science fiction in 1988, Fert and Grünberg's groundbreaking work helped make them science fact.

---

In this close-up of the interior of a hard disk drive, the tiny head at the end of the actuator arm glides above the reflective platter where data is stored. (Photo © Andrew Magill 2006.)

itself as the leading provider of complete information management solutions. On February 2, 1998, "The EMC Effect" campaign was launched via a three-page advertising spread in the *Wall Street Journal*. The goal of the campaign was to showcase EMC products as essential tools in the new information economy, tools that could help companies leverage knowledge and ideas to gain an advantage over competitors. The ads described how EMC's products could help companies manage and use their data more effectively and enable quicker access to more complete information. As a result, EMC offered companies the opportunity to make better business decisions and spot opportunities they might have otherwise missed.

Also during this period, EMC branched out into consulting with its new Professional Services unit. The unit, whose expertise focused on the design and implementation of storage systems, both expanded on EMC's strong reputation and took advantage of the burgeoning trend of outsourcing corporate IT services.[17] In 1998, IT consulting services served a $300 billion marketplace, a large share of which was controlled by Andersen Consulting, later renamed Accenture; Computer Associates International, now known as CA, Inc.; and Electronic Data Systems Corporation, acquired by HP.[18]

Within this marketplace, EMC focused its efforts on three areas: Enterprise Storage Architecture and Design, which helped companies find the storage systems best suited to their needs; Enterprise Business Continuity, which helped companies determine information availability requirements and implement data backup and restoration programs; and Enterprise Storage Network, through which companies could link together data from multiple servers.

In addition to an already impressive roster of resellers, in 1998, EMC established major reseller agreements with Silicon Graphics, Inc.; International Computers, Ltd.; and NEC Corporation.[19]

EMC's combination of hardware, software, and support service offerings gave the company a tremendous financial advantage, and the value of EMC's products allowed the company to sometimes charge twice as much as its competitors on a per gigabyte basis.[20] The new focus signaled a transition toward a more organized system for handling EMC's cash flow. As Irina Simmons, EMC's longtime treasurer, explained:

*Basically, during those first few years, obviously the company was growing very fast, and everything we did, we would outgrow six months later. So those first few years were really spent just keeping up with that growth, and then the second five years we spent getting to a place where we were more procedure oriented—more process ori-*

---

The company launched "The EMC Effect" campaign on February 2, 1998. The campaign described EMC's products as essential tools designed to help customers gain a competitive advantage.

Above: Irina Simmons, senior vice president and treasurer of EMC, joined the company in 1995 and is responsible for EMC's overall risk and liquidity management.

Below: An industry forecast in 1998 from market research firm IDC shows storage, as measured in terabytes shipped, growing at an accelerating pace. Most of this mushrooming information would be generated not by mainframes but by UNIX and especially Windows NT and Windows 2000 systems.

*ented. We put a lot of programs and systems in place to manage all of this money with the smallest number of people possible.*[21]

**Record Growth**

On the same day that "The EMC Effect" advertising spread hit the *Wall Street Journal*, and the same day that the Professional Services unit was announced, an EMC interoffice memo summarized the reactions of leading financial analysts to the company's recent gains. According to analyst Alex Brown:

*It is the range of robust storage management features available on EMC platforms that, we believe, provide strong and highly defensible competitive differentiation that positions EMC several years ahead of the competition.*

Meanwhile, analysts at Merrill Lynch stated:

*We continue to think that EMC may be the next franchise technology company. ... Maniacal focus on storage is the reason EMC can hold off newcomers such as Sun, IBM, and Compaq.*[22]

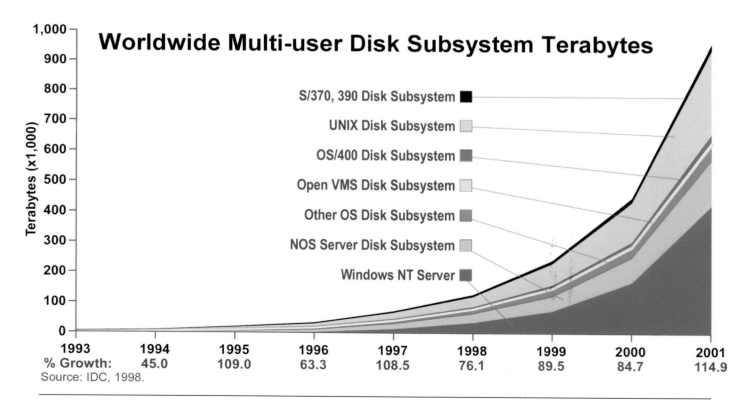

**Worldwide Multi-user Disk Subsystem Terabytes**

- S/370, 390 Disk Subsystem ■
- UNIX Disk Subsystem □
- OS/400 Disk Subsystem ▦
- Open VMS Disk Subsystem ▨
- Other OS Disk Subsystem ▩
- NOS Server Disk Subsystem ▧
- Windows NT Server ▦

Terabytes (x1,000)

| | 1993 | 1994 | 1995 | 1996 | 1997 | 1998 | 1999 | 2000 | 2001 |
|---|---|---|---|---|---|---|---|---|---|
| % Growth: | | 45.0 | 109.0 | 63.3 | 108.5 | 76.1 | 89.5 | 84.7 | 114.9 |

Source: IDC, 1998.

# PEACE OF MIND FOR THE NEW MILLENNIUM

IN THE LATE 1990s, THE MOVEMENT OF CORPORATE applications to smaller systems running Windows NT and UNIX operating systems was not the only thing that was shaking up data centers around the world. As the world headed toward a new millennium, a potential problem loomed for businesses and government agencies—a problem that caused widespread concern. In the early years of computing, when computer disk space was expensive and computer programmers relatively inexpensive, virtually all computer application programmers were taught as a "best practice" to use two digits instead of four digits to represent years in computer record fields in an effort to save disk space, and thus reduce costs. As the calendar shifted from 1999 to 2000, there were fears that the critical computer programs running everything from power grids to banking systems would generate erroneous data, and possibly even crash, if the systems interpreted "00" as any year other than 2000.

The problem became known as Y2K and it is estimated that up to $300 billion was spent updating and testing systems and applications to ensure compliance when the calendar rolled over into 2000. Once again, an EMC software product, appropriately named TimeFinder, would become an unsung hero, helping companies and governments make sure that heralding in the year 2000 would remain nothing but a big New Year's Eve celebration. It would also help EMC sell a lot of storage capacity.

EMC TimeFinder software enabled multiple copies of the same data to be created on a storage system—more copies of data required more data storage space. The original version of the data would remain in production and available to users, while another copy, for example, would be used for backup at the same time, without impacting performance. One of the uses of this software quickly became apparent to EMC and its customers. Using an exact copy of their data, customers could take a second version of their application and move the date forward to midnight on December 31, 1999, and see what happened and have proof that it was not an issue or correct any problems long before the actual changeover. All this took place behind the scenes while the production systems continued to be online and serving users. January 1, 2000, and the months and years that followed, came and went with no significant computer-related events and EMC played a major role in ensuring readiness for Y2K.

The list went on. Analysts across the board recognized EMC both for its consistent financial gains and for the soundness of its technology, helping the company achieve an amazing 30 percent year-over-year growth in revenue and income for eight quarters in a row by 1999.[23] EMC's financial growth was matched by an expansion of its operating facilities and a sizable increase in its employee population. In 1998, EMC opened a new 550,000-square-foot manufacturing facility in Franklin, Massachusetts. That expansion, along with a doubling in size of the company's Cork, Ireland, facility, was aimed at meeting increased worldwide demand for Symmetrix systems.

To shore up its position as a leading software provider, EMC also began acquiring companies with software expertise. One 1998 acquisition was that of the Conley Corporation, based in Cambridge, Massachusetts, a provider of storage management software for UNIX, Windows NT, and other platforms. Conley's Cambridge headquarters later became the EMC Cambridge Technology

Center, and its flagship product became EMC PowerPath, one of the company's most widely installed software products ever.

As EMC entered the new millennium, the company also embarked on a hiring binge. By October 2000, it had added 6,500 new employees to its ranks, 2,000 of them in Massachusetts—amounting to a pace that year of 125 new hires per week.[24]

**Introducing CLARiiON**

In October 1999, EMC completed the largest acquisition in its history, purchasing Data General, a minicomputer manufacturer based in nearby Westborough, Massachusetts. In addition to the AViiON server line, which EMC subsequently phased

CLARiiON gave prospective customers a less expensive storage solution that proved especially popular with smaller e-commerce start-ups.

out, Data General had created the CLARiiON line of midrange storage systems, launched in 1992 and later resold by Hewlett-Packard, Silicon Graphics, StorageTek, and other original equipment manufacturers.[25] CLARiiON fulfilled the needs of prospective customers from midsize companies interested in advanced, yet inexpensive, storage products. Such products would become particularly important for smaller e-commerce start-ups that had yet to achieve the scale of eBay or Amazon and did not need Symmetrix. "It was important for EMC to have a much less expensive product line as well," explained Jim Rothnie, former vice president of software development at Data General and retired senior vice president and chief technology officer at EMC.[26]

The Data General acquisition also proved significant for EMC because of the lessons learned while integrating the two company cultures. Data General had once been a hot start-up like EMC. It had its own strong culture, though years of decline had taken its toll. A key issue was gaining the trust

of those employees who remained with EMC. Bryan Fontaine, former vice president of manufacturing for North American operations, recalled working to smooth the transition during the merging of four former Data General plants:

> In one month, we had formulated the go-forward strategy, and within the span of three months, we had transitioned all the system activity into one site at Apex, North Carolina. So the challenge was making sure that we had a vested interest in their success.
>
> I asked them to put together a transition team of some of the most valuable people in the organization. ... I met one-on-one with each of them. I wanted them to know the value EMC placed in each of them, that the process was going to move forward and we really needed a leadership team to execute that, so their future at EMC was still bright. There were many opportunities that they could be integrated into, and I would personally make sure they received those opportunities. Then I had to ask them to put their trust in me, because they didn't know me. Leaving that room, I had already started to make connections with those

individuals, and they recognized it as a commitment. I wasn't just trying to use those folks.[27]

The Data General acquisition provided a window into EMC's culture, as new employees saw it from the outside. Erin Motameni, Data General's vice president of worldwide human resources, became vice president of worldwide staffing at EMC. She described an infectious enthusiasm from the moment she first stepped in the door:

> When I went to meet with my colleagues at EMC during the very early stages of the acquisition, I waited for a meeting in the lobby, and I started talking to the lobby guard.
> "Oh, who are you here to see?" he asked.
> "I'm with Data General. Just got acquired."

Left: Jim Rothnie was a senior vice president and longtime chief technology officer.

Below: Erin Motameni serves as a senior vice president in human resources.

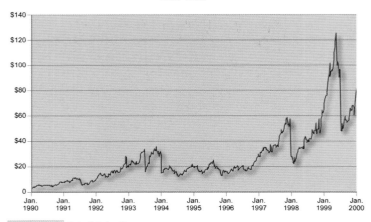

**EMC Stock Performance**
(Adjusted for Splits)
1990-1999

Data includes the effects of stock splits.
Source: Yahoo Finance, 8/25/2008

Above: During the 1990s, EMC achieved the highest single decade performance of any listed stock in the history of the New York Stock Exchange.

He said, "Let me tell you about EMC."

He went on, and he did this 10-minute overview of the company. … It really made a huge impression on me, and you'll find that everywhere in EMC, people can talk to you about EMC's business, and that's because of the commitment to communication here.[28]

That enthusiasm played out in employees' day-to-day functioning as well, Rothnie explained:

One of the things that was really striking culturally is that Data General, at that time, was in a long losing streak of declining revenue and declining market share, and it was really a struggling enterprise. That, in so many ways, affects the way that people operate in their day-to-day work. If you were part of a committee looking at some product idea, and I may be exaggerating just a little, you had to deal with [the idea that] this product was probably not going to be successful and [wonder] how you could make sure you didn't get blamed for it. EMC was really on a long winning streak and had a winner's culture. If you're talking about doing something new, the feeling was, "Hey, this is going to be a big hit. How can I get on board with this thing and make it happen?"[29]

In the years that followed, as EMC continued with an impressive string of acquisitions, integration would become a prominent issue, and executives remained devoted to providing extra support during the transition period.

### Stock of the Millennium

By the end of the millennium, EMC had become the New York Stock Exchange's (NYSE) best-performing single-decade stock ever, placing second overall for the 1990s to the NASDAQ-listed Dell. At EMC, only 20 years old at the time, it was the fulfillment of a once seemingly unattainable dream. Polly Pearson, who headed investor relations at the time, recalled the dramatic achievement:

It was a race toward the end of the 1990s. Mike Ruettgers and I watched [the developments] very closely because we had spent a lot of time out on the road talking to investors. … I remember being in a room and saying, "Mike, we've got 12 days left in the year. Do you think we're going to make it to No. 1 on the New York Stock Exchange?"

Mike said, "Polly, I want to ring the bell on the Exchange on the last day of the year."

I replied, "Mike, you want to ring it on the first day of a new century, right? This is just the beginning for us."

He said, "See what you can do."

Everybody around the room just started laughing [at the idea] of calling the NYSE and saying, "I want to ring the bell on this particular day."

Still, I called [then NYSE Chairman] Dick Grasso, and he said, "Gee, Polly, let me look into it."

Their whole team came back and said, "We're really sorry. We want you to ring the bell. You deserve to ring the bell. You are No. 1, but we've got Rudy Giuliani ringing the bell that morning."

Of course, he was running for office in New York at that point, but … we replied, "Listen, this is not an option. Help us out here."

So they actually bumped Rudy for us! The Ruettgers family and I went down there and rang the bell on the first day of the new millennium.[30]

The company's sizzling finish to the millennium was preceded by another impressive string of accomplishments. By 1999, EMC had become the most valuable company in Massachusetts, surpassing razor titan Gillette, which just a year earlier had been worth three times as much as EMC.[31] Ruettgers, in a January 2000 interview with *CBS MarketWatch*, announced that several fledgling dot-com companies had individually spent more money on EMC products in 1999 than all of the revenues from the entire 1994 mainframe marketplace combined.[32] The *Boston Globe* named EMC the Massachusetts-based company of the decade, and *FORTUNE*® magazine ranked it on its first list of leading Internet companies.[33] Salomon Smith Barney Inc. named EMC its top pick for 2000.[34] With such momentum, it is no wonder why, on September 20, 2000, the share price for EMC would hit an all-time high of $103.25, resulting in a market value of about $214 billion.[35]

**New Directions**

In January 2000, EMC enhanced its leadership team by hiring Joe Tucci as president and chief operating officer. Tucci, a high-tech veteran, captured the industry's attention after engineering a spectacular

Joe Tucci (left), former NYSE Chairman Dick Grasso (right), and a cape-clad troop of EMC employees leverage EMC's continued high standing on Wall Street to promote the announcement in December 2000 of new networked storage systems and software that bring NAS and SAN platforms into a unified network.

turnaround at Wang Laboratories, where he had served as CEO and chairman since 1993.

As Wang headed toward bankruptcy and needed to line up financing for protection against creditors before filing for Chapter 11 protection, Tucci gave the go-ahead to file, confident that he could secure the needed funding within the mandatory 60-day period. Not only did he succeed, but he did so in only 30 days.[36] He saved roughly 10,000 jobs in the process and transformed the former minicomputer manufacturer into a computer services company. Tucci's turnaround skills would prove more useful to EMC than anyone realized at the time.

Tucci, a native of New York City who grew up in Albany, New York, earned a business degree from Manhattan College and worked briefly on Wall Street before being hired as a systems programmer by RCA. At the time, he knew nothing

### 20 Most Valuable Companies (U.S.)
Market Value ($B)

| | | | | |
|---|---|---|---|---|
| ($496) GE | 1 | 11 | Am. Int'l Group ($184) | |
| ($457) Intel | 2 | 12 | IBM ($179) | |
| ($455) Cisco | 3 | 13 | Lucent ($177) | |
| ($426) Microsoft | 4 | 14 | Merck ($173) | |
| ($293) Pfizer | 5 | 15 | EMC ($162) | |
| ($272) Exxon-Mobil | 6 | 16 | SBC Comm. ($148) | |
| ($257) Wal-Mart | 7 | 17 | Verizon ($146) | |
| ($216) Citigroup | 8 | 18 | Coca-Cola ($146) | |
| ($215) Oracle | 9 | 19 | OraSuncle ($139) | |
| ($204) Nortel | 10 | 20 | Johnson & Johnson ($139) | |

**EMC Added $100B in Last 12 Months**

Source: Bloomberg, 7 July 2000

Above: In 2000, EMC became one of the 20 most valuable companies in the United States.

Below: Off-site, employees attend a team-building meeting with members of the EMC E-Lab team.

about programming, although other attributes made him an attractive hire.

"I guess I got the job because I played an instrument, I got A's in math, and I was a good baseball player," Tucci told the *Boston Globe*.[37] At the time, RCA's district manager wanted the company's baseball team to win its local league, which it did the year that Tucci joined.[38]

Shortly after Tucci joined RCA, rival Sperry bought the company. After the acquisition, Tucci moved into sales and gradually ascended through management ranks. When Sperry merged with computer-maker Burroughs in 1986 to form Unisys, Inc., Tucci was named president of Unisys U.S. Information Systems Operations. He remained with Unisys until he was hired as Wang's chief operating officer in 1990.[39] Tucci's directness and lack of flash earned the respect of his employees and peers within the industry.[40]

Given its more holistic emphasis on information management, it was inevitable that EMC chose to once again rebrand itself. In early 2000, it changed

Joe Tucci serves as EMC chairman, president, and CEO.

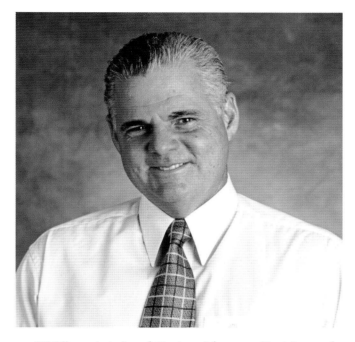

its tagline from "The Enterprise Storage Company" to "where information lives." Intended to convey EMC's role in a world becoming increasingly dependent on digitized information, this tagline has underlined the EMC logo for almost a decade as the company continually evolved. The word "lives" carries both the legacy of EMC's storage leadership and the vibrancy of an active verb that describes much more than "where information sleeps."

EMC's "where information lives" campaign was guided by the company's belief that the new century would bring a new era of building businesses out of information and that EMC would take responsibility for helping organizations channel the information torrent for greater productivity and a decisive competitive advantage. That April, the company rolled out its Symmetrix 8000 systems, with a higher-than-ever 19.1-terabyte capacity, and its new CLARiiON FC4500 systems and software.[41]

Yet, for the first time since the late 1980s, clouds began gathering on the horizon. The high-tech market had begun to slow in 2000, even as EMC maintained its torrid pace. But in early 2001, potential clients began eschewing EMC's systems in favor of lower-priced competitors. The company would soon enter a period that would test its mettle, forcing it to reorganize its strategy beyond storage.

Representatives of longtime EMC customer Siemens visit EMC's Executive Briefing Center in Singapore.

### CHAPTER SEVEN

# A SENSE OF URGENCY: EMC's SALES CULTURE

*There's nothing more important you can do than to be with a customer.*

—Jeff Goldberg

EMC WAS FOUNDED BY TWO ENGI-neers who not only understood the importance of the selling process, but were natural salesmen themselves. Dick Egan considered sales to be the most underrated profession and treated this discipline with great reverence. So it was not surprising that EMC made a point of striking a balance between its engineering and sales functions early on. Sales and marketing help a company understand what's truly important to its customers and how to conceptualize solutions for them. Engineering innovates to quickly develop the knowledge, technology, and products that solve customers' challenges and help advance their businesses. EMC became widely known for this unusual dual strength.

### The Art of Selling Value

EMC's "customers-first" ethos was really a founding principle. As the late Jeff Goldberg, who joined EMC in 1988 and served as a mentor to many in the early sales force, observed, "EMC's co-founder Dick Egan always said, 'You have two ears, one mouth. Use them in that proportion and you'll be OK.' Dick's philosophy has always been to talk to your customers. Listen to what they say. We have the money. We have the talent. If we listen carefully, then our customers will tell us what to do."

"The DNA embedded by Dick Egan, Mike Ruettgers, [Dick's oldest son] Jack Egan, and Roger Marino was this: You don't walk past a ringing telephone. You answer it. You don't transfer calls. You answer the question or tell the caller that you will get back with the answer," Goldberg said. "I could walk into a meeting with Dick or with Mike and say, 'Sorry I'm late, I was at the Executive Briefing Center with a customer.' No more questions asked. The word 'customer' carried that kind of meaning when I arrived at EMC—and it has ever since. There's nothing more important you can do than to be with a customer."

By natural extension, the next-most important priority for any EMC headquarters personnel or support function is to be responsive to the needs of the sales force. This attitude pervades EMC. The company's most senior executives will drop everything to help support the field sales force or meet directly with a customer or partner. As Goldberg put it, "We'll go through a wall for a customer."

---

The late Jeff Goldberg was one of EMC's earliest employees. He joined the company in 1988 and was extremely influential in establishing EMC's sales culture, serving as a mentor to many in the early sales force.

EMC's distinctive and intensely competitive approach to selling was evident early in its history. According to Bill Raftery, senior vice president of Global Product Sales, who has been part of EMC's sales culture for about 18 years, "EMC salespeople were hungrier than their peers in other companies. Most of the salespeople we brought into EMC had played competitive sports in high school and college and didn't come from high-income families. I came from a middle-income family myself. We were hungry to succeed. We hated to lose. We had great camaraderie. And we loved making money."

In 1986, Bill Scannell was one of those EMC recruits. He became one of EMC's most successful sales managers, and today he is an EMC executive vice president, running Americas Sales as well as Global Sales Programs. "I was finishing up college at Northeastern University," recalls Scannell. "I was bartending nights. One of the guys I bartended with had a brother who was with EMC back when it was a small startup company, and he knew I wanted to get into sales. He encouraged me to chat with his brother, and he convinced me I should come interview with the company. And so I did."

"When you first joined EMC sales back then right out of college, you went into the telemarketing organization, which was kind of a six-month training program where they trained you on the company, the products, how to sell, how to sell over the phone, with the assumption being that if you could sell over the phone, it's going to be a lot easier to sell face-to-face. And they got you with no preconceived notions about what the real business world was all about and how many hours a week you were supposed to work."

For Scannell, hard work was already understood. "As I had gone through high school and col-lege, I worked anywhere from 40 to 60 hours a week, balancing full-time jobs with getting an education. So the hard work wasn't new to me, but the culture was exciting because everybody did it. You wanted to try to outwork everybody else."

"In the training program," Scannell continued, "everyone wanted to be the first person in and the last person to leave. And besides that, I was leaving the office to go bartend at night. That was a skill from Dick Egan and Roger Marino and every time they walked through the building, they also were fighting to be one of the first in and the last out. So it wasn't as though the management was saying 'do as I say and not as I do.'"

In the late 1980s and early 1990s, EMC was selling expansion memory for many IT vendors' computer systems, including IBM, DEC, HP, Prime, and Wang. When competing against IBM in particular, EMC was subject to a classic IBM marketing tactic—scare customers away from a competitor with FUD, which stood for fear, uncertainty, and doubt. Explains Raftery, "Our sales guys always managed to overcome this FUD. They were very professional. They were business thinkers. They knew what to say to customers. In the memory business, for example, we proved to customers that IBM had been charging them a huge premium for a long time, taking advantage of the lack of competition in the aftermarket. We leveraged IBM's own programs against them."

Raftery relates a story that conveys how relentless, nimble, and creative EMC salespeople were in winning business, involving one of EMC's customers based in Boston:

*The customer had told IBM that EMC had won the business, and they were going to do the deal with us. But IBM kept returning to this customer, and each time would drop its price lower. I heard about this from one of our Boston-based guys, a legendary sales rep named John Hand. He and I discussed the situation, and I said: "Let's tell the customer to buy IBM's storage systems, and then we'll come in soon after IBM installs them. We'll de-install the systems, take them back, and return a few*

Bill Scannell was one of EMC's most successful sales managers, and later became an EMC executive vice president, leading Americas Sales. (Photo © George Disario 2009.)

*hours later and install all EMC systems. The customer will be happy because we're now able to double his storage capacity for the original price."*

*So, IBM came in at midnight. They installed the equipment. We showed up with our customer engineers at 6 o'clock the next morning. And with the customer's permission, we deinstalled IBM and installed EMC equipment. The next day the IBM rep showed up at the customer's site with his divisional manager, to show off his new account and the fact that he had beaten EMC. The customer conveyed the startling news: "This morning we swapped out all of your equipment for EMC." The customer made out very well. And we made a lot of money reselling IBM's equipment because IBM had lowered its price so much. This was how EMC's sales operated. Our sales culture embodied Dick Egan's mantra of "never, never, never give up."*

Goldberg echoed this point. "When people hire, they tend to look at two factors—one is maturity, the other is willingness. Many companies would rather the heavy emphasis be on experience.

EMC's model was the exact opposite. We put most of the emphasis on willingness. You can teach experience but you can't teach willingness. We used to say that the only difference between an EMC sales rep and a pit bull is that eventually the pit bull will let go. That speaks to the tenacity of our sales culture. We put a lot of attention on ensuring we hired the right kind of people."

One of those people was Adrian McDonald. He joined EMC in 1988 in his native England. After 15 years of sales management roles in different countries, he finally went home to run EMC's UK and Ireland business in 2003. "I had 10 international moves," said Adrian. "I'm not sure there is anyone else in the company with that many."

"I was always inspired by the fact that with EMC, anything was possible," said McDonald. "If you talked to a European company, they would refer to restrictions. In EMC, anything was possible. My first job at EMC was selling the Digital product line. The orthodoxy was that you bought your big system, and then you basically were shackled in all ways to the mother company of that system. We challenged the orthodoxy. At the time, Digital would sell you a memory board for £60,000. We could provide in some cases double the memory with added functionality for let's say £50,000. We would sell the memory and often times install the memory ourselves. We literally would have some of these products in our car trunks. On occasion I actually had some under my bed, which were worth more than the house I was living in."

McDonald boils it all down this way: "When people ask me what is the essence of EMC, I always give them the same answer, which is the ability to change. No. 1, we have always been inspired by great leaders. Dick, Jack, Roger, Mike Ruettgers, all were great leaders. Joe is a great leader. The thing I found most amazing of all was when we would get together every January, normally in Boston. One of these gentlemen, or a combination of them, would discuss what EMC was going to be like this year. There would be gasps about two things. One was the ambition, because the numbers they were pro-

Adrian McDonald, vice president and general manager for UK & Ireland, joined EMC in 1988.

jecting always seemed far bigger than could be achieved, and secondly the kind of company that we needed to be this year. I've never seen an organization that was open enough to embrace change so quickly. We went from that January meeting to training, and two weeks later we were out serving as the new company. We didn't wake up as unique sales guys. We went out, and we saw a bunch of customers, we talked about the new things that we heard. We learned as much from the customers as we did from internal training."

Creating and sustaining leadership in each of its addressable markets have always been an imperative for EMC. As it was building its storage business in the early 1990s, EMC had to figure out how to remove a barrier that most new technology companies face in trying to establish momentum in a market dominated by a much larger and more established rival. In the early 1990s, for example, IBM dominated mainframe storage—it had a 76 percent share of all the capacity shipped in 1990, when EMC's share was essentially zero.

One sales campaign that helped to turn the tide for EMC was called "Sweep the Floor in '94," which referred to swapping out IBM and Hitachi storage equipment in customers' data centers and replacing these systems with EMC equipment. A sales representative able to sweep the floor of any Hitachi or IBM storage would be paid double commissions. In the first 180 days, EMC swapped out more than 100 terabytes of IBM and Hitachi equipment for EMC systems. In addition, IBM and Hitachi sometimes wound up buying back all of their own equipment from EMC. Jack Egan, who was running worldwide sales at the time, called "Sweep the Floor in '94" one of the most successful programs EMC ever ran.

By the end of 1995, EMC's market share had soared to 41 percent of mainframe storage capacity shipped, surpassing IBM's, which had fallen to 35 percent. Enabled by the technology advantages of Symmetrix, the EMC sales organization played an essential role in successfully taking on such a large competitor.

### Sell Value

Goldberg is widely credited within EMC for shifting the focus of the sales force to value selling and encouraging salespeople to call higher up in the organizations of their customers and prospects. "We went from a purely financial sell to differentiating EMC's products based on their broader value to a customer's business, including playing to the rapidly emerging demand in the early 1990s to use information more competitively."

The first differentiator that EMC used was the size of the footprint—a smaller footprint would mean savings in power and cooling. IBM's comparable systems had substantially larger cabinets. Customers could fit some of EMC's early storage systems under a desk. "One of the justifications we used with customers was that with EMC storage systems you wouldn't have to build a bigger computer room. You could recover a good portion of the space inside your computer room," said Goldberg.

Another early product differentiator that EMC stressed was speed—specifically, rapid access to critical data regardless of hardware or software limitations. The speed of EMC's systems would enable customers to change the way they scheduled their jobs. It helped them lengthen the business day, develop new services for their customers, and enter new markets.

"Value propositions never go out of style," said Goldberg. "The only question is what do you emphasize at a given time? The financial impact? The operational impact? The business impact? We changed our emphasis as economic conditions changed." For example, EMC sales built powerful total-cost-of-ownership and return-on-investment tools. The company was able to show customers potential cost savings of millions of dollars related to reduced cooling, footprint, power use, and more.

And when EMC introduced Symmetrix in 1990, customers were able to do things that were appreciably different. They were able to get their own new products into the marketplace faster. They were able to change the way they serviced their customers. EMC created the concept of enterprise storage—storage not simply for customers' mainframe or midrange systems but for every type of computing platform they might have. It was all about ensuring that EMC could make a compelling case to customers about why it was strategically relevant.

Building lasting relationships with its customers and developing an understanding of their total business were very important to the sales organization. In 1994, EMC launched its Executive Briefing Center (EBC), a place where the company could bring in customers and deepen relationships with them. The EBC was Goldberg's brainchild. As he recalled, "We sought to create a center where there are few if any distractions, where we can talk with customers about their business and what we can do to make them successful, where we can bring in EMC experts and discuss the value propositions we can bring to a customer's company. We saw the center as a chance to discuss potentials with customers and how we can realize them by working together. We would also use these customer visits to give customers a tour of our facilities—our integration labs, demo and solution centers, our manufacturing floor—to convey that EMC was a very substantial company. EMC always came away from these sessions knowing a great deal more about its customers."

### Turn Selling into a Discipline

Raftery says there was and is a lot of pressure for salespeople to perform. "You had to be on top of your game. You had to be a top performer. The way it worked was we did 'drill-downs.' I remember when Harry Dixon took over North American sales. Harry said to me, 'We're getting on a plane.' We traveled for two weeks straight and inspected dozens of the company's sales districts. In each district we visited, we inspected every single sales rep. Every rep had to get up and talk in detail about every one of their accounts. We did a drill-down. We asked each rep: 'Who are you calling on? What's the current storage on the floor? What applications are they using their storage for? What's the compelling event that is making the customer buy now? Have you brought them to the Executive Briefing Center?' "

EMC's sales organization continues to do these drill-downs and inspections. In fact, in keeping with its disciplined approach to sales, EMC has established best practices for inspection. Long experience has shown EMC that a thorough inspection and the ability to drill down and ask the right questions ensure that the sales team is aligned, focused on the priority opportunities, and driving toward the same closing schedule. For EMC, the ultimate

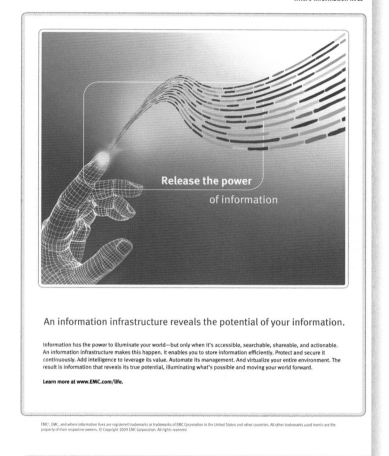

In 2008, EMC launched a series of ads to convey the importance of having the right information infrastructure in place to release the power of information by making this information accessible, searchable, shareable, and actionable.

goal of inspection is to find out how to improve the end result and the deal.

A force behind every major deal that EMC sales closes is the company's technology consultants—also known as TCs, the people who help sales reps "engineer" a sale. TCs, known over the years as "systems engineers," "sales engineers," and other titles, work alongside a sales rep or channel partner before a sale closes to help a customer understand how and why products being proposed will best meet that customer's requirements. TCs traditionally work in the field and are devoted to specific customers, sales territories, technologies, or partners. EMC's nearly 3,000 TCs handle the technical discussions as sales reps concentrate on learning the customers' business requirements.

Howard Elias, EMC's president of Information Infrastructure and Cloud Services, explains: "A technology consultant's job is incredibly important. Our TCs must first help our customers make the right technology choices to solve their business problems and get the most value possible out of their EMC investment. Then our TCs must ensure an integrated solution is properly architected and can be implemented and sup-

Bill Raftery, senior vice president of Global Product Sales, has been part of EMC's sales culture for the better part of two decades.

ported. With one foot in Sales and the other foot in Global Services, our TCs are the trusted advisors to our customers."

EMC works incessantly to ensure that its sales force understands its increasingly broad and rapidly changing product line. For example, in 2007 it introduced a mandatory sales accreditation program to ensure that everyone in its sales organization understands and can fully articulate the value of EMC's comprehensive product portfolio. The structured program creates a consistent baseline of expertise throughout its selling organization as well as more cross-selling leverage across the company's functional groups. "This program," says Bill Teuber, EMC's vice chairman and also head of Customer Operations, "goes to the heart of putting customers first and differentiating EMC."

EMC's super-competitive spirit and playfulness often merged. Raftery relates a story about Scott McNealy, a Silicon Valley legend who was chairman and CEO of Sun Microsystems, one of several large computer companies with which EMC competed directly for storage footprint and market share. "Several of our senior sales guys were out at Pebble Beach at the AT&T Pro-Am golf championship. We found out where McNealy's house was, and we lined up 100 golf balls that had EMC logos imprinted on them. We hit the golf balls onto his property. Now, we didn't break any windows—or we would have paid for them. We heard that McNealy went out to his backyard the next day and saw EMC golf balls all over the place." Just a friendly hello from the company that kept winning storage business from Sun's accounts.

Even today EMC is using the same strategies it began honing in the 1980s to take market share from the competition. Raftery concludes, "Our sales culture really has not changed at all as it relates to customers. It's all still the do-whatever-it-takes mentality. Never, never, never give up. The one thing that has changed for the better is that our sales organization is far more diverse. There's so much talent globally—and our customer base is so global—that we've made a concerted effort to recruit and build a diverse sales organization. We have been bringing in new talent from around the world and really listening to new ideas and continuing our entrepreneurial spirit."

한국이엠씨컴퓨터시스템즈 (주)
www.emc2.co.kr

모든 정보가 살아 숨쉬는 곳 – EMC

전 세계 100대 기업 중 95개 기업의
주요 정보는 EMC로 관리됩니다

EMC²
where information lives

## Success on a Global Scale

Adrian McDonald tried to build on all he had learned in his various stops when he took over EMC's UK and Ireland business in 2003. "The business was about $250 million at the time," he recalled. "We were not the largest EMC country subsidiary. We set ourselves the objective of being the first EMC subsidiary globally to reach $1 billion in sales by 2008. We reached that goal in 2008, and we were the first EMC country subsidiary to break the one billion dollar mark."

Another place where EMC has excelled, far from Hopkinton, is in South Korea. Kevin Kim joined EMC Korea in 1999. He rose from leading the marketing team to become country manager in 2003. Korea was one of the first countries outside the U.S. where EMC gained the No. 1 market share position in storage. That share reached nearly

In 2000, EMC launched a new global branding campaign. The EMC Orb, shown here in a Korean version of the campaign, is the visual representation of EMC's identity tagline "where information lives." It weaves together all forms of information delivered over every medium and network. The Orb said to customers, "There is a way to get your arms around all your information and accelerate all your business initiatives."

40 percent in the first quarter of 2009. It is no coincidence that Korea is also one of the weakest countries for EMC rival NetApp. "NetApp's market share is less than single digits in Korea, and it has been for years," said Kim. "We know they have done well in many countries, so when they first came to Korea, we decided to try and stop them. That was five years ago."

Innovative sales leaders devise novel ways of motivating and preparing their teams. In Korea, most Monday mornings begin with a voluntary education and training session, an hour earlier than the normal start of the workday. "We cover every new training topic, from Symmetrix VMax to RSA," explains Kim. "Sometimes we set up challenges that our partners are experiencing. We invite all EMC sales, pre-sales, TCs, engineers, and managers. It has become kind of a ritual to EMC Korea people. Attendance is more than 95 percent in every session. It starts virtually every week with learning something. I love the EMC culture."

Left: Kevin Kim, president of EMC Korea, joined EMC in 1999.

Below: In 2004, EMC Chairman and CEO Joe Tucci (left) met with Gee-Sung Choi, who would later become the president and CEO of Samsung Electronics, at a hotel in Seoul for the Signing Ceremony of OEM Partnership between Samsung Electronics and EMC. That year, Samsung began OEMing all CLARiiON products with the Samsung label in Korea.

삼성전자-EMC 사업 협력 조인식
■일시:2004년 2월 4일(수) 11:00~13:00   ■장소:조선호텔 2층 코스모스룸

Steve Leonard joined EMC in 2006, with extensive experience leading selling organizations in both Asian and European markets, most recently leading Veritas and then Symantec in Asia. Now the president of EMC Asia Pacific/Japan, Leonard's challenge has been to meld the classic EMC sales DNA with a wide variety of cultures that sometimes react negatively to aggressive approaches.

"My perception of EMC, as an outsider in the industry, was of a highly competitive, focused, aggressive selling company, very dedicated and passionate. That style does not always play effectively in Asia. We are trying to be as Asian a company as an American multinational can be. We try to listen to our customers and act in a way that is familiar and comfortable for them and still, at the same time, build on the EMC legacy of success and winning."

Leonard has also hired local "homegrown" leaders in these countries, which include some of the world's fastest-growing markets. "Customers in Japan or China or India want to see a leader who will be with them for a long period of time, ideally someone who grew up in that country and has language and culture in common."

All told, EMC has built a value-creation sales force—one of the most respected in the global

Steve Leonard, president of EMC Asia Pacific/Japan, joined EMC in 2006 and is responsible for driving EMC's growth and leadership, enhancing partner and channel relationships, and furthering product development throughout the region.

IT industry. Its customer loyalty ratings attest to this. Customers clearly see EMC delivering the value it promises, from the technology through the relationships.

Bear Stearns specialist Michael Mulroy (left) and EMC CEO Joe Tucci (right) at the New York Stock Exchange in late 2000.

CHAPTER EIGHT

# A DRAMATIC TRANSFORMATION

## 2001–2003

*I've seen the economy this bad, but I have never seen it turn this bad this fast.*

—Joe Tucci[1]

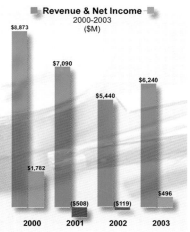

**Revenue & Net Income**
2000–2003
($M)

$8,873 · $7,090 · $5,440 · $6,240

$1,782 · ($508) · ($119) · $496

2000 · 2001 · 2002 · 2003

THE YEAR 2001 SEEMED TO START well for EMC. Even though high-tech markets had begun to soften, EMC roared into the year off its best quarter ever.[2] Revenues, which stood at $8.9 billion at the end of 2000 after 50 percent growth in the fourth quarter, were expected to reach $12 billion by the end of 2001.[3]

However, as 2001's first quarter unfolded, EMC could not remain immune to the first worldwide recession since 1975 and the worst annual decline in U.S. spending on IT since 1958. Shortly after announcing its plans to hire 10,000 more employees in 2001, EMC was forced to reverse course and reduce employee ranks by more than 4,000.[4] That same month, EMC lowered its growth forecast for the year, acknowledging that orders from dot-com customers had ground to a halt, while its stock price plunged more than 50 percent to a new 52-week low.[5] The road to $12 billion had encountered its first bumps.

During 2001, EMC's revenues dropped 20 percent from the previous year. Its market capitalization of $225 billion at the end of 2000—more than the aggregate share value of the world's six top automobile manufacturers—dropped 90 percent over the next nine months.[6] At the end of the year, the company's revenues stood at $7.09 billion—a far cry from EMC's original $12 billion target—and a net loss of $508 million on the bottom line.

### The Turnaround Artist

In January 2001, a year after he joined the company, Joe Tucci was named EMC's CEO, and Mike Ruettgers became executive chairman of the board. Dick Egan, meanwhile, "took a step back," as he phrased it, to serve as chairman emeritus of the board of directors. At this point, Egan was 64 years old and had, for more than 21 years, poured his heart and soul into the company he had co-founded. In May 2001, U.S. President George W. Bush appointed Egan ambassador to Ireland. A letter to Egan in the company's 2000 Annual Report described some of the personality traits that had made him such a successful leader:

> *The raw energy. The tireless devotion to customers. The passionate insistence on being the best. And the unshakable conviction that roadblocks are just thrills in disguise.*[7]

By 2003, EMC's income had begun to improve after a decline in the early part of the 21st century.

At EMC Analyst Day 2001, held in Boston, Massachusetts, more than 400 portfolio managers, Wall Street analysts, and journalists learned how EMC was riding out the economy and leading the way to a new generation of information storage technology. Left to right: Joe Tucci, Mike Ruettgers, Jim Rothnie, Dave Donatelli, Frank Hauck, and Bill Teuber.

Egan's letting go, and Ruettgers turning over the CEO duties after nine historic years, clearly signaled a new era. Tucci, as a leader, was known for his forthrightness. He explained EMC's reversal of fortune in terms of both the downturn in IT spending and the degree to which EMC had depended on the Internet boom for its growing revenues.

"We got very addicted to that boom and the Y2K boom," he admitted. "And when that went away, there went a big chunk of our business."[8]

Because Tucci had made a name for himself by turning Wang Laboratories around, observers wondered if the selection of Tucci, in 1999, for a leader-

ship role at EMC signaled some prescience on the part of Ruettgers, Egan, and the Board. EMC's situation, however, would prove very different from what Tucci faced at Wang. As Tucci explained:

*The restructuring and turnaround of EMC and Wang were totally different.*

*Wang was a company with no money, no cash, and that had lost its market position in e-mail, word processing, and office automation. ... There's no way you could rebuild the company into what it was. Basically, we rebuilt the company into something totally different. ... EMC had a big restructuring here, too, but the company obviously remained king of storage. Storage was still growing, and we still had $4 billion in cash, so it was a very different kind of turnaround.*"[9]

### A New Course

Reviving EMC first required unseating the enshrined conviction that storage could remain relatively immune to market downturns. The belief that storage needs would grow so long as there were enough people creating information was countered by the losses EMC experienced in the wake of the dot-com bust.[10] Taking into account sales to e-businesses, telecommunications providers, and service providers placed more than 20 percent of EMC's revenue at risk.[11]

Facing mounting uncertainty within the industry, Tucci sought to better understand the changing realities of the storage market to help him predict the future demand for EMC products. As part of his efforts, he spoke directly to the CEOs and chief financial officers of potential customers. EMC also hired consulting firm McKinsey & Company to help the company understand its products in relation to an ever-changing marketplace. According to Mark Quigley, senior vice president of operations for the RSA Security Division of EMC:

*They helped us come up with different thoughts on how we might want to structure the organization and how we might want to sell. ... We actually worked with them to brainstorm how and where we should change, [then] debated it amongst ourselves, agreed upon a direction, and then moved on to implementation and execution.*[12]

With new knowledge and a fresh perspective, Tucci began the difficult task of purging EMC of unprofitable areas of business, and the even more difficult task of downsizing. EMC reduced its head count from approximately 24,500 at its

Above: Mark Quigley, formerly EMC's head of sales operations and its chief information officer, later served as senior vice president of operations for the RSA Security Division of EMC. *(Photo © George Disario 2003.)*

Left: As early as 2002, EMC planned to reduce its dependence on system sales by focusing on increasing its software and services offerings. The mantra became "50-30-20."

### EMC's Business Model
Information Storage Revenue

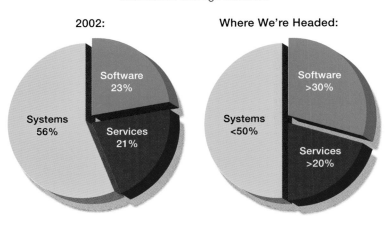

2002:
Software 23%
Systems 56%
Services 21%

Where We're Headed:
Software >30%
Systems <50%
Services >20%

peak to 20,140 at the end of 2001, with the target of 19,000 by mid-2002.[13]

During the process of scaling back EMC, Tucci focused on rooting out bad behavior within the company. Certain members of the sales force, he learned, had become known for overconfidence verging on arrogance, and in the process had damaged extremely valuable customer relationships.

"We had a reputation for having the most aggressive sales force on the planet, which was great and not something we were going to throw away," he explained. "But customer after customer told me that we were crossing the line. It was clear to me that there were some deep pockets of pure arrogance."[14]

In May 2001, EMC sponsored the world's largest women's leadership conference at the Simmons Graduate School of Management (GSM) Leadership Conference. There were 2,600 attendees, including 140 women from EMC. Pictured are EMC employees (back row, left to right) Rebek Duhaime of engineering, Heather Lowre of global events, Sarah Adamsky of engineering, Kim Santillo of global alliances, Debbie Snow of engineering, Christine Carlson of marketing, Jane Pingalore of engineering, (front row, left to right) Jane Eldredge of global alliances, Keri Sefton of engineering, and Kathy Klotz of global alliances.

Tucci fired the worst offenders among the sales force, demonstrating in the process that disrespectful tactics would not be tolerated. However, only a small number of the employees lost their jobs as a result of bad behavior. More were let go because their jobs were eliminated with Tucci's restructuring plan. He remained dedicated to ensuring they were treated well throughout the process. "People are entitled to honor and respect," Tucci said. "Most of them had contributed significantly to the company but were not the right people to take us to the next level."[15]

After he had streamlined and stabilized the company's operations, Tucci next embarked on the path toward renewal, engaging in a strategy revolving around a new revenue model for products and services. He sought to align EMC with a firm grasp of market realities, including a greater focus on the mid-tier storage market to attract financially squeezed customers who had grown less willing to spend money on high-end systems. The result was a reconfiguration of the company's revenue targets:

- Hardware (storage systems), which had comprised 75 percent of revenue, would eventually comprise 50 percent or less.
- Software, which had accounted for 16 percent of revenue, would be boosted to 30 percent.
- Services, which previously represented 9 percent of revenue, would be raised to 20 percent.[16]

To facilitate the shift in revenue makeup, Tucci brought in executives with experience in software and services. Michael Gallant, senior director of analyst and media relations, recalled the transition:

*Joe Tucci did a classic turnaround move: a third, a third, and a third. He kept about a third of the existing management team, promoted a third up, and brought in a third from outside. That seems to have worked, because the third that he'd brought in from the outside had heavy service and software experience. So he didn't break the culture, but he shocked it a little.*[17]

The mix of old and new executive leadership ushered in changes to EMC's partnership strategies. "We decided we really had to change our market strategy, because back then, we were pretty much a high-touch, direct sales organization, selling into the FORTUNE® 1000," Quigley said. "However, it became pretty clear that a lot of the growth was going to come out of the lower end of the marketplace."[18]

In the spirit of partnering, Tucci began relying more heavily on distribution channels. On October 22, 2001, as part of a strategy to increas-

Above: Joe Tucci shakes hands with former Dell President and CEO Kevin Rollins (left) in celebration of a new distribution contract between their companies. As part of the deal, Dell bundled CLARiiON storage systems with its industrial networking sales packages.

Left: In 2002, CEO Joe Tucci illustrated EMC's distinctive will to win by walking across hot coals. The EMC Fire Walk Experience, in which new sales hires walk across a bed of hot coals, was aimed at showing new recruits that they could overcome a fear of going beyond their comfort zones by being prepared.

ingly target small and midsize businesses, EMC signed a deal with Dell, the world's leading manufacturer of personal computers and a company trying hard to revamp its business model to sell more to enterprises. Under the terms of the contract, Dell agreed to sell EMC's CLARiiON storage systems as part of its computer networking packages. In 2003, the two companies agreed to a five-year extension.

Although the agreement represented a change of tactics by both companies, as Dell had already been selling its own line of storage products, the benefits were mutual. "This agreement has delivered proven results for our business and our clients' businesses," explained Michael Dell, founder of Dell. "We have the ability to offer them new products, improve the supply chain, and increase industrial capacity."[19]

## Storage Evolution = EMC Evolution
### Building on the Shoulders of Giants

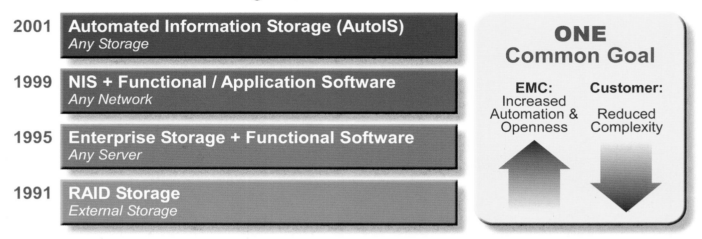

In the fourth quarter of 2001, EMC announced its open storage management software initiative and introduced the first set of AutoIS products. By year's end, AutoIS was widely hailed by the media as one of the year's most significant developments in information storage management.

### A Shift in Identity

As part of EMC's expansion into the mid-tier market, the company began to reduce its dependence on Symmetrix systems to shift more of its focus to software and mid-tier SAN and NAS systems.

In late 2001, Tucci announced the creation of three units that would align the company's operations with its new strategy:

- Storage platforms operations, led by David Donatelli, encompassed development efforts aimed at EMC's Symmetrix, CLARiiON, and Celerra systems and the rich software functionality that runs directly on these systems.
- Open software operations, led by software architect Erez Ofer, accelerated the company's efforts in developing storage management software compatible with competitors' hardware.

- Customer operations, led by Frank Hauck, oversaw distribution and support of EMC storage platforms, services, and open software technologies, as well as customer service.

Additionally, EMC's sales organization began dividing operations according to large, commercial, and small customer segments, leading to enhanced targeting of products and services as well as superior customer relationship management.[20]

In his talks with CEOs, chief financial officers, and consultants, Tucci learned that customers had grown weary of proprietary software and wanted software capable of working with storage devices from different manufacturers. Recognizing that customers would seek out the products and solutions that suited them best—regardless of the manufacturer—EMC began releasing software and hardware specially designed to support network devices and storage arrays from other companies. EMC's Automated Information Storage (AutoIS) strategy was directly aimed at developing products that managed competitors' systems, allowing customers to organize and control information across various IT environments.

Joe Tucci explained the value of AutoIS:

*Until now, complex and growing information infrastructures have been difficult and expen-*

*sive to manage. Just as information technologies such as spreadsheets have automated time-consuming work, AutoIS automates the management of information in less time at lower costs. By managing competitors' systems as well as our own, AutoIS opens up a whole new market for EMC.*

Although AutoIS did not have a long run as a central EMC strategy, it served two important purposes. First, it signaled to the market that EMC was committed to being an "open" software provider—making its key software offerings valuable for customers even when they weren't running all-EMC storage environments. And second, it heralded the beginning of an era in which Joe Tucci's EMC would invest billions in developing and acquiring software for information management, protection, security, and virtualization.

Despite the many changes in EMC priorities, Tucci refused to waver on his commitment to increasing funding for storage-focused research and development. Even in the midst of financial challenges, in 2002, EMC's investment in research

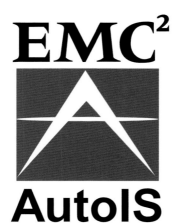

and development remained several times larger than that of its nearest competitor.[21] Tucci did, however, change research priorities to focus two-thirds of EMC's engineers directly on software development by 2003.[22]

**Building Trust**

Guiding EMC during a time of financial difficulties while supporting a substantial shift in priorities and steering the company toward a radically different course required a strong sense of trust between Tucci and his employees. His leadership style differed in many ways from Ruettgers', perhaps reflecting their differing backgrounds. Ruettgers came from a military background and strongly favored order and process, even going so far as to institute a dress code policy. Tucci, on the other hand, favored less hierarchy in a work environment and decided against a company-wide dress code, believing employees would "feel empowered to let common sense be their guide."

According to Ruettgers, those differences helped make Tucci a less intimidating leader. "Employees are more comfortable approaching him," Ruettgers admitted.

However, despite their different styles, the two leaders worked well together, and Ruettgers continued to meet with customers and represent EMC at

Above: Although short-lived, EMC's Automated Information Storage (AutoIS) strategy marked the beginning of the company's commitment to developing open software compatible across multiple platforms.

Left: Bill Teuber, EMC Vice Chairman, assists CEO Joe Tucci in the day-to-day management of EMC and leads EMC Customer Operations, the company's 9,000-person sales and distribution organization. Teuber joined EMC in 1995 and served as chief financial officer between 1997 and 2006, leading the worldwide finance operation with responsibility for the company's financial reporting, balance sheet management, foreign exchange, audit, tax, and investment banking programs. *(Photo © George Disario 2009.)*

public events. Tucci, meanwhile, continued to build on the founding values that his predecessors had used to lead EMC to its leadership position within the industry. According to William Teuber, Jr., vice chairman and longtime chief financial officer:

*What Joe Tucci has done is taken the best attributes of EMC that Dick Egan started with and Mike Ruettgers really nurtured, and he's further nurtured them. He hasn't changed the character of the place; he's enhanced it, and with Tucci style. ... What made this place great were the people and the energy and the attitudes, and what we didn't need was someone to tell us that it's all going to be different now. What Joe said is, "I'm going to take that energy, and I'm going to harness it in my own way and make it even better."*

A team from EMC customer DoCoMo (seated) visits EMC's Executive Briefing Center in Hopkinton, Massachusetts. Among the EMC executives in attendance were CEO Mike Ruettgers (seated in the center of the DoCoMo team) and several executives from EMC engineering and customer service.

*And that's what he's done. He's really stood on the shoulders of Mike and Dick. He hasn't reinvented the wheel. He's taken the wheels that were created for him.*[23]

Tucci, like Egan and Ruettgers, placed great value on communication and made extensive use of meetings and videoconferences. He also made a point of answering every e-mail he received from customers and employees.[24] Tucci also believed strongly in consensus building. Whereas Ruettgers led the company through many individual discussions, Tucci favored meetings where everyone had a chance to speak.[25]

His frank and open communication style earned him the trust of investors and analysts—a critical component of EMC's strategy to regain lost ground. While this trust undoubtedly required faith on the part of investors, Tucci won them over with his vision and confidence. As Tucci explained:

*We kept telling the analysts what we were going to do even if they didn't like it. I told them point-blank. I said we're going to do this in three phases.*

*We've got a first stage. We're going to do a lot of cost cutting and stabilize the company. The second phase is we're going to rejuvenate it. We're going to put our strategies in place to grow and tell you why we're going to differentiate ourselves. The third phase is growth. We're going to produce growth."[26]*

The fact that Tucci chose candor over trying to paint pleasant pictures was appealing to analysts, recalled Tony Takazawa, vice president of global investor relations: "Being as open as Joe is, he earns tons of credibility with the investor base when he speaks with them because they can tell that he's not spinning anything and not trying to keep anything back."[27]

### Renewal

Such trust from outside and within the company proved necessary, as EMC's climb back was a long one. Its 2002 revenues only reached $5.44 billion, down almost 25 percent from $7.09 billion in 2001. Yet EMC employees remained determined to continue rolling out new products. In 2002, EMC released its Celerra NS600 network server, which combined Celerra's NAS capabilities with the cost advantages of more affordable CLARiiON systems.

As EMC and all companies struggled in the post-9/11 economy, the company quickly recognized that changes in the way businesses were being regulated were creating another major data storage opportunity. The Public Company Accounting Reform and Investor Protection Act of 2002 was sponsored by Senator Paul Sarbanes and Representative Michael Oxley in response to several major corporate accounting scandals that had captured headlines. Sarbox, as it became known, required corporations to meet many strict new requirements and implement new controls and practices on how they managed and retained information.

In April 2001, EMC had purchased FilePool NV, a Belgian software company. Its technology would form the foundation of another major storage system launched in Brussels a year later, one that was designed from the ground up to manage fixed-content data that does not and could not change over its lifetime. The system, EMC Centera, created a new class of storage called CAS for content-addressed storage. Unlike other EMC systems, which stored

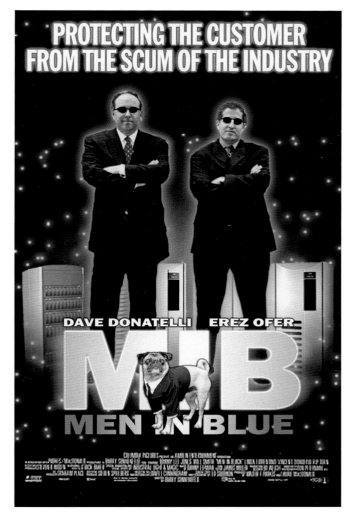

This tongue-in-cheek poster was created for one of EMC's major storage systems product launches. Pictured are (left) Dave Donatelli, head of EMC's storage systems business, and Erez Ofer, head of EMC's open software business.

transactional data, Centera would store data as objects, each with a unique identifier—a signature with a date and time stamp—which could prove its immutability. If a record was changed, it would create a second object with its own date and time stamp signature, leaving a digital paper trail. This unique system allowed records and images to be stored and recalled quickly if needed with digital proof that they had not been altered since they were stored. This was valuable to public companies to meet compliance requirements and quickly became popular in other industries, including healthcare, where it was used to store medical images such as X-rays. Inspired by the life sciences boom and the mapping of the human genome, as well as by the Sarbanes-Oxley Act of 2002, Centera quickly became EMC's fastest-growing system.

According to Chuck Hollis, vice president and global marketing chief technology officer:

*Since we've always been in a leadership position, we can define the criteria and chart the progress of the industries we play in. We have a very powerful capacity to define the progress of the industry. ... We were able to define a new category of storage called CAS and then launch that product into the category. Only market leaders can define new categories. Some of the terms that are just bandied about the industry, EMC developed, such as enterprise storage and business continuity. These are now broad industry concepts, but EMC actually created the concepts and the first substantiation of the technology.*[28]

According to International Data Corp., in 2002, EMC served as the world leader in networked storage, including open NAS systems as well as SANs.[29] EMC also led the storage management software

market in 2002 for the fourth straight year, according to Gartner, Inc., even as the market itself experienced an overall decline.[30]

Some of EMC's newfound growth was built on a string of acquisitions. The technology EMC gained through its acquisitions undeniably made it a stronger competitor, particularly in the software market. Besides FilePool, EMC acquisitions during 2001 and 2002 included Luminate Software Corporation, which gave EMC the technology to develop performance monitoring software for storage-intensive applications, and Prisa Networks, a provider of storage management software that enabled EMC to better serve customers with small to midsize SAN environments.

While Tucci firmly believed that acquisitions were of little help unless a business had a very solid foundation, he also remained convinced that to successfully shift its focus to highlight software and services, EMC would need to "acquire smartly."[31] According to Tucci, his decision to acquire a particular company came down to its ability to success-

Pictured is EMC's Six Sigma training Kaizen team.

Left: Former sales executive Tammy Osterman was with the company for more than a decade.

Right: Diane Russell is a senior sales executive in EMC's Mid-Atlantic Enterprise Division and has been with the company since 1988.

fully integrate with EMC's established culture, as well as the rate at which its core business was growing in relation to the market it served.[32] As EMC rebounded and made even more significant acquisitions in the years ahead, this philosophy would play an important role in the company's success.

### Customer Focus

As they had during EMC's hard times at the end of the 1980s, many customers remained loyal throughout the rough period following the dot-com crash. However, retaining that loyalty and support required EMC to first respond to customers' needs—one of EMC's consistent strengths.

As Tucci explained:

*I think in a way, customers rebelled against us in 2001 and part of 2002 because we had been charging a pretty big premium over market. ... In a lot of cases, customers felt that premium was too big, and then our approach to justifying that premium made us look arrogant, and I was getting that feedback almost everywhere. We had to change those two perceptions, and after we changed those two perceptions, customers loved the service. They loved what EMC stood for. Once we changed those two areas that they pointed out, customers started voting for us again, and the way customers vote is with their dollars.[33]*

Like Egan and Ruettgers before him, Tucci made customers his top priority. He became known for crossing the Atlantic twice a week when business from important clients was at stake. In late May 2003, during a French air traffic controller strike, Tucci insisted on attending an important client meeting in France. "He was even prepared to land in Brussels and drive to Paris to be there," recalled Frédéric Dussart, vice president and EMC regional country manager Europe South.[34]

Tucci dedicated an average of 40 to 50 percent of his time to dealing directly with customers. As he explained, "If it goes over 50 percent, I find that I can't keep up with my operational duties; if it goes below 40 percent, I feel out of touch."[35]

To keep a customer relationship going over many years, "the No. 1 thing is you have to be there for your customer through the good and the bad," said Tammy Osterman, a sales executive who has been with EMC since 1999. "Being there when you're selling them something—that's expected. But when you're there when you're not selling something—that is what creates the long-term relationship. The customers knew they could always reach us, even if it was 2 o'clock in the morning. They knew we were on their side. They knew we were getting our best people to fix their problems. They knew we cared."

"I'll tell you what I'm most, most proud of," said Diane Russell, an EMC sales executive who joined EMC in 1988, initially on a part-time basis while she was a junior at Boston College. "I have customers I first spoke with in 1990 and that are still my customers today or that I continue to stay in touch with. Most of the customers I have today I've worked with for anywhere from seven to 15 years—and I haven't even been married that long."

EMC has always listened to and learned from its customers. In fact, one of its core values is customers first. Years of pursuing customer loyalty have continually earned EMC accolades, and in June 2001, *Fast Company* magazine named EMC "The World's Most Customer-Centric Company."

The three CEOs in EMC's history (left to right), Mike Ruettgers, Joe Tucci, and Dick Egan, commemorate two-and-a-half decades of growth at EMC's 25th anniversary celebration.

### CHAPTER NINE

# REBIRTH

## 2003–2004

*I was riding a horse better than anybody. Got knocked off, learned a few lessons, and dusted myself off. I'm back on, and I'm riding like hell again.*

—Joe Tucci explaining EMC's comeback approach[1]

ONE OF THE MOST IMPORTANT traits any business can have is resilience. The more resilient a company is, the more change and disruption it can withstand and still recover. The years 2001 and 2002 were especially tough ones for EMC. The economic downturn had hit the IT industry hard. But undeterred by the slow economic cycle in 2002, EMC managed to deliver on the most aggressive schedule of new product introductions up to that point in its history.

The company designed a new series of Symmetrix systems based on its revolutionary new Direct Matrix storage architecture, reasserting high-end technology leadership. It introduced an entire family of new mid-tier CLARiiON and Celerra platforms to take EMC further into fast-growing markets. It broadened its industry-leading line of storage software and also invented a new category of storage for fixed content, such as e-mail archives and medical images, creating a promising market segment that did not exist before. "Never underestimate the power of a great new product cycle," said CEO Joe Tucci.

As the company entered 2003, it did so with the building blocks of a promising future fully in place. By streamlining its operations without sacrificing its heavy investment in innovation, and by broadening its product portfolio dramatically, EMC had evolved from a primary focus on high-end storage platforms to become the only company to offer a full range of open, integrated, automated networked storage solutions designed to simplify storage management. As Tucci said at the time, "We are helping our customers network their entire information base, assuring easy, ubiquitous connectivity to this information from all applications. The value proposition for automated networked storage is compelling. It provides the foundation for business flexibility, information safety, and significant cost effectiveness—addressing three of the top issues facing organizations today."

Beginning in mid-2003, EMC extended its strategy once again, evolving to information lifecycle management (ILM). Here's how Tucci described EMC's continuing evolution to investors in July 2003:

*Going back to the beginning, it was direct attached storage where it was at one array, one*

EMC developed this emblem to convey the elements of its information lifecycle management strategy, which focused on helping customers get the maximum value from their information at the lowest total cost.

# Information Lifecycle Management at Work Within a Hospital

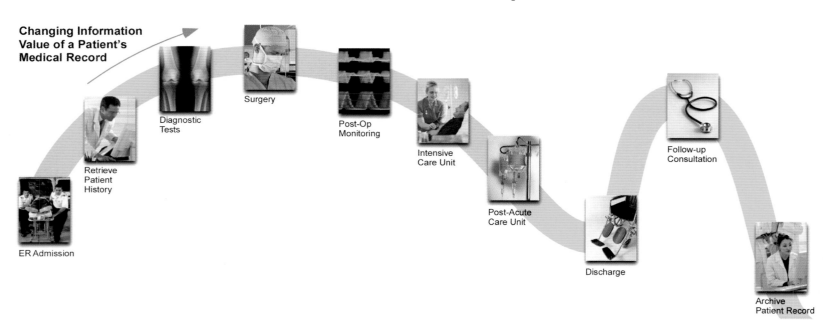

**Changing Information Value of a Patient's Medical Record**

ER Admission

Retrieve Patient History

Diagnostic Tests

Surgery

Post-Op Monitoring

Intensive Care Unit

Post-Acute Care Unit

Discharge

Follow-up Consultation

Archive Patient Record

Above: The fundamental concept behind information lifecycle management is that the value of information changes over time. In this instance, a patient's accumulated medical record becomes extremely important at key junctures during the course of the patient's treatment—very high during surgery, less critical after the patient has been discharged.

Below: EMC employees based in Sydney, Australia, promote information lifecycle management. From left: Steve Redman, Stephen Lloyd-Jones, and Graham Pullen.

*server—one array attached to one server. We then went to enterprise storage. Now we had one array attached to dozens of servers. We then went to network storage. Now you could have dozens of storage arrays attached to hundreds, and maybe even thousands in our bigger customers, of servers. And, of course, once you get multiple hundreds and into the thousands of servers attached via a storage network to storage, the amount of information that proliferates is immense. Customers were clamoring for tools and automation in software to help manage all that, hence we introduced Automated Network Storage. So as we introduce the next one, it'll be very much based on everything that we did with Automated Network Storage. But the interesting thing to note here is we're really going into the next segment ... the information management business. So we're going to collect a lot of information about information and help customers manage that proliferation across the whole lifecycle.*

It had become increasingly clear to EMC that chief information officers at companies large and small needed better ways to manage and protect information, reduce cost and complexity, get the most out of their IT assets, and meet regulatory compliance requirements—all while making their information more accessible. EMC's answer was information lifecycle management (ILM). Through ILM, EMC would help organizations get the maximum value from their information at the lowest total cost at every point in the lifecycle of information. EMC's goal was to become the ultimate information lifecycle management company. ILM solutions soon proved an indispensable information management approach for organizations and companies throughout the world of business and government.

Hospitals, clinics, and doctors' offices use the ILM approach to economically manage patient records, including diagnostic test results, past surgeries, and recommended follow-up treatments, allowing medical professionals to comply with increasingly stringent legal requirements to keep patient data for many years. CareGroup Healthcare Systems and Harvard Medical School, for example, employed ILM infrastructure to move data across multiple systems in a multi-tier storage approach. Recently created and frequently accessed data is stored on Symmetrix systems. Data migrates to CLARiiON once it becomes less relevant in daily interactions, until it is finally archived in a Centera system for long-term storage.[2]

Many companies found the ILM strategy appealing, especially given the escalating volumes of information and increasingly rigorous regulations for how to handle it. As the late Jeff Goldberg, then vice president of customer programs, explained:

*How many customers are consolidating their information? All of them. How many of them are dealing with business continuity concerns? All of them. How many of them are struggling with issues of information control? All of them. How many of them are struggling with content?*

# THE ART OF ACQUISITION

INSTILLING EMC'S EMPHASIS ON ACCOUNTABILITY and customer service has always remained a key component in merging company cultures. As part of its effort to ensure a smooth transition after an acquisition, EMC invited employees of acquired companies to attend Total Customer Experience summits. During the summits, various EMC departments staged presentations describing the status of individual products and services, focusing on how customer service shaped their development.

Because many of the companies EMC acquired did not have comparable product control mechanisms in place, attending Total Customer Experience summits allowed new employees to learn about EMC's inner workings and share in the excitement of joining a supportive, devoted workforce.

"They see other people ... asking for help, showing great results," explained Frank Hauck, executive vice president. "Employees of acquired companies say, 'We want in. We want to be able to take advantage of what you've built, and you can hold us accountable in the same way.'"[1]

The summits also help define the quality of service that new employees will be accountable for. "It's important for them to ratchet up their level of support, service, availability, and reliability so that they can continue our long-standing business relationships," Hauck said.[2]

As EMC continued its trend of acquisitions and global expansion, Joe Tucci began emphasizing the unifying message of "One EMC." The phrase was intended to drive home the importance of integration and presenting a more unified company to its customers, ensuring fewer touchpoints and simpler interactions.[3] Although some acquired companies were completely absorbed into EMC's established divisions, others continued operating as relatively autonomous units, including Documentum, VMware, and RSA Security.[4]

*All of them. How many are struggling with cost? All of them.*[3]

The company also meticulously tracked outages and problems using the Six Sigma quality control system, first introduced at EMC in 2003. Six Sigma uses stringent mathematical guidelines to reduce product defects and variations in processes. As EMC expanded the scope of its Six Sigma implementation throughout the middle of the decade, the company remained committed to extending the tradition of quality initiated under Mike Ruettgers.

Jim Pearson, vice president of customer advocacy, worked closely with Tucci to implement the corporate-wide rollout of EMC's Lean Six Sigma initiatives. He recognized that employees would need empirical data to make decisions, instead of taking the more anecdotal approach that had often characterized the company. "If a customer had an

Members of the EMC executive management team gathered for a day-and-a-half of "Green Belt" training in 2004 to learn the principles of Lean Six Sigma. Left to right: Dave DeWalt, Mike Ruettgers, David Wright, Jack Mollen, Mark Lewis, Bill Teuber, Joe Tucci, Howard Elias, and Paul Dacier. Teaching the course was Mark Kiemele, president and co-founder of Air Academy Associates, a world leader in helping organizations apply Lean Six Sigma methodology.

issue, everything stopped, and we'd go right out and try to fix things," he explained. "We had a hero mentality, but it was very reactive. We needed to be much more proactive."

By focusing on quality while continuing to fulfill the needs of the high-end storage market, as well as the mid-tier market, EMC's executives believed the company could meet the needs of an increasingly broad range of potential customers.

The strategy produced impressive results. First quarter earnings for 2003 were higher than expected, and that upward trajectory continued throughout the year as EMC's revenues reached $6.24 billion, up 15 percent (counting acquisitions) from the previous year, compared with a worldwide storage market that grew about 4 percent. Net income for the year was nearly $500 million compared with a net loss of more than $100 million for 2002.

### Symmetrix Reloaded

Along with EMC's increased emphasis on software and services, the company continued making improvements to its flagship storage system. In February 2003, EMC released Symmetrix DMX. The system took three years to develop and was based on Direct Matrix technology, a flexible architecture that employs a network of dedicated, point-to-point connections instead of traditional buses or switches.[4] Symmetrix DMX vastly increased the speed of information flow over previous versions. Analysts declared DMX four to five times faster than competitors' products.[5] With prices ranging from $409,000 to $2.5 million, the largest Symmetrix DMX systems were capable of storing enough information to fill 4 million books.[6] The transformed system proved appealing to major corporations, and on the very day EMC unveiled Symmetrix DMX, General Mills purchased six of the units to help manage financial operations and human resources, among other functions.[7]

Symmetrix built EMC's reputation for engineering and innovation leadership and became the platform on which most of the company's accelerating growth was based during the 1990s and early 2000s.

# The Evolution of Symmetrix
## Two-Decade Tradition of Innovation

| Symmetrix 4400 | Symmetrix 5500 | Symmetrix 3000/5000 | Symmetrix 8000 | Symmetrix DMX-1/-2 | Symmetrix DMX-3 | Symmetrix DMX-4 | Symmetrix V-Max |
|---|---|---|---|---|---|---|---|
| World's first integrated cached disk array | World's first terabyte disk array | "Open Symm" stored data from all major server types | 3-4 times faster than competitors' systems | Direct Matrix Architecture breaks new ground | World's first petabyte disk array | World's highest-performing, most cost-effective, secure, and energy-efficient high-end array | World's first high-end array purpose-built for the virtual data center |

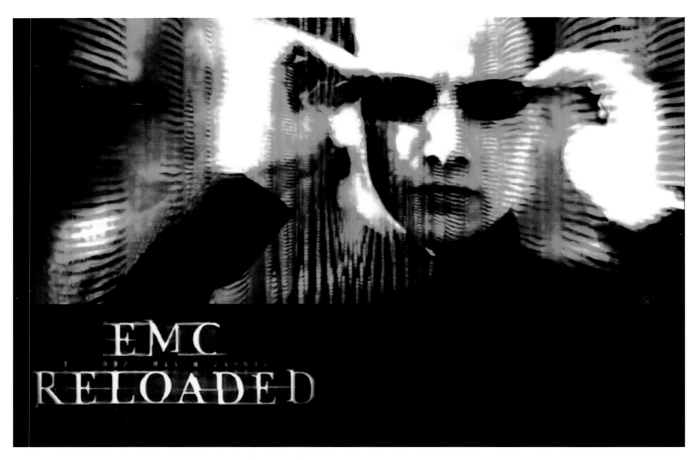

EMC
RELOADED

To add more excitement to the product's release, EMC invited more than 5,000 customers, business partners, and members of the press from across the U.S. to sneak previews of *The Matrix Reloaded.*

In May 2003, EMC invited more than 5,000 customers, business partners, and members of the press to sneak previews of the film *The Matrix Reloaded* to promote its new Direct Matrix Architecture.

### Growing ILM

In October 2003, EMC acquired Legato Systems, Inc., a backup software and services provider based in Mountain View, California, with approximately 1,500 employees worldwide. It was the company's 10th software-related acquisition since January 2000 and EMC's largest acquisition of any kind since Data General in 1999.

EMC had been evolving from a vendor of storage platforms at the high end of the market into the leading provider of comprehensive, integrated storage solutions for the full range of customer needs. Legato, too, had been undergoing its own evolution, building on its traditional strength in backup and recovery to position itself for promising growth

areas such as e-mail and content management. This is key, said Joe Tucci, "because acquisitions have less to do with what the other company has done in the past than how that company fits into your future. Legato has great growth potential in these rapidly growing markets and significant value to EMC as EMC becomes the place where more information lives."

Then in December 2003, EMC acquired Documentum, a leader in the growing market for enterprise content management software. Already a strong EMC partner, Documentum helped organizations manage the explosion of digital content that drives business, everything from Web pages and spreadsheets to medical records and audio and video. As Joe Tucci told employees at the time, "If you've heard us speak about the coming 'content wave' in information technology, then think of Documentum as one of the dynamic surfers best positioned to catch the wave."

Documentum's software functionality filled a key component of EMC's information lifecycle management strategy: giving customers information about their information (or "metadata") so they could formulate policies that will automatically migrate data to the right place, and even dispose of it, at the right time. Coupled with the acquisition of Legato, Documentum accelerated EMC's software business and solidified its ability to become the ultimate information lifecycle management company.

In January 2004, EMC pulled off what would become its most important acquisition yet, capturing VMware, the world leader in Intel-based virtualization software. Based in Palo Alto, California, VMware was widely viewed as one of the most exciting companies in all of technology. VMware, as its CEO and President Diane Greene noted, "had established a new layer of infrastructure software that would allow customers to take a pool of servers and treat them as a single resource, consolidating and managing their applications across that pool of physical machines." Customers were using VMware's innovative software to virtualize and provision IT resources in the compute layer to drive up utilization rates, minimize downtime interruptions, and reduce

# EMC's Starring Role

WHEN *THE MATRIX* SEQUELS WERE RELEASED in 2003, EMC seized the opportunity to promote its newly released Symmetrix Direct Matrix Architecture. However, the company had earned its place in show business years earlier. Through a partnership with Massachusetts-based Avid Technology, Inc., a leading supplier of digital editing hardware and software, EMC systems contributed to the production of blockbuster films such as *The Perfect Storm, The Cell, Mission Impossible 2*, and the original *Matrix* movie, as well as television shows such as *Survivor*.[1]

After EMC acquired Data General in 1999, it took over an equipment manufacturing agreement combining the capacity of CLARiiON's mid-tier storage capabilities with the editing prowess of Avid's digital media tools. The collaboration created state-of-the-art systems that allow editors to easily store, rearrange, and manipulate digitized video. Clint Eastwood praised the system for its "slickness" compared to older film-editing methods.[2]

Since the collaborative system bypasses the video transfer step that was part of older editing products, it has proven instrumental for broadcasters replaying highlights of heavily watched events just after they happen. NBC Sports took advantage of this capability during the 2000 Summer Olympics in Sydney, Australia.[3] Live footage was sent directly to disk for broadcasters to replay, allowing viewers to see Australian swimmer Ian Thorpe's record-breaking finishes, along with other Olympic highlights, within seconds.

The system also found its way to the island of Pulau Tiga, near Borneo, during the filming of reality TV smash hit *Survivor*, which premiered in 2000. The show was produced with help from four Avid Media Composer 1000 systems and three CLARiiON systems. Footage was edited daily on the island and then sent to California, where editors used seven more integrated Avid and CLARiiON systems to perfect each episode.[4] CLARiiON systems have also been used in the Los Angeles offices of Beantown Productions, which produces original programming content such as documentaries for cable television and promos for shows such as *The Simpsons* and *Seinfeld*. In 2008, EMC storage systems appeared in two thrillers, *Body of Lies* and *Eagle Eye*.

# LESSONS LEARNED DURING THE DOT-COM BUST

IN AUGUST 2004, *BARRON'S* DUBBED EMC CEO Joe Tucci the "Makeover King." Tucci, former head of Wang Laboratories, had once again proven his ability to turn companies around.[1] Reviving EMC from the doldrums of the dot-com bust required Tucci's keen ability to listen to different sets of customers and adjust to new market realities.[2]

Tucci encouraged employees and executives to take a fresh look at the facts, challenging some of the long-standing beliefs about EMC's customers and markets. In the early part of the decade, investors and high-tech companies alike believed that the growth of information would perpetually increase, creating a constant stream of sustainable business. However, the subsequent collapse of countless businesses within service provider and Internet business sectors proved that even the newest revolutions in cyberspace could prove just as fallible as the previous technological booms of the past.

Carefully calculating and predicting the true effects of the downturn in 2001 allowed Tucci to recognize how much of EMC's cost structure to trim back. "It's incredibly difficult," Tucci said of downsizing.[3]

costs. This complemented the way customers were using EMC information infrastructure software to virtualize and provision storage to realize similar benefits. By using VMware's technology with its own, EMC could enable organizations to abstract both the storage layer and the compute layer. That allowed them to go from virtualized storage to a virtualized information infrastructure—the foundation for next-generation information lifecycle management solutions. This gave companies the ability to configure and reconfigure their compute and storage environments dynamically, with no downtime, as their business needs changed.

In recounting the technology momentum provided by the acquisitions of Legato, Documentum, and VMware, Joe Tucci observed, "I'm really proud of what we've built here at EMC. We now have a company that is again redefining and leading the networked storage marketplace. We have expanded into information and content management. And now we are the company best positioned to deliver on the Holy Grail of IT, namely the virtualization of open systems server, network, and storage environments."

EMC has a reputation for being very deliberate, thoughtful, and careful in its approach to acquisitions. And for nearly all of them, EMC followed a three-step process. The first step is always, "Don't break it." In Tucci's words, "When you buy a company, you want their technology, you want their customers, and you want their people—above all, their people." The second step is to apply what Tucci calls "the EMC effect," by which he means ensure that this company is able to grow faster under the EMC umbrella than it could as an independent company. The third step is to tightly integrate the acquired company with EMC. The one exception to this three-step approach was VMware. Right from the start, EMC made it clear that it would operate VMware in a community source model, providing even its fiercest competitors with access to VMware's technology—all with the aim of encouraging VMware's rapid growth. EMC's sustained success in buying and integrating companies prompted *BusinessWeek* to write in its July 10, 2006, issue, that "Tucci has quietly put together one of the most successful mergers and acquisitions records in the tech industry."

During 2002 and 2003, Tucci also realigned the company's operations according to shifting market realities, relying less on the high-end Symmetrix systems that had made EMC famous in the 1990s and focusing more on mid-tier hardware, software, and services.

The shift in focus also entailed sustaining EMC's significant investments in research and development. Tucci considered R&D absolutely essential to EMC's ability to thrive and always worth the expenditure, despite the lean times.[4] From 8.8 percent of its revenues in 2000, EMC's R&D expenditures rose to 14.4 percent in 2002 and 11.5 percent in 2003.[5]

The deep structural changes at EMC required a substantial shift in the company's culture as well. Tucci recognized that EMC's exceptional culture had been flourishing long before his tenure with the company. Changes could only be implemented incrementally, allowing enough time to bring about a deeper shift in the long run.

Toward this end, he took steps to eliminate the preexisting hierarchy at EMC. After EMC moved its corporate headquarters to a single building at 176 South Street in Hopkinton, Massachusetts, Tucci favored a layout with similar offices designed to emphasize equality.[6] In addition, during meetings and conferences, Tucci preferred to place a greater prominence on building consensus, allowing every participant an opportunity to speak.

Perhaps most significantly, Tucci sought to drive change by serving as an example to his employees. Tucci always took the time to answer his own e-mails. He remained approachable, making sure to spend personal time listening to EMC's customers and spanning the globe to meet with important prospects.[7] "These little things make a big difference when you're in the middle of a transformation," Tucci explained.[8]

### Merging Cultures

EMC's pace of acquisitions meant the continual integration of employees, business practices, and technology. To help weather the challenges of merging disparate companies into one corporate culture, EMC developed an integration plan focusing on three key operating principles. David Gingell, then vice president of marketing for Europe, the Middle East, and Africa, lived through such a transition himself. He arrived at EMC in 2003 after eight years at Documentum.[8] Gingell described EMC's three-pronged strategy:

*We ensure that we follow what we have called the three A's. ... We try to ensure that the organization we acquire remains accountable to the greater EMC, the mother ship, for [proper] execution and continued successful growth. ... There's also an autonomy that we need to maintain. ... Documentum remained an autonomous group in order to ensure that we made the right decisions based on the whole content management space. The third A is alignment, ensuring that [acquisitions] support the core EMC sales force and core EMC strategy.*

Accountability proved a vital feature in linking acquired companies to EMC, as EMC's own no-excuses culture encouraged all employees to complete what they say they are going to do. At the same time, EMC executives remained careful not to disregard the business philosophies of acquired companies, maintaining the distinctive atmosphere to which longtime employees had grown accustomed. That balancing act was complicated by the fact that, global growth notwithstanding, EMC remained a New England company, forged in a different place and time in technology history compared with many of the supposedly more "laid-back" California companies it had acquired.

Erin Motameni, senior vice president of human resources, spoke of that cultural difference as a diversity that EMC needed to embrace while keeping its core values intact:

*I have absolutely seen openness to learning from acquired software companies. Yet I think that as we've managed those acquisitions, we've been very careful about not just dumping them into EMC's culture and "EMC-izing" them, but really learning what we can from them about the software business. ...*

*We're really trying to appreciate their strengths and learn from them.*[9]

### Winning Again

By the end of 2003, Tucci had lived up to his reputation as a transformation artist. "I think that Joe has done an outstanding job. He walked into a hornet's nest," said Paul Dacier, executive vice president and general counsel.[10] "We could have either died or changed. He forced change."

Even facing economic adversity, EMC's employees worked very hard to keep their attention fixed squarely on what matters most: how to provide customers with the best total experience in the

industry. That determination, along with the ability to roll with market changes, also attracted new employees. Becky DiSorbo, hired as director of marketing for the Asia Pacific/Japan region in early 2006, said she was first drawn to the company during its transformation stage. As DiSorbo explained, "It was a fast-growing company, but unlike other companies of its size, the great thing about EMC is its ability to transform, and keep things moving forward, but also be nimble and quickly adapt to changes in the marketplace."[11]

Part of that confidence came from EMC's innovative, supportive spirit. As Mary Bracoloni, senior director of event marketing, explained:

*I think the biggest thing at EMC [is that] you can be anybody you want to be. I mean, no one is pigeonholing you. You're not walking in going, "This is the job today. Congratulations." It's more like, "This is your baseline job." You can do whatever you want with it as long as you get that baseline job*

---

EMC has a long and successful track record of acquiring and integrating outstanding companies, enabling it to strengthen its core business and extend its market to new areas.

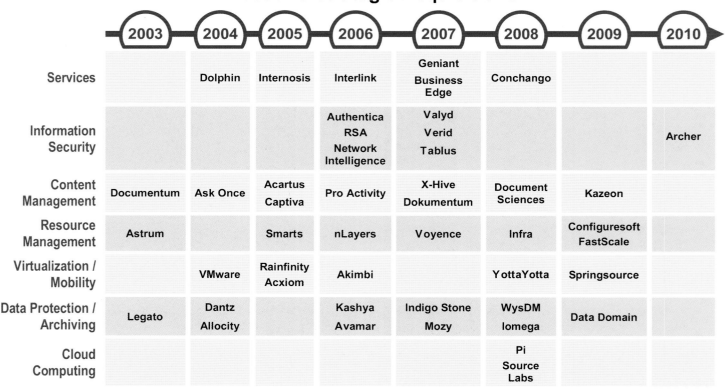

## Since 2003, EMC has Invested ≈$11 billion in About 45 Strategic Acquisitions

| | 2003 | 2004 | 2005 | 2006 | 2007 | 2008 | 2009 | 2010 |
|---|---|---|---|---|---|---|---|---|
| Services | | Dolphin | Internosis | Interlink | Geniant Business Edge | Conchango | | |
| Information Security | | | | Authentica RSA Network Intelligence | Valyd Verid Tablus | | | Archer |
| Content Management | Documentum | Ask Once | Acartus Captiva | Pro Activity | X-Hive Dokumentum | Document Sciences | Kazeon | |
| Resource Management | Astrum | | Smarts | nLayers | Voyence | Infra | Configuresoft FastScale | |
| Virtualization / Mobility | | VMware | Rainfinity Acxiom | Akimbi | | YottaYotta | Springsource | |
| Data Protection / Archiving | Legato | Dantz Allocity | | Kashya Avamar | Indigo Stone Mozy | WysDM Iomega | Data Domain | |
| Cloud Computing | | | | | | Pi Source Labs | | |

Above: The EMC event marketing team is the program management center point for EMC's hundreds of annual events. Some of its members include (left to right) Dan Preiss, leader Mary Bracoloni, Nancy Gallagher, Jim Robert, and Chi Huey.

Below right: Named by *Sports Illustrated* magazine as "the greatest winner of the 20th century," basketball legend Bill Russell visited EMC in January 2004 to talk about the power of teams. In addition to meeting with EMC CEO Joe Tucci, Russell met with a team of EMC employees. Standing left to right: Mike Murphy, Steve Bardige, Laurie Lober, Carter Wilkie, Mark Fredrickson, Terri McClure, and Peter Schwartz. Seated left to right: Paul Dacier, Bill Russell, and Elisa Gilmartin.

in networked storage markets, including network-attached storage and storage area networks.

Meanwhile, EMC continued solidifying its alliances with other leading companies. In April 2003, EMC and Microsoft reached a deal to share software code and designs, collaborate on sales and customer service, and jointly market products.[13] Under the terms of the agreement, EMC licensed Microsoft's Windows Powered NAS to deliver a new network-attached storage product called NetWin for the fast-growing lower end of the NAS market. Around the same time, Cisco and EMC announced that EMC would sell, service, and support Cisco's MDS 9000 series of switches and directors for storage area networks and work jointly on developing the next generation of storage networking technology.[14] In June of that year, EMC extended its agreement with Dell into 2008, enabling Dell to continue manufacturing EMC's CX300 (CLARiiON) systems under the Dell/EMC name.[15] The arrangement also included provisions permitting Dell to serve as an authorized dealer of high-end Symmetrix systems, leading to increased sales.[16]

All of that change, confidence, and cooperation proved invaluable to EMC's astounding turnaround. EMC's revenues rose 32 percent to $8.23 billion in 2004, and net income grew 76 percent. In 2004, the company achieved another breakthrough: For the first time ever, software and services accounted for more than half of the company's revenues.

In January 2005, *BusinessWeek* magazine named Tucci to its list of best managers, noting, in particular, his expansion into software and services

*done, and it's almost like a challenge that people get a chance to rise to. ...*

*If you want to give it a shot, give it a shot. EMC allows employees to experiment a little bit. It's that ability to be able to just say, "I want to make a difference." No one has ever stopped me.*[12]

As an extra assurance to employees, customers, and stockholders, the company maintained its investments in R&D, kept broadening its product portfolio, and remained the front-runner in the field of information storage and management. In 2003, EMC led the external controller-based disk storage market for the sixth consecutive year. It also led

Above: In 2003, EMC opened its first software development center in South Asia, in Bangalore, India. Pictured are some of the employees at the new location.

Below: Pictured at EMC China's first Solution Center opening in Beijing, China, in 2003 are (left to right) former EMC executive Gary Jackson, then vice president of sales in Asia Pacific/Japan; Steve Fitz, former president of EMC Asia Pacific/Japan; Bill Teuber, vice chairman and, at the time, chief financial officer; and former EMC executive Patty Chang, who was the country manager of EMC China/Hong Kong.

and his efforts to boost the visibility of EMC's mid-tier storage offerings.

## A Growing Global Economy

Along with dramatically expanding its product portfolio, EMC had begun stepping up its investment in international markets to drive its revenue growth in regions where it was underrepresented either from a direct presence or a market share perspective. In August 2003, EMC opened a storage solutions center in Beijing, its first in China and third in the Asia Pacific/Japan region.[17] In February 2004, EMC announced plans to establish its third logistics and services support center in India and plans to double its presence in Russia.[18]

As EMC aimed to capitalize on opportunities presented by growing economies, it also focused on expanding its horizons in terms of its corporate culture. As Steven Fitz, then president of Asia Pacific/Japan, explained:

*The Asia Pacific/Japan region is home to some of the fastest-growing GDPs in the world. So it was a tremendous opportunity for us to jump in and take advantage of the hyper-growth that's happening in this part of the world ... which creates some unique challenges as well as opportunities.*

Navigating this challenge led to a greater emphasis on nurturing diversity within the company. In 2004, EMC senior management launched a "Living Inclusion" strategy, a partnership with employees around the world to strengthen diversity within individual locations and throughout EMC as a whole. As part of this strategy, employee groups such as the Women's Leadership Forum, Black Employee Affinity Group, Asian Circle, and Indian Subcontinent Employee Circle were created to make it easier for employees of different nationalities and backgrounds to support each other and take a more active role in the company.

By mid-2004, people born outside of the United States made up 30 percent to 40 percent of EMC's engineers.[19] According to Motameni:

*We've always seen that as a rich source of talent for us and a strength of the company. In the technology [field], there is a rich history of diversity and of valuing differences and being focused on what people contribute to the work and really nothing more.*

*I think in other parts of the organization, as our strategy has changed, we've become more diverse. … We have much more of a partner focus, and we really want to understand our customers better, to make tighter connections with our customers, so there is much more of an appreciation for the diversity of EMC's sales teams. I think the appreciation for diversity has grown along with the maturity of the business and the complexity of the business.[20]*

EMC's growing worldwide staff was attracted to the company's distinct vision and clearly defined goals. Prospective employees found themselves wanting a role in helping EMC thrive.

A former longtime Microsoft executive, Sanjay Mirchandani joined EMC as senior vice president of Singapore-based global alliances and international development and later became chief information officer. He said the

specific strategy EMC laid out after the rough post-dot-com period attracted him to the company. He added:

*EMC built out a strategy that said, "Hey, we're going to focus on software. We're going to focus on services. We're going to focus on technology."*

*I looked at some of the acquisitions, and I spoke with Joe Tucci and Bill Teuber and some of the other executives. It became clear to me that the company had a deep vision, and I guess the best thing was that I really felt that this would give me a chance to … be part of the decision-making process as we moved forward to the next stage of growth.[21]*

### 25 Years of EMC

On August 23, 2004, the company reached its silver anniversary. From the early days when Dick Egan and Roger Marino ran the company from a basement office, EMC had grown to employ 21,000

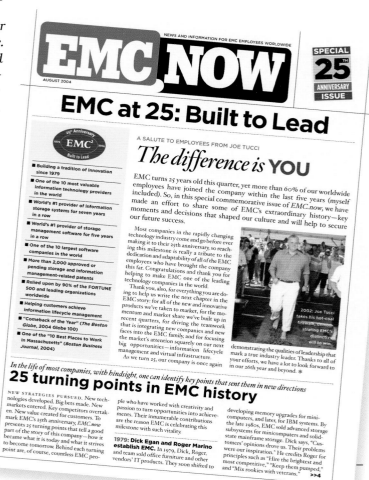

This special 25th anniversary edition of the award-winning publication *EMC.now* was released in August 2004.

Right: At the celebration of EMC's 25th anniversary, then chairman Mike Ruettgers and founder Dick Egan walked toward the stage, accompanied by a standing ovation from more than 4,000 employees.

Below: EMC commemorated its 25th anniversary with an ad in the *Boston Globe* celebrating the hard work, dedication, and spirit of innovation that have led the company toward increasing success.

people in more than 50 countries.[22] Although 60 percent of EMC's staff had joined the company within the previous five years, many longtime employees remained, fondly remembering the hard work, innovation, intimate working environment, and strong personal relationships.[23] As Kathie Lyons, vice president of global customer operations, explained, "Being comfortable around the people you work with, and liking them very much, becomes a big reason to stay."[24]

According to Bill Teuber, then chief financial officer, the interpersonal connections among EMC employees have helped nurture a strong sense of community:

> *You know, there's an energy within the doors of EMC. That's what I could feel then, and I still feel it today. I hope all of the other 21,000 people feel it too. I feel that's one of the things I'm trying to make sure happens. I've become a storyteller here. I've become one of the old guys. I am part of the history, not talking about the history.[25]*

On July 22, 2004, at the company's anniversary celebration at its Southborough, Massachusetts, facility, Dick Egan addressed the thousands of

When EMC celebrated its 25th anniversary in 2004, Dick Egan spoke to thousands of EMC employees about his affection for the company and its people as his wife Maureen appeared on the screen behind him.

employees in attendance and thanked them for their contributions to the company.

"I'm often known for saying, 'It's the products, stupid!'" he said. "But let me tell you—I've known all along that it's really the people. All of you—and all of your colleagues around the world—have built something lasting and remarkable—a company that tens of thousands of companies in every industry rely on to keep their operations running. I love this company, and I love you all."[26]

Egan, serving as chairman emeritus, recalled meeting with analysts and prospective investors in 1986, shortly after deciding to take his young company public. In New York, Egan, Marino, and then chief financial officer W. Paul Fitzgerald met with an IBM investor from a bank that EMC had eliminated from its underwriting syndicate. "Not the most friendly fellow," Egan said. "His question was 'Mr. Egan, as we know, all companies eventually go out of business. What is it that will cause EMC's demise?'"

As Egan recalled, he had not considered that idea in 1986: "I had never even really thought about it, and, standing here today, I can't see why I ever will!"[27]

As EMC expanded globally, it recruited top talent from around the world. From left to right: K. C. Fung, director of technology solutions at EMC Hong Kong; Edwin Wan, sales director at EMC Hong Kong; T. Rajah, chief information officer of EMC customer CLSA; and Gabriel Leung, general manager of EMC Hong Kong.

### CHAPTER TEN

# EMC TODAY

## 2005 AND BEYOND

*The EMC story continues to impress people.*

—Steven Syre, business columnist for the *Boston Globe*[1]

THROUGHOUT ITS HISTORY, EMC has grown and developed by building on its considerable strengths. These strengths include a passion for helping its customers succeed, a willingness to invest heavily in market-focused innovation during good and bad economic times, and an unrelenting focus on storing, protecting, and managing information. The company has also maintained the ability to attract, develop, and retain highly talented individuals, and the resolve to make change and continuous learning the norm at EMC.

The result is a FORTUNE® 200 information infrastructure solutions leader that, at age 30, marshals the diverse talents of more than 40,000 employees in more than 80 countries to help individuals and organizations bring the power of their information to life. EMC operates with a diversified portfolio of hardware, software, services, and solutions that goes far beyond storage. It generates more than 50 percent of its revenues from software and services. It conducts its investment activities in R&D and acquisitions on a global scale. And the company now considers nearly every user of digital information—from the largest global organization to the individual consumer—to be a potential customer.

The year 2005 proved to be one of the most successful and important in EMC's history. On a purely financial level, 2005 marked EMC's third year in a row of profitable, double-digit revenue growth, gaining significant market share and expanding the market opportunity for its products and services. Revenues for the year grew 17 percent to $9.7 billion, and for the first time since 2000, EMC's net income exceeded $1 billion.

The executive management team and the EMC board of directors believed so strongly in the company's strategy, direction, and future opportunities that they invested more than $2.7 billion in the company during 2005. More than $1 billion of this investment was directed to R&D; about $680 million was used to strengthen the core business, through acquisitions; and more than $1 billion was used to buy back EMC stock.

Most significant for the long term, EMC saw the full flowering of its information lifecycle management (ILM) strategy. ILM shaped every aspect of its business—the talent it hired, the investments and acquisitions it made, the products and solutions it designed, and the partners it worked with. For customers, ILM proved to be a great information strategy, and for EMC's business, it proved to be a great growth strategy. In fact, EMC's sustained focus on

CEO Joe Tucci speaks at the opening of EMC's R&D center in Shanghai in November 2006.

At the 2005 North American International Auto Show in Detroit, Michigan, longtime EMC customer DaimlerChrysler honored EMC for outstanding performance in quality, system costs, technology, and delivery. Left to right: Heinrich Reidelbach, DaimlerChrysler vice president of international procurement services; Frank Hauck, EMC executive vice president; and Thomas Sidlik, the DaimlerChrysler Board of Management member responsible for global procurement and supply.

ILM served as a catalyst in transforming EMC from an information management and storage company into what it is today—a trusted information infrastructure and virtual infrastructure provider. And with that transformation, the strategic direction of the company broadened from ILM into IT infrastructure. In EMC's hands, information infrastructure helps organizations and individuals intelligently and efficiently store, protect, and manage information so that it can be made accessible, searchable, shareable, and ultimately actionable.

Spurring EMC to broaden its strategic direction were three trends. First, digital information was quickly becoming one of the most important assets in nearly all organizations. Second, the sheer growth of information was surpassing even the most optimistic forecasts. For example, market research firm IDC forecast that by 2011 the digital universe would be 10 times the size it was in 2006. And third, while IDC estimates that about 70 percent of this information will be created by individuals, the responsibility for managing 85 percent of it—overseeing its security, privacy, reliability, and compliance with regulations—will belong to businesses and other organizations.

In response, EMC substantially broadened its capabilities, product portfolio, and strategic partnerships to put all the pieces in place to bring the power of its information infrastructure strategy to life. EMC combined its strengths in storage, content management and archiving, security, and virtualization, with the breadth of a 14,000-person-strong Global Services organization to help customers activate the power of their information.

Underlying its information infrastructure is the company's unwavering commitment to delivering the best Total Customer Experience (TCE) in the IT or any industry. TCE was not simply a new phrase for an old, if timeless, concept: customer satisfaction. As Frank Hauck, executive vice president, wrote to employees in mid-2005:

> *In the old days, a focus on product features and functions, bolstered by passion and commitment from our field organizations, was enough to make EMC the global leader in our industry. Those days are long gone. Today we need to raise the bar to be not only the best in the business for products and solutions, but the best in everything that touches a customer. EMC's Total Customer Experience initiative that is rolling out with increasing speed around the world is the differentiator that will keep us No. 1 and widen our lead over everyone else.*[2]

What EMC recognized is that customer loyalty goes far beyond customer satisfaction. It's not uncommon for companies to have customers who say they are "satisfied" with their products and yet purchase the same products from another company if offered something only slightly better or cheaper.

**Total Customer Experience**

EMC created its own rigorous definition of customer loyalty. Its definition gets at the whole picture of what its customers value about its products and services and their interactions with its people. In other words, EMC resolved to pay attention to and improve customers' total experience with the company.

For EMC, loyalty became the sum of its customers' points of view on three questions:

- Overall, how satisfied are you with EMC's people, products, and services?
- Given your experience with EMC's offerings, how likely are you to continue as a customer and repurchase?
- How likely are you to recommend EMC's products and services to others?

With that in mind, EMC launched a major company-wide effort, which continues to this day, to

## The Voice of the Customer Drives EMC Action
### Lean Six Sigma: Data Drives the Process

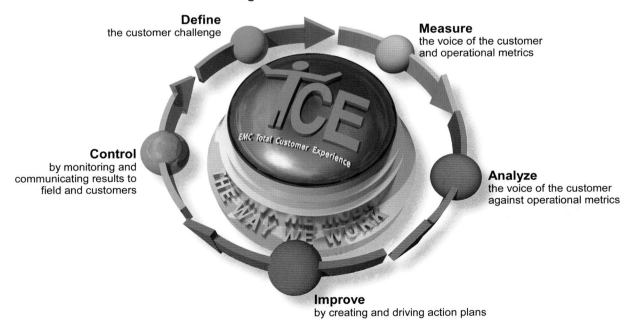

**Define** the customer challenge

**Measure** the voice of the customer and operational metrics

**Analyze** the voice of the customer against operational metrics

**Improve** by creating and driving action plans

**Control** by monitoring and communicating results to field and customers

ensure that customers get reliable products, feel good about the support they get before and after they buy from the company, and have a knowledgeable partner to work with to keep their businesses in tune. Behind those straightforward goals were complex processes and initiatives that extended to every corner of EMC—to sales and services operations, engineering, IT, manufacturing, and marketing.

### Symmetrix DMX-3

By the middle of the decade, EMC had become one of the most trusted brands within the data center. One of the reasons for this is EMC's ability to continually redefine high-end information storage and take it to new heights. For example, in July 2005, EMC announced the world's largest-capac-

The DMX-3 was unveiled in August 2005 as the world's most scalable storage array, with a 1 petabyte capacity in a single array and almost three times the processing power of its nearest competitor.

ity, fastest, most scalable storage array to date: Symmetrix DMX-3. Capable of scaling to support 1 petabyte of capacity in a single array, the system also had almost three times the processing power of its nearest competitor.

DMX-3 customers consisted of some of the most information-intensive enterprises that EMC serves, including banks, security trading firms, telcos, airlines, retail chains, Internet service providers, and government agencies. They run transaction-intensive applications and store massive amounts of information while working under stringent record-retention regulations. Commenting on the new storage system, industry analyst Charles King from Pund-IT Research noted, "Overall we believe EMC's DMX-3 stands out as a singular high-end solution that also complements the rest of the company's all-star storage lineup."

During 2005 and 2006, EMC was not only opening new chapters in high-end storage, it was investing heavily to dramatically expand its product line, to innovate in new areas of technology, and to extend its market to new areas by acquiring and integrating innovative software companies. EMC

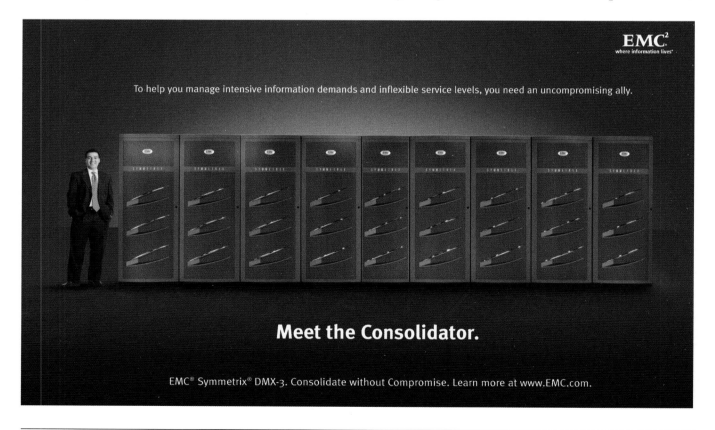

EMC²
where information lives

To help you manage intensive information demands and inflexible service levels, you need an uncompromising ally.

**Meet the Consolidator.**

EMC® Symmetrix® DMX-3. Consolidate without Compromise. Learn more at www.EMC.com.

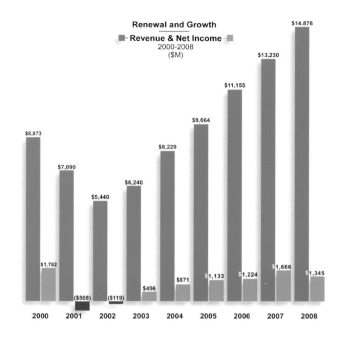

**Renewal and Growth**

■ Revenue & Net Income ■
2000-2008
($M)

$8,873

$7,090

$5,440

$6,240

$8,229

$9,664

$11,155

$13,230

$14,876

$1,782

($508)

($119)

$496

$871

$1,133

$1,224

$1,666

$1,345

2000 2001 2002 2003 2004 2005 2006 2007 2008

Above: EMC has undergone a dramatic and highly successful transformation in its business, resulting in year after year of balanced and consistent financial performance.

Right: Howard Elias, president and chief operating officer, EMC Information Infrastructure and Cloud Services, has overall responsibility for setting the strategy and creating the best practices that create an exceptional total customer experience, and help customers plan, build, manage, and support their information infrastructures. *(Photo © George Disario.)*

was intent on bringing more value not only to the way organizations manage their information, but also to the way they optimize their IT infrastructures.

One of these new and highly productive areas of technology is virtualization. At the most fundamental level, virtualization is about making complex technologies simpler to use and manage. EMC's offerings for virtualizing storage and file systems, together with the offerings of VMware for virtualizing x86 infrastructures, collectively gave EMC by far the strongest and broadest virtualization portfolio in the IT industry.

Another new area EMC began investing in during the middle of the decade was model-based resource management—the ability to have a common, simple, and cost-effective way to manage the

resources within a large data center. To achieve this, EMC began building on its strengths in storage resource management, a market the company created and continues to lead, and on its expertise in model-based management technology, which came to the company with its 2005 acquisition of Smarts, a private company specializing in event automation and network systems management software.

**Smarts**

Integrating Smarts software into EMC's already robust offerings enabled customers to even more effectively monitor and safeguard their information storage networks.[3]

Smarts represented a revolution in network management, simplifying the network error detection process by using modeling, correlation, and root cause analysis technologies. Previous solutions for detecting problems within large computer networks typically involved compiling error incident statistics into databases and frequently relied on pattern matching to test the system for inadequacies.

# STRENGTH IN NUMBERS

As EMC HAS GROWN, IT HAS BUILT A ROBUST AND impressive roster of alliances and partnerships with other leading IT companies. Given the highly diversified nature of the technology field, it is impossible for any one company to go it alone. Partnerships are essential to survival, and EMC's long partner list includes companies of all sizes, from start-ups to giants such as Microsoft, Oracle, Cisco, and Dell. "This is a big environment, and others have to win, too," Joe Tucci explained.[1]

Partnering with companies has allowed EMC much greater access to products and customers through alternate business channels. Since 2001, EMC's successful partnership and reselling agreements with Dell have proven invaluable in increasing CLARiiON sales. As EMC diversified into software and services, partnerships helped give EMC an edge in new markets, providing the company with expertise and expanding its opportunities. Agreements with Microsoft, for example, have allowed EMC to offer enhanced support in implementing ILM solutions for Microsoft application users. In the late 1990s, EMC entered into a partnership with Oracle that has fostered the joint development of information infrastructures that are exceptionally efficient, scalable, and secure, helping customers reduce costs and maximize profitability.[2]

Small companies specializing in cutting-edge technology have also been a boon to EMC. Before acquiring file virtualization provider Rainfinity, EMC partnered with the company, reselling its software alongside EMC's own offerings.[3] Such

However, traditional methods proved incapable of handling the daily realities organizations faced as they increased in size and complexity.

As Howard Elias, president and chief operating officer, EMC Information Infrastructure and Cloud Services, explained:

*In very large, complex environments, those methods become tremendously challenging, if not ultimately impossible, because now there are literally hundreds of thousands of devices and millions of events that are occurring, with relationships going on across a company's worldwide network.*

*Let's say a company has 100,000 employees, running literally thousands of applications—to just collect a whole bunch of data, throw it in a database, and pattern match is just unwieldy. So Smarts utilizes a model-based approach, which is essentially turning that problem on its ear. ... Smarts actually goes out and ascertains the specifics of that environment, understands the connection points of relationships and the behaviors, and then, most importantly, models those. Smarts builds a model of that environment, so that as all of these*

*error events start occurring, organizations know what to ignore and what to pay attention to based on the model's behavior.*[4]

The Smarts model provides a more intelligent way of identifying the root cause of problems, allowing end-to-end automated IT management services for intricate network, application, server, and storage infrastructures. In contrast to traditional systems, where IT professionals might receive multiple alerts from dozens of affected systems, forcing them to pore over error reports before determining the cause of the problem, Smarts technology offers sophisticated real-time analysis tools designed to isolate problems, making it easier to determine the root cause.

"We have really assembled an entirely new paradigm of management that we refer to as model management," said Elias.

### Acquisitions and Partnerships

In the middle of the decade, EMC continued to steadily develop its identity as a complete informa-

partnerships are clear wins for both parties, as EMC gains expertise in new fields, while partners gain access to much larger markets than they would otherwise. As Rainfinity co-founder Charles Fan commented, affiliation with EMC earned his company's products a much larger market share than they ever could alone.[4]

Some of the greatest lessons EMC has learned about partnerships have come from abroad. EMC currently conducts nearly all of its business in Korea and China through partnerships, although that has not always been the case. According to Steve Leonard, president of EMC Asia Pacific/Japan operations:

*Historically, EMC had chosen not to work much with partners in Asia, but the market here really does survive and thrive on a leveraged model, meaning that partners can reach many hundred times more customers than any one company can. One of the things we've been working hard on over the past year is to change our profile with partners so that they know we want to work with them, and [we want] to change our programs to make it more rewarding and profitable for partners to work with us.[5]*

EMC has harnessed its partnerships into a number of successful customer-oriented programs. The EMC Select Program offers customers EMC-tested, third-party products such as tape libraries, host bus adapters, and data security products that help enhance the EMC hardware and software that make up their ILM solutions.[6] The Velocity Partner Program, open to industry and software partners and original equipment manufacturers, among others, offers customers the use of EMC's products, skills development programs, and lead-generating tools.[7] In addition, the Velocity Technology and ISV Program allows customers to more seamlessly integrate their activities with EMC's ILM solutions, supporting new projects and helping them grow revenue.[8]

tion solutions provider through partnerships and acquisitions. After buying Legato, Documentum, VMware, and Smarts, EMC aimed to strengthen its presence in new areas of the information technology marketplace while expanding on its preeminent lead in the field of computer storage.

In August 2005, EMC acquired California-based Rainfinity, which specialized in virtualization and network file migration software—offering customers enhanced data mobility across multiple networks and storage devices with minimal downtime, data loss, or security risks. That same year, EMC added to its ILM offerings with the acquisition of Captiva, a software vendor offering expert solutions for converting, indexing, and processing paper files into easily accessible digital formats.

EMC purchased ProActivity Software Solutions in 2006, another important step in the evolution of EMC's ILM strategy. Working in concert with Documentum, ProActivity gave EMC customers the ability to monitor, analyze, and optimize business processes, providing up-to-the-minute multidimensional analysis and graphical process maps.

## Global Services

In mid-2006, EMC formed a new organization—EMC Global Services. More and more of its customers were looking to EMC to provide end-to-end ILM capabilities that would include expert services for helping customers plan, build, manage, and support their ILM solutions and information infrastructures. Howard Elias was given overall responsibility for setting the strategy and creating the best practices to create a seamless services experience for EMC customers. Overall, Elias' new organization began helping EMC deliver its growing portfolio of services in a more powerful, consistent, and focused way—ensuring that EMC looked like one company to its customers and delivered the highest levels of customer satisfaction to accelerate the adoption of ILM and EMC's growth.

Elias explained the importance of Global Services to EMC:

*Services enable customers to better manage the inherent and increasing complexity of their IT environments. Services help our customers get the most value possible from EMC's platforms, software, and solutions. In fact, services are essential for providing the end-to-end ILM capability that customers now require. In addition, services are making an increasing contribution to EMC's growth and are helping accelerate EMC's transformation into a more solutions-oriented technology company.*

EMC Global Services began rapidly expanding its portfolio of professional and support services, solutions, and training to help customers through every stage of the information management lifecycle—plan, build, manage, and support.

For example, in 2006, EMC acquired Interlink and Internosis, two companies that specialize in professional services for establishing operationally

Joe Tucci (second from right) lays out his vision for EMC in Shanghai alongside Wang Shenghong (fourth from left), president of the prestigious Fudan University, during a trip to inaugurate EMC's first research and development center in China. EMC executives Sanjay Mirchandani and Steve Leonard are second and third from left.

efficient infrastructures, automating business processes, and integrating enterprise applications. These acquisitions enhanced EMC's existing Microsoft services capabilities around strategy, infrastructure and application development, and managed services. EMC has built a very strong Microsoft services practice because so much of EMC's technology is deployed in Microsoft environments. As Elias noted, "What we've been able to do is assemble a lot of expertise around Microsoft technologies. Having this knowledge in how to design an optimal information infrastructure for Microsoft environments is something customers value greatly."

A major part of EMC Global Services' growth strategy is based on the ability to provide world-class consulting and solutions integration capabilities that leverage EMC's information infrastructure technologies to help customers get more value from their information and clear business impact from their IT investments. To accelerate its commitment to this strategy, in 2007, EMC acquired BusinessEdge, a privately held, industry-focused business and technology consulting firm. BusinessEdge is a highly regarded industry consulting services organization that has established multi-year relationships with

blue chip clients in the financial services, telco/ media/entertainment, and life sciences vertical industries. This acquisition strengthened EMC's ability to be a trusted advisor to its largest customers in these markets and is enabling earlier and more strategic entry into customer accounts to drive purchase decisions to EMC's portfolio. There is significant synergy between BusinessEdge and EMC services and focus in helping customers at the intersection of business and information infrastructure challenges in the three targeted vertical industries.

### More International Growth

As part of EMC's continued expansion, the company kept focusing on emerging international markets. Although the United States continued to account for more than a quarter of the world's gross domestic product (GDP), the budding economic powerhouses of Brazil, China, India, and Russia had grown to account for a quarter of overall GDP growth in their own right.[5] With such rapid growth came a larger, more competitive information marketplace, along with impressive technical talent, providing EMC with plenty of room to grow.

"Worldwide IT spending is 60 percent outside of North America and 40 percent inside of North

Following the opening announcement of the Shanghai R&D center in November 2006, EMC established another R&D center in Beijing at the Tsinghua Science Park. Tucci officially unveiled the center in November 2007, providing an additional location for talented EMC engineers. From right: Charles Fan; Steve Leonard; Joe Tucci; Jeff Nick; Denis Yip; and Gus Amegadzie, general manager of the EMC China R&D Center in Beijing.

America," said Sanjay Mirchandani, senior vice president of global alliances and international development, who later became EMC's chief information officer.[6]

In India, the site of EMC's largest offshore software development center, the company doubled its software development staff from 500 to 1,000 as part of a plan announced in 2006 to invest $500 million in the country by 2010.[7] Part of that growth included the opening of a new research center in Bangalore.[8] EMC also announced plans to invest $500 million in China by 2011. In 2006, EMC opened an R&D center in Shanghai, and a year later, increased its planned Chinese investments to $1 billion, which included the opening of an R&D center in Beijing.[9]

"The talent availability in China has been amazing," explained Charles Fan, vice president and general manager of China R&D. "For example, in 2006, when we started, there were 4 million college graduates. ... In 2007, there were 5 million, and next year, there will be 6 million. So not only is it a huge number, but it's also growing very rapidly."[10]

The need to keep pace with rivals such as IBM and HP drove EMC, the leading storage software vendor in China even before it opened its Shanghai R&D center, toward continuous growth throughout Asia.[11] As EMC grew in China, Hong Kong, and Taiwan, its TCE and Lean Six Sigma initiatives proved essential in facilitating a unified approach to customer relations.[12] Introducing a "TCE mindset," with its universal emphasis on providing the best customer experience possible, helped create streamlined, consistent process standards.

The company also fortified its presence in other countries where it already had a strong foothold. In May 2006, EMC purchased Israel-based Kashya, a leader in continuous data protection technology as well as disaster recovery and remote replication solutions. The acquisition helped pave the way for EMC's Israel Software Development Center.

EMC's international R&D centers played a pivotal role in the development of new products, leading to a number of new patents for the company.[13] According to Rona Newmark, senior vice president of global sourcing and development, "The global development centers are some of the few locations at EMC where engineering teams from

# FOLLOWING THE BOOM

AT THE TURN OF THE 21ST CENTURY, COUNTRIES LATE to the information technology boom caught up in a hurry. As the economies of Brazil, Russia, India, and China (coined the BRIC) headed toward rapid rates of growth, accounting for a quarter of global gross domestic product growth in 2007, the number of Internet users worldwide received a tremendous boost. Within a few years, the number of Internet users in China has grown to equal or surpass the number of users in the United States, according to Charles Zhang, chairman and CEO of Sohu.com, a Chinese news site.[1] China's external storage market seems to be growing at twice the worldwide rate.[2] In India, Brazil, and Russia, growing online populations have led to an ever-increasing need for information storage and management. EMC is well positioned to follow that boom.

China's rapid growth and strong emphasis on science and technology has drawn many high-tech companies. By 2001, the country awarded almost as many science and engineering degrees as the United States, and a few years later, its burgeoning semiconductor industry placed it among the world's largest producers of digital technology.[3] In late 2007, EMC announced it was doubling its $500 million investment in China, to $1 billion by the end of 2012. As part of EMC's additional investments in China, the company expanded its research and development centers in Beijing and Shanghai while strengthening its sales and service operations.[4]

In India, which claimed about 60 million Internet users in 2007 and has a vast pool of technical talent, EMC announced it would invest $500 million to expand the country's information management market and bolster the company's R&D presence.[5] By strengthening its partner network there, EMC enabled customers in the 60 largest cities in India to purchase its products and services more easily. The company also announced plans for a Center of Excellence for e-Governance in the country, designed to help government agencies build a more cohesive and accountable information infrastructure.[6]

EMC's expansion allowed the company to tap into a vast global reservoir of talent as the number of available scientists and engineers throughout the world skyrocketed. By 2003, estimates placed more engineers in Bangalore than

multiple product lines work side by side, share laboratory space, share office space, and do it in a way that we think is going to help increase our 'One EMC' integration capabilities."[14]

Those international centers evolved into comprehensive Centers of Excellence, teams of software developers and customer service professionals that design, develop, test, and deploy global core EMC products and that serve as an integral part of EMC's global R&D network.[15]

EMC opened its St. Petersburg, Russia, Center of Excellence in June 2007. Like most of the other centers, its focus is on software product development.[16] EMC's presence in Russia capitalizes on the country's long-standing emphasis on mathematics and science education, the number of scientists and

engineers per capita (Russia ranks third worldwide), and an economic and political climate ripe for high-tech companies. IT spending in Russia increased by 30 percent in 2006, and EMC's revenues in the country grew at a rate four times that of its overall global business.[17]

By the end of 2007, EMC had Centers of Excellence in China, India, Israel, and Russia.[18] As the evolution of technology erased barriers and crossed borders, available business opportunities skyrocketed, as did access to the most capable employees across the globe. An increasing number of EMC's staff lived and worked outside of the United States, up to 44 percent in 2009.[19] "To build the best information infrastructure solutions in the world, we need to recruit the best talent in the world,"

Employees of EMC's R&D center in Shanghai—the company's first such facility in China. It opened in November 2006.

in Silicon Valley.[7] In China, there were 4 million college graduates in 2006, according to Charles Fan, vice president and general manager of the EMC China R&D Center in Shanghai.[8] When EMC opened its first R&D center in Shanghai, more than 12,000 people applied for 80 openings.[9]

In Russia, EMC benefited from a long-standing emphasis on mathematics and science

education, equaling India's rate of 200,000 new science and technology graduates every year, even though its population is 80 percent smaller.[10] In terms of software exports, Russia ranks third worldwide, after China and India.[11]

Business in China is conducted almost exclusively through partners, and the company continues working to sign up more partners. To take advantage of the growth in China, as well as in other countries, EMC must effectively leverage its partner networks, particularly in Asia, where, according to Steve Leonard, president of Asia Pacific/Japan operations, "partners can reach many hundred times more customers."[12]

Above: The employees of Kashya, an Israeli company that developed sophisticated data replication and protection solutions, formed the basis of EMC's software R&D center in Israel.

Below right: Art Coviello, executive vice president and president of RSA, the security division of EMC, is responsible for delivering EMC's global vision of information-centric security.

Newmark explained shortly after the St. Petersburg center opened.[20]

### Securing Information

Although EMC had already established itself as the leader in information infrastructure solutions, including significant technology and software to protect information, it found that information security was repeatedly topping the list of chief information officers' priorities. As Joe Tucci put it:

*We need to make sure that the information itself is protected. We need to make sure that the information itself is secure. We need to make sure it is encrypted, wherever it lives. ...*

*We fundamentally believe that the technology company that seamlessly integrates information storage and information management, while keeping information protected with information security, as well as centrally managing and orchestrating this information infrastructure, will be a huge winner in the technology marketplace.*

In September 2006, EMC paid $2.1 billion to acquire Bedford, Massachusetts–based RSA Security, the industry leader in protecting and managing identities and digital access.[21] "The customers were demanding an element of information security protection, and Joe Tucci responded," explained RSA Security President Art Coviello. He would later go on to head the RSA Security Division of EMC following the acquisition.[22]

With a long history of innovation, RSA traces its origins to a Passover seder in 1977. During the seder, a traditional Jewish holiday dinner involving symbolic foods and the ceremonial drinking of four glasses of wine, Massachusetts Institute of Technology (MIT) faculty members Ron Rivest, Adi Shamir, and Leonard Adelman began discussing the Diffie-Hellman key exchange protocol.

Invented in 1976, the Diffie-Hellman protocol uses cryptographic algorithms to allow the exchange of private, encoded information across unsecured networks. Unfortunately, although it does successfully protect against most eavesdroppers, the Diffie-Hellman protocol leaves messages vulnerable to man-in-the-middle attacks, allowing a third party to effectively impersonate both the sender and receiver of encrypted data to gain access to important information.

Above: EMC opened its first Russian R&D facility on St. Petersburg's Vasilyevsky Island in June 2007. *(Photo courtesy of Corbis.)*

Left: From left, EMC executives Joel Schwartz, Sanjay Mirchandani, and Jack Mollen attend a news conference for the opening of the St. Petersburg R&D facility.

That evening, as they had many times in the past, Rivest, Shamir, and Adelman considered new ways of implementing the Diffie-Hellman protocol and overcoming its inherent weaknesses. At the end of the seder, the three friends went their separate ways. However, that night, back at home, Rivest continued to think about the problem. As he went over the exchange of ideas that had taken place at the seder, Rivest suddenly imagined a new algorithm, utilizing both digital signatures and encryption to provide added security against third party attacks. He called Adelman right away, and the very next morning, the three friends began work on the RSA public key cryptography algorithm,

named for their combined initials.[23] Considered one of the greatest advances in the history of computer cryptography, the RSA algorithm is still widely used in Web sites and in computer networks around the world.

Founded in 1986, RSA Security set the industry standard for implementing data security utilizing computer cryptography, digital signatures, and SecurID authentication tokens. Purchasing RSA helped EMC protect its current customers while anticipating upcoming trends in the market. According to Coviello, firewalls and antivirus protection products, while still indispensable tools, were "not going to be adequate for the future of computing, since increasingly, businesses want to let more people into their networks."[24]

After the acquisition, RSA's far-reaching security technology allowed EMC to offer customers new ways to protect their data. As Coviello explained:

> *They came up with this concept of information-centric security that relies on understanding risk, protecting the people who get access to data, and protecting that data from people who shouldn't get access. That's where the authentication comes in. It protects the data itself, first through encryption, but also through things like digital rights management and monitoring, and enforcement of policy. Then they added to this information-centric approach the ability to prove that you were in compliance with not only regulations, but your own internal policies concerning security as well.*[25]

RSA, like EMC, had a strong company culture—one that was team oriented, employee friendly,

Above right: EMC's RSA Security Division utilizes advanced computer cryptography to help keep customer data secure and private. *(Photo courtesy Getty Images.)*

Below: In September 2006, EMC purchased RSA Security for $2.1 billion—its largest acquisition to date. RSA was well known for the security conferences it held each year, such as this one in 2007.

and careful to recognize employee contributions.[26] As a result, even though RSA remained a distinct division, the two cultures blended well—a testament to EMC's careful acquisition strategy. "We have walked away from acquisitions because there would not have been a good cultural fit," Elias said. "Even if we liked the technology, even if the financials worked or could be made to work, if we felt the leader or the leadership team didn't have the right principles, the right sort of DNA to be successful here, we would walk away."[27]

### VMware

Since EMC acquired VMware in 2003, the virtualization software provider has continued to operate independently in its Palo Alto, California, headquarters as an EMC subsidiary. VMware was founded in 1998 by Mendel Rosenblum, an expert in operating systems, and his wife, Diane Greene, a veteran of Silicon Valley start-ups, alongside computer scientists Scott Devine, Ed Bugnion, and Edward Wang. The team focused on x86 server virtualization technology. Virtualization is a proven software technology that is rapidly transforming the IT landscape and fundamentally changing the way that people compute. VMware software is a pioneering approach to computing that separates the operating system and the application software from the underlying hardware to achieve major improvements in efficiency, availability, flexibility, and manageability.[28]

One of the fastest-growing public software companies, VMware is the leading provider of virtualization solutions from the desktop to the data center. Its solutions are used by more than 170,000 customers to reduce costs. VMware software has consistently been used in large corporate data centers, allowing customers to save electricity, hardware, and maintenance costs by simultaneously executing multiple applications on each server. For example, utilizing VMware software, International Truck and Engine Corporation was able to run 230 applications spanning many of its corporate functions on just 18 computers, at a considerable cost savings.[29]

In February 2007, EMC announced plans to sell 10 percent of VMware in an initial public offering (IPO). Industry watchers and EMC executives had no doubt the stock would be hot. "I'm 59 years old, and VMware is the best investment I ever made in my life," Tucci told the *New York Times*.[30]

That August, the IPO brought in $1.1 billion, the biggest technology offering since Google in 2004.[31] EMC continued to own about 80 percent of the company, with small percentages held by Cisco Systems, Inc., and Intel Corp.[32] From an initial price of $29 per share, the stock price briefly climbed above $100.[33]

The intent of this IPO was to unlock more of VMware's tremendous value to EMC shareholders in a way that would provide the greatest potential benefit to both EMC and VMware. As Joe Tucci told employees at the time, "By improving the transparency of VMware's performance and growth relative to the marketplace, we believe that investors will be better able to gauge the significance of VMware's contribution to EMC. Additionally, this IPO helps reinforce EMC's commitment to VMware's open platform strategy, a model that has enabled the growth of virtual infrastructure as a platform-neutral, industry-standard layer that benefits all customers and partners. In fact, VMware has the opportunity

Employees attend the 2008 Women's Leadership Forum (WLF) launch in Cork, Ireland. Back row, from left: Karen O'Sullivan, controller of international finance and accounting and WLF treasurer; Marie Downey, senior manager of the Manufacturing Portfolio Group and WLF president; Jackie Murphy, training and development manager, and WLF founding member and launch coordinator; and Gillian Bergin, senior IT applications developer and WLF vice president. Front row, from left: Kate O'Connor, director of human resources Ireland; Joe Tucci, EMC chairman and CEO; Jack Mollen, executive vice president of human resources; and Erin Motameni, senior vice president of human resources.

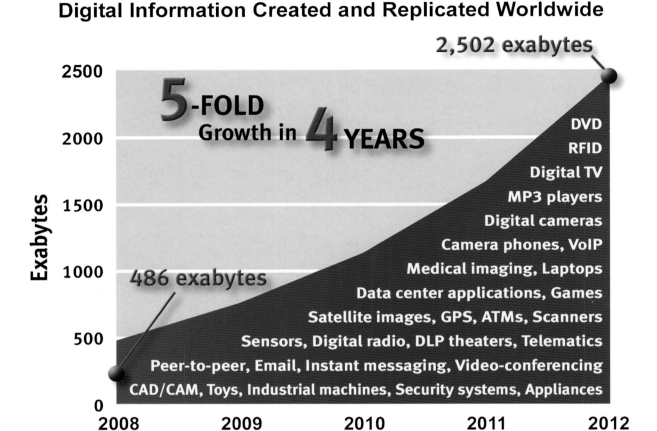

## Digital Information Created and Replicated Worldwide

**2,502 exabytes**

**5-FOLD** Growth in **4** YEARS

DVD
RFID
Digital TV
MP3 players
Digital cameras
Camera phones, VoIP
Medical imaging, Laptops
Data center applications, Games
Satellite images, GPS, ATMs, Scanners
Sensors, Digital radio, DLP theaters, Telematics
Peer-to-peer, Email, Instant messaging, Video-conferencing
CAD/CAM, Toys, Industrial machines, Security systems, Appliances

**486 exabytes**

*Exabytes* (y-axis): 0, 500, 1000, 1500, 2000, 2500

*(x-axis):* 2008, 2009, 2010, 2011, 2012

to be an industry-standard technology layer, one that will be ubiquitous in customer information technology infrastructures across the globe."

In April 2009, VMware introduced vSphere, which, according to VMware CEO Paul Maritz, "is in a very real sense the world's first operating system for the cloud, whether that be an internal or an external cloud."

The term "cloud" refers to IT infrastructure and services delivered as a service via the Internet. Cloud computing is changing the way IT resources are used. Companies want the ability to access infrastructure resource pools how and when they choose. IT teams are asked to accommodate this shift in the consumption model, but still deal with the security, compatibility, and compliance issues associated with delivering that convenience to application business owners. The private cloud, which leverages VMware vSphere, "federates" computing between on- and off-premise environments. This gives IT

According to IDC's forecast of worldwide global information, 2,502 exabytes of information are expected by 2012, a fivefold increase in just four years.

teams the cost savings and efficiency cloud computing promises with the flexibility, security, and control needed for production applications. VMware vSphere delivers resources, applications—even servers—when and where they're needed. VMware customers typically save 50 percent to 70 percent on overall IT costs by consolidating their resource pools and delivering highly available machines with vSphere. VMware's value proposition is so strong that it has grown at an explosive pace. Its revenues have soared from $218 million in 2004 to $2 billion in 2009.

EMC continued to perform very well overall in 2008. As Joe Tucci told the financial community in

April 2008, "I love our strategic position today and even more so for tomorrow."[34]

### Contributing to a Better World

As EMC regained its financial strength and made inroads into a greater number of markets worldwide, it stepped up its long-standing civic commitments—especially in the field of education, a tradition stemming from Dick and Maureen Egan's early philanthropy in the Hopkinton public schools and at Northeastern University.

The sign that once hung over Egan's desk said, "It's the Products, Stupid." He, of course, knew

Above: In November 2005, Hellmut Seemann, president of the Weimar Klassik Foundation, and Malte Rademacher, marketing director of EMC Germany, signed a sponsorship agreement with the Duchess Anna Amalia Library. EMC donated two Centera systems to help the library digitally archive its materials.

Left: EMC's mission is to lead customers on a journey to the private cloud, a dramatically more efficient and effective model for delivering IT as a service.

## THE JOURNEY TO THE PRIVATE CLOUD STARTS NOW

### A Next-Generation IT Infrastructure that Delivers Efficiency, Control, and Choice

**The Private Cloud is a next-generation IT environment under the control of the IT organization.**

**It is built differently: dynamic pools of virtualized resources**

**It is operated differently: low-touch and zero-touch models that span traditional IT disciplines**

**It is consumed differently: a convenient consumption model**

that without the hard work and innovative efforts of talented engineers, there would be no products to sell. To help maintain a steady stream of intelligent, well-trained information specialists, EMC has consistently worked to improve science and mathematics education in the United States and to help close the achievement gaps that persist among children in the U.S. EMC has also partnered directly with colleges and universities to train students for careers in information storage technology. Through the company's Academic Alliance program, EMC offers schools a comprehensive curriculum that includes courses in the specific technologies and principles needed to succeed in the highly competitive IT field.[35] To augment that curriculum, EMC's storage experts wrote and, in collaboration with John Wiley and Sons, published the industry's first definitive resource on information storage and management technologies.

# THE WORKING MOTHER EXPERIENCE

*T*HE WORKING MOTHER EXPERIENCE, PUBLISHED in 2009 by EMC, contains real stories written by EMC women (and one man) from around the world. These stories provide candid perspectives on being working mothers in a fast-paced business environment. The book showcases the unique choices, daily challenges, and victories these working moms encounter in today's business world and in their personal lives. The essayists are the perfect examples of individuals who each day creatively and successfully manage the balancing act that is the working mother's experience. Ninety-six contributors from 15 countries on five continents provided the content for the 239-page book. EMC's working mothers are skilled professionals who bring a wealth of talents to their work. At the same time, they also skillfully manage their homes, enriching their own and their families' lives.

In the foreword to *The Working Mother Experience*, EMC Executive Vice President Frank Hauck, who has served as the executive sponsor of the Hopkinton, Massachusetts, chapter of the Women's Leadership Forum, which is dedicated to the personal and professional growth of women at EMC, wrote:

*I'm glad that women all over the world took the time to participate in this effort. Like the working mothers themselves, this book is strong, authentic, and sincere. In their own words, through their very personal stories, they help us to appreciate our differences, similarities, and cultural perspectives. Perhaps the ultimate gift of their contributions is the new, extended community that has been created; it is one that consists of EMC women—and men—around the world.*

For several years, Tucci served as the head of the education task force of the Business Roundtable, an association of American CEOs dedicated to promoting public policies that ensure economic growth and a productive American workforce. In conjunction with his fellow Business Roundtable CEOs, Tucci issued a statement in August 2005 emphasizing the need to engage children in science and mathematics to regain ground lost to other countries in high technology fields.[36]

EMC has also dedicated considerable resources to help protect precious historical archives and cultural artifacts. Through the EMC Information Heritage Initiative, the company strives to expand global Internet access to digital copies of historic

documents, preserving and safeguarding valuable information that could otherwise be lost, as was the case in 2004. That year, a fire at the renowned Duchess Anna Amalia Library in Weimar, Germany, destroyed thousands of irreplaceable archives, including rare first editions of *Faust* from the 1800s and original documents by author and playwright Johann Wolfgang von Goethe, as well as centuries-old maps and atlases.

In response, EMC donated two Centera systems with 36 terabytes of storage to help the library digitally preserve its remaining priceless artifacts.[37] EMC also donated $1 million to digitize and archive material in the John F. Kennedy Presidential Library in Boston, Massachusetts, and in 2007, the company entered into a five-year partnership with Boston's Museum of African-American History, contributing equipment, software, and services to help preserve the museum's archives and make them available to researchers and students around the world.[38]

In addition to EMC's historical preservation efforts, the company has also taken concrete steps toward contributing to a cleaner planet. Its manufacturing facilities are ISO 14001 certified, a globally recognized standard of excellence in environmental management. In 2004, EMC was among the first companies to join the U.S. Environmental Protection Agency's Climate Leaders program, pledging to monitor and reduce greenhouse gas emissions from its facilities. EMC made a similar voluntary commitment to the Ireland EPA, and has maintained its greenhouse gas emissions at 10 percent below its annual allowance since 2005.

EMC estimates that the energy-conserving measures the company has adopted in its corporate facilities since 1987 have reduced its associated greenhouse gas emissions by 127,000 metric tons. Conservation initiatives include data center upgrades to implement best practices in energy efficiency. In its renovations and new buildings, EMC has installed high-efficiency lighting, heating, and cooling systems, including "free cooling" packages that rely on outside air to cool indoor facilities whenever possible. EMC also purchases only energy-efficient PCs, servers, printers, and photocopiers for its offices worldwide.

Recent product releases have continued EMC's 20-year leadership in energy-efficient products. In July 2007, EMC launched Symmetrix, CLARiiON,

In April 2008, the Simmons School of Management held its annual Leadership Conference in Boston, for which EMC was the lead sponsor. About 130 EMC women gathered with EMC CEO Joe Tucci (behind kiosk), who was one of the conference speakers, and with Jack Mollen, executive vice president of human resources.

As a future-oriented company, EMC maintains a firm commitment to environmental sustainability. The company has instituted many programs designed to reduce waste and energy consumption and is dedicated to battling climate change.

and Celerra storage platforms that use up to 33 percent less power than their predecessors, and the Centera 4 Low-Power, which uses up to 67 percent less power, but stores 50 percent more data. In January 2008, EMC was the first in the market to offer flash drives in high-end storage systems, which use up to 98 percent less energy per transaction.

Around the world, EMC employees are involved in volunteer initiatives to help improve communities. Through charitable walks and runs, building houses, donating holiday gifts for abused and neglected children, and mentoring students in area schools, EMC employees help respond to the chal-lenges facing their local communities. In China, for example, employees from EMC's Center of Excellence have built a special relationship with a local school and launched a weekend tutoring program. In Massachusetts, EMC employees participate in the Department of Social Services (DSS) Kids' Fund Snowman Project, donating toys, clothes, and other gifts to children in need. Employees are now partnering with local charities around the United States for holiday drives, and in 2007, EMC employees gave gifts to at least 10,000 children. EMC employees from across the nation contributed to the multiple "Soldier Drives" held in 2007. And annually, EMC employees in Massachusetts, North Carolina, California, New Hampshire, and Missouri participate in a Back-to-School drive. This drive collects backpacks, notebooks, pens, pencils, and other school supplies for children in need. EMC also offers all of its employees sponsored "Build Days" with Habitat for Humanity. Employees pound nails, paint walls, and complete other essential construction tasks on a new house for a family in need.

In 2008, EMC published its first full sustainability report to convey its deepening understanding of the interdependencies among its financial success, the health of the environment, and the well-being of people. The report details how EMC is contributing to a cleaner planet, developing its talented IT workforce, expanding access to education and IT, and operating with integrity.

### EMC in the Future

For nearly two decades, EMC, unlike virtually any other company, has placed its primary focus on the "I" in IT—the information. It has long been EMC's belief that while technologies may come and go, information persists and forms the permanent strategic core of an organization. Information, according to EMC, has the power to illuminate the world—but only when it's made accessible, searchable, shareable, and actionable. The right information infrastructure can make this happen.

According to Ken Steinhardt, chief technology officer for EMC's customer operations:

*It really is all about the information. It always has been about the information, and it should always be about the information. Instead of*

### EMC Culture Talk

**Overview** | **All Content** (221) | **Discussions** (171) | **Documents** (50)

## Welcome

**Welcome. This community is home to your story, ideas and beliefs about EMC. People, their ideas and actions make up a culture. Let's recognize, enhance and celebrate what is ours.**

## Leadership in Action!

Leadership in Action features EMC's senior leaders and strategic influencers in a series of candid video clips. **They are uncut, unplugged and unbelievably straightforward.** Get to know the person behind their work and join in the conversation!

## Latest Videos!

 +  + 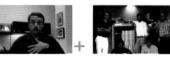 +

**Brian Gallagher** on leadership, FLASH, and a personal tour

View: 1 | 2 | 3
Released: 12/15/09

**Frank Slootman** on wellness and dedupe frenemies

View: 1 | 2
Released: 12/15/09

**Pat Gelsinger** on culture, VCE, and his first 45 days

View: 1 | 2
Released: 12/15/09

**Celebrate** the 20th anniversary of CLARiiON

View: 1
Released: 12/15/09

more

## Culture Talk

**EMC Acronyms**
6 hours ago in EMC Culture Talk — by Peter Walden

**Re: What perk would you choose or do you desire?**
21 hours ago in EMC Culture Talk — by Candi Imming

**LIA Graphics Repository**
1 day ago in EMC Culture Talk — by Brandi Hamlin

**Re: What would you want to see in an EMC Brand Ambassador Program?** — by Mark Zurlo

## Previous Videos

 +  +

**Joe Tucci** on building a bridge to the future

Released: 10/26/09
Length: 03:08

**Joe Tucci and David Goulden** on "a great quarter"

Released: 10/26/09
Length: 01:44

 +  +

**Sanjay Mirchandani** on IT and culture

Released: 10/26/09
Length: 04:17

**David Goulden** on cost mgmt and optimism

Released: 10/26/09
Length: 01:09

more

EMC | ONE is the internal, online network of EMC employees, a place where they can exchange ideas and best practices, support each other, and learn how their peers are doing.

# BUILDING A WORLD-CLASS LAW DEPARTMENT

EMC WAS ALREADY AN 11-YEAR-OLD PUBLIC COMpany when Dick Egan hired Paul Dacier in 1990 to be its first general counsel. Over the course of EMC's first decade, Dick and co-founder Roger Marino had built a culture of high performance, big rewards, and an intense work ethic. Sales was the dominant function, but the hiring of Mike Ruettgers brought an immediate focus on product quality and customer service, and the arrival of Moshe Yanai raised EMC's engineering prowess.

The company was clearly in transition, and Dacier's task was to build a law department commensurate with the opportunities and challenges

---

EMC General Counsel Paul Dacier (center) was joined by Chairman and CEO Joe Tucci (left) and Vice Chairman Bill Teuber (right) when the Massachusetts Appleseed Center for Law and Justice honored Dacier with its 2010 Good Apple award for his support of the societal and charitable causes championed by Appleseed.

of an increasingly diverse and global business—one that, in his words, "always remained close to the roots of the business."

Dacier had been a staff attorney at another high-growth, Massachusetts-based technology company, Apollo Computer. When Hewlett-Packard acquired Apollo, he was ready for his next challenge. He brought to EMC an understanding of the importance of protecting intellectual property as a means of building competitive advantage.

EMC had one patent when Dacier joined the company. There were no other lawyers on staff. In a 2007 interview with *InsideCounsel* magazine, he recounted his early conversations with co-founder Dick Egan: "There hadn't been a lawyer working for the company for at least two years. Dick told me with great pride that he was handling or managing all the legal work for EMC at the time. They were putting all their efforts into building market share. But when the company grew really quickly, competitors started suing the company for patent infringement. It became evident that we

needed to build our patent portfolio so we could level the playing field."

Two decades later, Dacier now oversees a worldwide intellectual property (IP) empire of more than 2,300 granted patents and more than 1,500 pending applications, and manages a legal team of more than 100. EMC's law department has aggressively defended that portfolio, winning high-profile patent infringement battles over the years with HP and Hitachi relating to data-storage technology, and leveraging the portfolio to secure long-term licensing agreements with IBM that both benefit and protect EMC.

There are long walls inside EMC's headquarters building that are lined with plaques representing patents awarded to the company's engineers. "When we have patents issued, we give a bonus to the engineers responsible and put a bronze plaque for that individual in the hallway area near the engineering labs," noted Dacier.

Unlike the attorneys inside most major corporations, Dacier and his team routinely participate in customer meetings. "At EMC we all sell," he explained. "It doesn't matter what your role is. There is no better way to understand the business and appreciate the issues our sales people have to deal with than being out in the field and rocking and rolling with them."

Another trait that crosses all functions is the EMC work ethic. "We work very hard. We will stay up all night to resolve a legal issue," Dacier said. "We don't bog things down. We are relentless in our pursuit of the goals and objectives of the business, and we make great things happen. We also have fun."

In recent years, the EMC legal team has repeatedly been recognized for setting a standard of excellence in corporate governance and other areas. Susan Permut, EMC's senior vice president and deputy general counsel, leads a group whose work enabled EMC to be chosen by *Corporate Secretary* magazine as its Corporate Governance (Large Cap) Team of the Year in 2009. The magazine noted that EMC's directors are among the most open and accessible of any board in the U.S. and actively and intelligently engage shareholders, activists, advisers, and regulators to create

EMC was named Corporate Governance (Large Cap) Team of the Year in 2009 by *Corporate Secretary* magazine. Pictured at the ceremony are (left to right) David Drake, president of Georgeson, a global proxy solicitation firm, with EMC attorneys June Duchesne, Susan Permut, Rachel Lee, and Liz McCarron.

a highly non-adversarial working relationship. Permut also was elected to the Board of Directors of the Council of Institutional Investors. Krish Gupta, EMC vice president and deputy general counsel, was chosen as an "In-House Leader in the Law" by *New England In-House* and *Massachusetts Lawyers Weekly*.

In 2009, Dacier was recognized among *Massachusetts Lawyers Weekly's* list of the most influential attorneys in Massachusetts, and in 2010 he was honored by the nonprofit Massachusetts Appleseed Center for Law and Justice with its annual Good Apple Award for his contributions to the charitable and societal causes championed by the Appleseed Center.

Dacier and his team have clearly established the EMC law department as not only a world-class legal function, but a true competitive advantage for this growing global business.

Expanding its brand in the large Japanese market, EMC sponsored Major League Baseball's Japan Opening Series in 2008, which featured season-opening games played in Tokyo by the Boston Red Sox and the Oakland Athletics.

the word "storage," if we're successful in the future, I think the single word people will associate with EMC will be "information."[39]

In 2007, Mark Lewis, president of EMC's Information Intelligence Group, sketched out new ways for people to think about and interact with information in the future. Lewis suggested that information will be increasingly held separate from applications, allowing easier access and sharing across networks. He also proposed that, in conjunction with the rise of on-demand access to

unstructured information such as video, photos, and music, adding metadata will more easily allow this unstructured information to be indexed, queried, and searched. In response to such free and open exchange of information, security will be built into the information itself, rather than being dependent upon firewalls isolating information within organizations.[40]

In May 2009, IDC released its latest EMC-sponsored study describing the explosive growth of the digital universe.[41] Titled "As the Economy Contracts, the Digital Universe Expands," the study forecasts that the digital universe—which includes all information created, captured, or replicated—will double in size every 18 months, and in 2012, five times as much information will be created compared to 2008.

However, such growth is not without its challenges, according to Tucci:

*Society is already feeling the early effects of the world's digital information explosion. Organizations need to plan for the limitless opportunities to use information in new ways and for the challenges of information governance. As people's digital footprints continue growing, so too will the responsibility of organizations for the privacy, protection, availability, and reliability of that information. The burden is on IT departments within organizations to address the risks and compliance rules around information misuse, data leakage, and safeguarding against security breaches.*[42]

In light of today's diverse and expanding digital universe, thoughtful IT professionals are stepping back and asking:

- Who is responsible for my organization's information portfolio?
- Who is paying attention to the information's changing requirements and changing value as it moves through its life cycle?
- Who is stepping up to take on the important role of protector, manager, and optimizer of my business' core asset— its information?

The answer, says EMC, is the emerging role of the "informationist," who will manage an ever-increasing amount of information in a way that meets the business' shifting requirements, while keeping overall technology and operational costs to a minimum.

To help informationists—whether they work in large global corporations, medium-size and smaller businesses, or at home—and to capitalize on the many untapped market opportunities ahead, EMC has been investing in the expansion of its information management capabilities well beyond the enterprise, and in the development of next-generation information management technologies designed to leverage cloud computing and provide ubiquitous access to information.

With that in mind, in the fall of 2007, the company acquired Berkeley Data Systems, a provider of online information backup and recovery services and creator of Mozy, the premier online subscription service for the protection of data that resides on desktops, laptops, and remote office servers. Mozy was a natural extension of EMC's leadership in the protection and security of personal and business information.

Then, in February 2008, EMC acquired Pi Corporation, a Seattle-based developer of software and services for personal information management. Pi is an expert in developing technology that helps individuals control how they access, organize, and share their ever-increasing volumes of digital information. Pi's CEO, Paul Maritz headed the newly formed Cloud Infrastructure and Services Division, and in July 2008, he was named the new president and CEO of VMware, which, much like EMC, is one of the few companies in information technology that has been able to create a new industry.

As Joe Tucci noted:

*By combining the vision, leadership, and technical talent of the Pi management and engineering teams with EMC's vast engineering, development, and sales resources and expertise, I believe EMC is positioned on the leading edge of a new paradigm in cloud infrastructure and services and personal information management.*

Then, in the spring of 2008, EMC acquired Iomega, a market leader in data storage and protection for small businesses and consumers. EMC invested in Iomega because it has talented people, a strong brand, great products with a solid reputation, and wide-reaching channels to markets that are important to EMC's future. In other words, Iomega has consumer and small business expertise in its DNA. "By purchasing Iomega," said Tucci, "we bought a brand and a team who knows the consumer market extremely well."

"The proliferation of information in the hands of consumers, businesses, and organizations of all kinds has brought about massive digital information growth on a scale never imagined," Tucci said. "As the leading provider of information infrastructure, we are positioned to set a new standard for organizing, accessing, and deriving value from this information. Pi's technology is very complementary to our emerging cloud infrastructure strategy."[43]

In recent years, it has become increasingly clear to EMC that the state of IT is poised for a dramatic change. IT is widely regarded as inefficient. For example, a very small portion of each dollar spent

# EMC's Cost Transformation Program

EMC IS INTENSELY FOCUSED ON MANAGING itself for sustained and profitable global market leadership over the long haul. That means emphasizing not only growth but also efficiency. A strong advocate of operational excellence, EMC is always striving to continuously improve its operating efficiencies by driving productivity and finding new ways to optimize its non-people spending across the business, with the aim of using these savings to fund innovation and growth. As the global economy became increasingly more challenging during 2008, EMC resolved to do more than simply manage its expenses conservatively. Under the leadership of Chief Financial Officer David Goulden, EMC launched a systematic, company-wide effort to reduce its non-people-related costs in areas such as real estate, inventory, infrastructure, travel, purchasing, third-party contractors, and more.

As Goulden told employees in late 2008, "To emerge from this downturn in a position of strength, as an organization we need to grow fiscally fitter and stronger. We have several teams working very hard to review how we spend every single penny of our shareholders' dollars. We have

In 2008 and 2009, EMC Chief Financial Officer David Goulden led the effort to implement a company-wide Cost Transformation Program.

begun a number of initiatives throughout the company as we collectively strive to reduce our costs while minimizing the additional impact on jobs. At the corporate-wide level, we have implemented a Cost Transformation Program (CTP) that will focus on reducing our non-people-related costs."

According to Goulden, "What we are not doing is taking a generic approach and simply cutting every part of every budget. This might save us money in the short term, but it would hinder our ability to grow profitably over the long term. Instead, we are being thoughtful and deliberate with an eye on the future, which is why we are looking at new ways to approach our business so that we emerge from this slowdown an even stronger company than we are today."

EMC made a point of soliciting constructive ideas to save money from its employees around the world. They, in turn, submitted hundreds of creative ideas for helping EMC emerge from the economic downturn an even stronger, more resilient company, and many of their ideas have been incorporated into the Cost Transformation Program. The CTP is so named, said Goulden, because the goal is not simply to cut costs selectively in the short term but to "transform the way EMC spends money so we can achieve a level of improved operational efficiency that is self-sustaining and ranks with the very best in the IT industry."

on IT today delivers new business value. The vast majority is spent "keeping the lights on," or doing things that don't truly differentiate a company.

"The data center as we know it today will change," says Tucci. "What's wrong with today's data center? It's very static. The application or the device kind of owns the infrastructure. What's needed is a way to use these IT resources more dynamically, effectively, and efficiently. The key to doing so is to build a virtual data center operating system."

According to Paul Maritz, "What VMware is fundamentally about is making that plumbing, that complexity, disappear—in the data center, in the cloud, and on the desktop. We believe that we can do this in an evolutionary manner. We can take people from where they are today, in a series of steps, to where they really want to be. In fact, virtualization is the only way to get there without doing a wholesale rip and replace, and a rewriting of applications, which, by the way, no enterprise can do."

Where is this future of a fully virtualized IT world taking us? Chuck Hollis, EMC vice president and global marketing chief technology officer, puts it this way:

*Consider, for a moment, that you can ship stuff without needing to own any trucks, airplanes, or trains, but you'll still know where your stuff might be or when it's going to get there. The same will be true in the fully virtualized IT world. When you put important stuff, [applications and information], in a virtual container, you don't have to own the plumbing. You could ship your applications to a compatible service provider if you wanted—or take them back again if things change. This isn't true only for server applications; it's true for desktop devices. Imagine being able to use any desktop device, anywhere, any time, and get the exact same user experience with your applications and your files.*

EMC and other vendors have started to use the term "private cloud" to describe this new model.

All information, applications, and desktops live in virtual containers. Enterprise IT organizations can choose either to pool their owned IT assets or "federate" with external service providers. Tucci and Maritz have now publicly committed EMC and VMware to this vision. They have also identified Cisco as a key partner in this journey.

Hollis continued: "Is this private cloud model really new? Yes and no. It's new to IT but not to other forms of infrastructure. This model is how we use telephones, how we power homes and factories, how we ship products globally. The transformation of infrastructure into a service is finally catching up to IT. That's pretty exciting!"

For organizations that want to speed their journey to virtualizing their entire infrastructures and then implement private cloud computing, EMC and Cisco, together with VMware, established a first-of-its-kind collaboration in 2009 called the Virtual Computing Environment (VCE) coalition. This powerful coalition will help EMC move its customers along the path to their preferred future. In essence, EMC is telling customers that "next starts now," that they can get to the future they want sooner with the VCE coalition's help.

After delivering its sixth year in a row of double-digit annual revenue growth, EMC entered 2009 with what Joe Tucci called "a firm grasp on what's required to thrive in tough times and emerge even stronger in the next growth cycle." EMC is well positioned in the markets that will remain top IT spending priorities—storage, virtualization, security, compliant archiving, eDiscovery, governance, risk, and compliance. EMC is committed to investing heavily in R&D to extend its technology lead and maintain rapid product rollout cycles. EMC remains intensely focused on customers' top priorities—saving

Former Microsoft executive Paul Maritz headed EMC's Cloud Infrastructure and Services Division before being named president and CEO of VMware in 2008.

# FORTUNE

## WORLD'S MOST ADMIRED COMPANIES

### Best in
### Quality of Products / Services

| Rank | Company | Industry Rank |
|------|---------|---------------|
| 1 | New York Times | 2 |
| 2 | Graybar Electric | 1 |
| 3 | Anheuser-Busch | 1 |
| 4 | Sysco | 1 |
| 5 | Walt Disney | 1 |
| 6 | Altria Group | 1 |
| 7 | Herman Miller | 1 |
| 8 | Nordstrom | 3 |
| 9 | Polo Ralph Lauren | 2 |
| 10 | EMC | 1 |

From the March 16, 2009 issue.

EMC is the only technology company among the World's 10 Most Admired Companies for Product and Service Quality, according to *Fortune*® magazine's prestigious annual ranking of the "World's Most Admired Companies." *(From* Fortune® *magazine. © March 16, 2009. All rights reserved. Used by permission and protected by the Copyright Laws of the United States.)*

money, attaining a faster return on investment, reducing risk, and preparing for the delivery of next-generation data centers. The company's commitment to quality has achieved notable results. In 2009, *Fortune*® magazine named EMC the No. 1 Most Admired Company in its industry, and the only technology company on its overall list of the World's 10 Most Admired Companies for Product and Service Quality.

What does the future of information hold? EMC believes the next wave of computing will be information-centric computing. Whereas today most information is trapped inside devices and applications, in the future people will have the abil-

ity to use and manage information across all their sites. Whereas today people often have only fragmented views of their information, tomorrow they will have consolidated views of their information. Whereas today policies for managing information, if they are applied at all, are applied haphazardly, tomorrow, common policies and safeguards will be followed everywhere.

EMC's dedication to pioneering trends in the marketplace has left the company in a prime position to take advantage of new opportunities. "Our long-term goal has really been to put EMC at the forefront as one of a handful of technology solution suppliers that the greatest companies in the world will look to as essential partners to help them navigate the future," said Mark Fredrickson, vice president of marketing strategy and communications.[44]

Accomplishing this is undoubtedly a tall order, and EMC has responded by strengthening and expanding its already solid network of alliances, maintaining an emphasis on innovation, and continuing its tradition of employing some of the most talented people in the world. "The thing that separates EMC, and always has in my opinion, is that they have more 'A-list' players than everybody else," said Steve Duplessie, founder and senior analyst at Enterprise Storage Group.[45]

According to Bill Scannell, executive vice president of Americas:

*This is just the most dynamic company I could ever imagine working for. ... I mean, people actually look forward to getting in here in the morning. You know, you look at neighboring companies, and no one has cars in the parking lot as late as we have at EMC—and that's not mandated. People do that by choice, because they know we're creating history, and they want to be part of it. People are as excited about joining EMC today as they were 10 years ago, 20 years ago, and 30 years ago.*

EMC turned 30 years old on August 23, 2009. In the rapidly changing information technology industry, most companies come and go long before their 30th birthday. Reaching this milestone was a tribute to the vitality, creativity, and adaptability of EMCers around the world, all of whom come together each day to help people and organizations bring the power of their digital information to life.

"I know we started from a family-like atmosphere and we've grown bigger," said EMC sales executive Diane Russell, who has been with EMC for more than 21 years. "But the 'never give up, never die' attitude, the mentality to keep working hard, that's what EMC is known for, and if you're someone who likes to always feel challenged, always feel like you're with a winner, then EMC is the best place to be."

EMC's pivotal role in shaping and leading the IT industry makes it a magnet for world-class executive leaders. In September 2009, Pat Gelsinger, a 30-year veteran of Intel, joined EMC to serve as president and chief operating officer, EMC Information Infrastructure Products, taking responsibility for EMC's entire technology and product portfolio. At Intel, Gelsinger had run the company's largest business group, whose enterprise-class products generated more than half of Intel's $38 billion in annual revenue. A holder of six patents, Gelsinger was deeply involved in the development of several generations of Intel's processors, including the award-winning Nehalem microarchitecture product. He reflected on what brought him to EMC:

*Over my long career at Intel, I led teams that changed the course of the IT industry. And that's pretty thrilling. I looked back on the role the microprocessor played and wanted to contribute to that level of industry-shaping impact once again.*

*EMC offers this opportunity. It's an exciting company, a product company that invests billions in R&D. And I am passionate about building great products. I like to be able to do large-scale engineering. In fact, building industry-shaping products is something I've done for nearly my entire career. I can do that here at EMC. Our mission is to build the world's greatest products in all of the categories that we serve. We are going to lead the industry in innovation and go to market.*

Pat Gelsinger worked at Intel for 30 years before joining EMC as president and chief operating officer, EMC Information Infrastructure Products, in September 2009. *(Photo © George Disario 2009.)*

*I was also eager to be part of EMC's leadership team. Well before I arrived at EMC, my role at Intel gave me the chance to get to know Joe Tucci fairly well. In speaking with him, I was struck by the clarity of his strategic vision for the company and the prominent role virtualization would play in EMC's future. I really see Joe as an intuitive strategist: He identifies key trends and technologies, tests them thoroughly, and then is able to make significant strategic leaps from these insights. When I talked to my contacts across the industry, it was clear that people like Joe, people trust Joe, people give him credit for his strategic intuition, his insight, and his long track record of success.*

*I was also excited by my meetings with EMC's Board and the executive management team. I saw unanimous support across the team and from the Board for EMC's strategy, vision, and direction. People at all levels of the company*

*quickly made me feel welcome and part of the EMC family.*

*With our strategy and our expertise in virtualization and cloud computing, we're going to be one of the companies to transform the state of IT infrastructure. In fact, I believe we can be the fundamental disruptive entity in the future of the IT industry—one of the true powerhouses of the IT industry of tomorrow. And now we are off to create the next chapter of EMC's wonderful history.*

Six months after recruiting Gelsinger from Intel, EMC again reached into the Silicon Valley talent pool and hired software industry veteran Jeremy Burton as executive vice president and chief marketing officer—the first EMC executive to hold that title. Burton had served in general management and senior marketing roles at Oracle, VERITAS, and Symantec, and then as president and CEO of a software start-up. At EMC his mission is to extend EMC's presence and relevance on the world stage; help EMC build, manage, and guide its global reputation and brand; increase the consistency, discipline, and distinctiveness of its marketing; and ensure that marketing produces measurable results.

Burton's first area of intense focus has been to ensure that EMC's mission of leading customers on a safe and swift journey to the private cloud—a dramatically more effective and efficient way to consume and deliver IT as a service—is broadly and deeply understood by employees, customers, partners, the media, and analysts. To that end, he orchestrated EMC's presence, messaging, and advertising at its largest customer event of the year, EMC World. In fact, he made certain that it would be impossible for any of the 5,000 customers, 750 partners, and 300 analysts and members of the press attending the May 2010 conference to miss the theme—"The Journey to the Private Cloud Starts Now."

Burton's view is that "marketing is all about story, simplicity, sizzle, sales, and strategy." By virtue of its vision, technologies, products, and partnerships, EMC has a compelling story to tell. Burton is leading EMC's worldwide marketing organization to fully operationalize EMC's private cloud message, making sure that customers understand not only why to make the journey to the private cloud now,

Jeremy Burton, executive vice president, joined EMC in 2010 as the company's first chief marketing officer.

but also why EMC is the best company in all of IT to lead them successfully on this journey. "Marketing fills the gap between today's reality and tomorrow's vision," he says. "My job is making sure people understand the sum of EMC's parts. Marketing's job is to join the dots. Marketing can move the needle."

A future-oriented company, EMC is looking forward to its next 30 years. The company intends to thrive for decades to come. And it is determined to make an even greater contribution to the world, not only in the realm of its customers, partners, and suppliers but also within society as a whole.

EMC knows that these long-range aspirations are possible only if it keeps looking outward and acts in a way that acknowledges its absolute dependence on all forms of capital—human, financial, social, physical, and natural—to keep its business strong and growing. This deep-seated belief in the interdependencies that are inescapable for all businesses explains why sustainability is at the heart of EMC's strategy.

As Joe Tucci put it in his March 2009 letter to shareholders:

*EMC's long-term success depends on recognizing and acting upon the interdependencies between our financial health, the health of the environment in which we operate, and the health of the society in which we live. Our financial health stems from the profitable growth of our business and the creation of shareholder value. Out of our commitment to the health of the environment, we're reducing the energy consumed by our products, our operations, and our supply chain, and targeting the environmentally friendly use and disposal of materials throughout the lifecycles of our products and packaging. From a business and societal perspective, we maintain a fully inclusive workforce—we are an organization that strives to reflect the diversity of our global, multicultural marketplace.*

EMC is better positioned for the future than ever before. Its product and service quality levels are the highest they have ever been. Its reputation for helping customers succeed has never been more positive. Its business is focused on high-growth markets around the world. EMC will continue to build on its three-decade–long tradition of innovation and growth.

"To put it simply," says Tucci, "we all believe EMC's opportunity has never been greater."

# NOTES TO SOURCES

### Chapter One

1. Richard Egan, speech, EMC's 25th Anniversary Dinner, 22 July 2004.
2. Sam Hill and Glenn Rifkin, *Radical Marketing: From Harvard to Harley, Lessons From Ten That Broke the Rules and Made It Big*, (New York: HarperBusiness, 1999), page 182.
3. Ibid.
4. "Richard J. Egan," EMC Web site, http://www.emc.com/about/management/egan.jsp/.
5. "The Early Days: Dick Egan Remembers," EMC Web site, http://www.emc.com/about/emc_story/early_days.jsp/.
6. Egan interview.
7. Ibid.
8. Ibid.
9. Ibid.
10. Ibid.
11. "The Early Days: Dick Egan Remembers."
12. Ibid.
13. *Radical Marketing: From Harvard to Harley, Lessons From Ten That Broke the Rules and Made It Big*, page 196.
14. "The Early Days: Dick Egan Remembers."

### Chapter One Sidebar: Founding Values

1. Richard Egan, interviewed by Jeffrey L. Rodengen, digital recording, 22 June 2004, Write Stuff Enterprises, LLC.
2. Ken Steinhardt, interviewed by Jeffrey L. Rodengen, digital recording, 7 June 2007, Write Stuff Enterprises, LLC.
3. Egan interview.
4. Mark Fredrickson, interviewed by Jeffrey L. Rodengen, digital recording, 22 June 2004, Write Stuff Enterprises, LLC.

### Chapter Two

1. "EMC Corporation," Harvard Business School case study, page 1.
2. Richard Egan, interviewed by Jeffrey L. Rodengen, digital recording, 22 June 2004, Write Stuff Enterprises, LLC.
3. "EMC Corporation," page 7.
4. "EMC Corporation," page 5.
5. EMC 1986 Annual Report, page 1.
6. EMC 1990 Annual Report, page 12.
7. EMC Prospectus, 4 April 1986, page 15.
8. "The Early Days: Dick Egan Remembers," EMC Web site, http://www.emc.com/about/emc_story/early_days.jsp/.
9. EMC Prospectus, page 19.
10. Paul Noble, interviewed by Jeffrey L. Rodengen, digital recording, 24 September 2007, Write Stuff Enterprises, LLC.
11. Egan interview.
12. "EMC Corporation," page 6.
13. Ibid.
14. Jack Egan, interviewed by Jeffrey L. Rodengen, digital recording, 21 February 2008, Write Stuff Enterprises, LLC.
15. Tom Heiser, interviewed by Jeffrey L. Rodengen, digital recording, 22 June 2004, Write Stuff Enterprises, LLC.
16. Mark Fredrickson, interviewed by Jeffrey L. Rodengen, digital recording, 22 June 2004, Write Stuff Enterprises, LLC.
17. Ibid.
18. Ibid.
19. Brian Fitzgerald, interviewed by Jeffrey L. Rodengen, digital recording, 22 June 2004, Write Stuff Enterprises, LLC.
20. Heiser interview.
21. Jeffrey Goldberg, interviewed by Jeffrey L. Rodengen, digital

recording, 22 June 2004, Write Stuff Enterprises, LLC.

22. Brian Gallagher, interviewed by Jeffrey L. Rodengen, digital recording, 23 June 2004, Write Stuff Enterprises, LLC.
23. Ibid.
24. Ibid.
25. "EMC Corporation," page 5.
26. Celeste Rippole, interviewed by Monya Keane, digital recording, 3 June 2004, EMC Corporation.
27. EMC Prospectus, page 18.
28. "EMC Corporation," page 5.
29. EMC 1990 Annual Report, page 8.
30. EMC Prospectus, page 17.
31. David Donatelli, interviewed by Jeffrey L. Rodengen, digital recording, 28 December 2005, Write Stuff Enterprises, LLC.
32. EMC Prospectus, pages 16–17.
33. EMC Prospectus, page 5.
34. Ibid.
35. "EMC Corporation," page 10.
36. EMC Prospectus, page 11.
37. Ibid.
38. "EMC Corporation," page 9.
39. EMC 1987 Annual Report, page 2.
40. EMC Prospectus, page 19.
41. "The Early Days: Dick Egan Remembers."
42. EMC 1987 Annual Report, page 4.
43. Ibid., page 5.
44. EMC 1990 Annual Report, page 7.
45. EMC 1987 Annual Report, page 1.
46. "EMC begins first day of trading on NYSE with ribbon cutting ceremony," Business Wire, 22 March 1988.
47. EMC 1988 Annual Report, page 3.
48. Danny Fitzgerald, digital recording, interviewed by Monya

Keane, 11 June 2004, EMC Corporation.
49. Jim Callahan, digital recording, interviewed by Monya Keane, 21 June 2004, EMC Corporation.
50. Maureen Clancy, interviewed by Jeffrey L. Rodengen, digital recording, 23 June 2004, Write Stuff Enterprises, LLC.
51. Ibid.
52. Mark Fredrickson, interviewed by Jeffrey L. Rodengen, digital recording, 22 June 2004, Write Stuff Enterprises, LLC.
53. Ibid.
54. Donatelli interview.
55. "Boom!" *Forbes*, 2 October 2000, page 146.

**Chapter Two Sidebar: "Yes, Folks, It Snows in New England."**

1. David Donatelli, interviewed by Jeffrey L. Rodengen, digital recording, 28 December 2005, Write Stuff Enterprises, LLC.
2. Ibid.
3. Ibid.
4. Maureen Clancy, interviewed by Jeffrey L. Rodengen, digital recording, 23 June 2004, Write Stuff Enterprises, LLC.
5. Donatelli interview.
6. Ibid.
7. Ibid.

**Chapter Three**

1. Chuck Loewy, interviewed by Monya Keane, digital recording, 11 June 2004, EMC Corporation.
2. "How a Hot Company Overheated," *BusinessWeek*, 23 May 1988, page 126.
3. Leo Colborne, interviewed by Jeffrey L. Rodengen, digital

recording, 26 April 2005, Write Stuff Enterprises, LLC.
4. Richard Egan, interviewed by Jeffrey L. Rodengen, digital recording, 22 June 2004, Write Stuff Enterprises, LLC.
5. Egan interview.
6. Ibid.
7. Colborne interview.
8. Clarence Westfall, interviewed by Monya Keane, digital recording, 16 June 2004, EMC Corporation.
9. Tim Mulvihill, interviewed by Monya Keane, digital recording, 17 June 2004, EMC Corporation.
10. Colborne interview.
11. Sam Hill and Glenn Rifkin, *Radical Marketing: From Harvard to Harley, Lessons From Ten That Broke the Rules and Made It Big*, (New York: HarperBusiness, 1999), page 182.
12. EMC 1988 Annual Report, page 2.
13. "EMC Financial Results," Business Wire, 29 April 1988.
14. EMC 1988 Annual Report, page 1.
15. Ibid., page 2
16. EMC 1989 Annual Report, page 1.
17. *Radical Marketing: From Harvard to Harley, Lessons From Ten That Broke the Rules and Made It Big*, page 197; EMC 1988 Annual Report, page 2.
18. *Radical Marketing: From Harvard to Harley, Lessons From Ten That Broke the Rules and Made It Big*, page 197.
19. "How a Hot Company Overheated," page 126.
20. "EMC Corp.'s Founders Vow to Go Without Pay Until Company Shows Profitability Again," Business Wire, 15 May 1989.

21. *Radical Marketing: From Harvard to Harley, Lessons From Ten That Broke the Rules and Made It Big*, page 197.
22. "EMC Corporation (A): From Inception Through 1998: The Rise to Market Leadership," Babson College case study, 2001, page 2.
23. Ibid.
24. Ibid.
25. Egan interview.
26. "EMC Corporation (A): From Inception Through 1998: The Rise to Market Leadership," page 26.
27. Ibid.
28. *Radical Marketing: From Harvard to Harley, Lessons From Ten That Broke the Rules and Made It Big*, page 198.
29. Egan interview.
30. Ibid.
31. "The Early Days: Dick Egan Remembers," EMC Web site, http://www.emc.com/about/emc_story/early_days.jsp/.
32. "EMC: High-Tech Star: The inside story of how Mike Ruettgers turned EMC into a highflier," *BusinessWeek*, 11 September 1999.
33. Ibid.
34. Ibid.
35. Loewy interview.
36. Ibid.
37. Ibid.
38. EMC 1989 Annual Report, page 2.
39. John Walton, interviewed by Monya Keane, digital recording, 15 June 2004, EMC Corporation.
40. "EMC: High-Tech Star: The inside story of how Mike Ruettgers turned EMC into a highflier," *BusinessWeek*, 11 September 1999.
41. EMC 1988 Annual Report, page 3.

42. Ibid.
43. "EMC Corporation (A): From Inception Through 1998: The Rise to Market Leadership," page 2.
44. "EMC Corporation Announces First Use of 4 Mbit DRAMS in IBM Mainframe Environment," Business Wire, 12 September 1989.
45. EMC 1989 Annual Report, page 3.
46. Don Watson, interviewed by Monya Keane, digital recording, 14 June 2004, EMC Corporation.
47. *Radical Marketing: From Harvard to Harley, Lessons From Ten That Broke the Rules and Made It Big*, page 195.
48. EMC 1988 Annual Report, page 4.
49. Ibid.
50. "The Early Days: Dick Egan Remembers."
51. Moshe Yanai, interviewed by Jeffrey L. Rodengen, digital recording, 19 October 2007, Write Stuff Enterprises, LLC.
52. Ibid.
53. "EMC Corporation (A): From Inception Through 1998: The Rise to Market Leadership," page 5.
54. Steve Cerand, interviewed by Monya Keane, digital recording, 1 July 2004, EMC Corporation.
55. David Donatelli, interviewed by Jeffrey L. Rodengen, digital recording, 28 December 2005, Write Stuff Enterprises, LLC.

**Chapter Three Sidebar: EMC Goes Global**

1. EMC Prospectus, 4 April 1986, page 17.
2. "Cork Facility," EMC UK & Ireland Web site,

http://uk.emc.com/local/en/GB/about/corp_profile/ireland.jsp/.
3 "EMC-UK Brings In Worldwide Deal Worth $575K," *Inside Information: News and Views of EMC Corporation*, Vol. 2, Issue 10, October 2001, page 5.
4. EMC Prospectus, page 7.

**Chapter Three Sidebar: A Focus on Quality**

1. 1990 EMC Annual Report, page 10.
2. Maureen Clancy, interviewed by Jeffrey L. Rodengen, digital recording, 23 June 2004, Write Stuff Enterprises, LLC.
3. Ibid.

**Chapter Four**

1. "Rising Revenue Doesn't Always Mean Profit; Bank of New England, Wang Had Worst Years Despite Hefty Sales," *Boston Globe*, 12 June 1990, page 27.
2. "Boom!" *Forbes*, 2 October 2000, page 146.
3. "EMC Corp.: High-Tech Firm Wins Gamble on Innovation," *Boston Globe*, 9 June 1992, page 57.
4. Steve Cerand, interviewed by Monya Keane, digital recording, 1 July 2004, EMC Corporation.
5. EMC 1990 Annual Report, page 5.
6. EMC 1990 Annual Report, page 7.
7. Sam Hill and Glenn Rifkin, *Radical Marketing: From Harvard to Harley, Lessons From Ten That Broke the Rules and Made It Big*, (New York: HarperBusiness, 1999), page 183.

8. "EMC Corporation (A): From Inception Through 1998: The Rise to Market Leadership," Babson College case study, 2001, page 6.

9. "EMC Corporation (A): From Inception Through 1998: The Rise to Market Leadership," Babson College case study, 2001, page 3.

10. *Radical Marketing: From Harvard to Harley, Lessons From Ten That Broke the Rules and Made It Big*, pages 183–184.

11. "Fast Data-Storage Systems Are EMC's Big Opportunity," *New York Times*, 27 January 1992, page D1.

12. EMC 1991 Annual Report, page 7.

13. "EMC Top Stock Pick for '92," Business Wire, 30 December 1991.

14. EMC 1991 Annual Report, page 2.

15. Paul Noble, interviewed by Monya Keane, digital recording, 4 June 2004, EMC Corporation.

16. Mike Sgrosso, interviewed by Monya Keane, digital recording, 7 June 2004, EMC Corporation.

17. EMC 1990 Annual Report, page 12.

18. EMC 1992 Annual Report, page 4.

19. "Up Close and Virtual," *CFO: The Magazine for Senior Business Executives*, April 1998, Vol. 14, No. 4, page 88.

20 "Unorthodox Rules Help EMC Double Sales," *Electronic Business Buyer*, December 1993.

21. Ibid.

22. Ibid.

23. "The Early Days: Dick Egan Remembers," EMC Web site, http://www.emc.com/about/emc_story/early_days.jsp/.

24. Maureen Clancy, interviewed by Jeffrey L. Rodengen, digital recording, 23 June 2004, Write Stuff Enterprises, LLC.

25. "EMC's Harmonix Leads Disk Array Race," *Computerworld*, 5 October 1992.

26. "Fast Data-Storage Systems Are EMC's Big Opportunity," page D1.

27. "EMC Corp.: High-Tech Firm Wins Gamble on Innovation," page 57.

28. EMC 1993 Annual Report, page 2.

29. EMC 1992 Annual Report, page 3.

30. "EMC to Open Research & Development Facility in Israel," Business Wire, 22 April 1993.

31. EMC 1993 Annual Report, page 4.

32. Peter Simmons, interviewed by Eileen McKeever, digital recording, 15 June 2004, EMC Corporation.

33. Lennie DeMarco, interviewed by Monya Keane, digital recording, 7 June 2004, EMC Corporation.

34. Josh Onffroy, interviewed by Monya Keane, digital recording, 1 July 2004, EMC Corporation.

35. Malte Rademacher, interviewed by Jeffrey L. Rodengen, digital recording, 9 October 2007, Write Stuff Enterprises, LLC.

36. EMC 1993 Annual Report, page 2.

37. Moshe Yanai, interviewed by Jeffrey L. Rodengen, digital recording, 19 October 2007, Write Stuff Enterprises, LLC.

38. "EMC At 25: Built to Lead," *EMC.now*, August 2004, page 4.

39. "EMC Launches CLARiiON, 19 TB Symmetrix Storage— CLARiiON 4500, Symmetrix 8000, Product Announcement," *ENT*, 24 May 2000.

40. Polly Pearson, interviewed by Jeffrey L. Rodengen, digital recording, 22 June 2004, Write Stuff Enterprises, LLC.

41. "EMC Corporation (A): From Inception Through 1998: The Rise to Market Leadership," page 8.

42. *Radical Marketing: From Harvard to Harley, Lessons From Ten That Broke the Rules and Made It Big*, page 187.

43. Ibid.

44. "EMC Corporation (A): From Inception Through 1998: The Rise to Market Leadership," page 9.

45. "EMC: High-Tech Star: The Inside Story of How Mike Ruettgers Turned EMC into a Highflier," *BusinessWeek*, 11 September 1999.

46. Ibid.

47. Doc D'Errico, interviewed by Jeffrey L. Rodengen, digital recording, 25 April 2005, Write Stuff Enterprises, LLC.

48. "A Conversation With Moshe Yanai: The Storage Software That Changed Everything," *EMC.now*, Vol. 4, Issue 2, February 2002, page 5.

49. "Memory, Megabytes and Megabucks: EMC Corp. Finds Bulging Profits in 'Electronic Filing Cabinets,'" *Boston Globe*, 17 May 1994, page 29.

50. "Symmetrix Sales Up Over 500 Percent to Telecommunications Industry," Business Wire, 8 September 1994.

**Chapter Four Sidebar: Investing in Research and Development**

1. EMC 1994 Annual Report, page 29.

2. EMC 2000 Annual Report.

3. "EMC To Open Software Development Center in China," EMC press release, 23 June 2006, http://www.emc.com/news/emc_releases/showRelease.jsp?id=4471/.
4. Rona Newmark, interviewed by Jeffrey L. Rodengen, digital recording, 8 June 2007, Write Stuff Enterprises, LLC.
5. Ibid.

**Chapter Four Sidebar:
The Rise of the
Information Enterprise**

1. EMC 1994 Annual Report, page 6.

**Chapter Four Sidebar:
Surveying the Storage Landscape
of the 1990s**

1. "EMC Is the One to Beat," *InformationWeek*, 1 May 1995.
2. "EMC Corporation (A): From Inception Through 1998: The Rise to Market Leadership," Babson College case study, 2001, page 3.
3. "Good Things Come in Small Packages," *InformationWeek*, 17 August 1992, page 24.
4. "Small Disks, Big Business: EMC Sees Future in Client-Server Data Storage," *InformationWeek*, 17 March 1994.
5. "EMC Corporation (B): 1999 and Beyond: Charting the Future," Babson College case study, 1999, page 4.
6. Ibid.

**Chapter Five**

1. "Why EMC Will Stay on Top," *Insight*, Vol. 1, Issue 1, First Quarter 1995, page 1.

2. "EMC Storms IBM Disk Drive Gates," *Computerworld*, 22 May 1995.
3. EMC 1995 Annual Report, page 1.
4. Ibid.
5. "IBM Product Delay Could Help EMC Boost Market Share," *Boston Globe*, 22 August 1995, page 35.
6. Sam Hill and Glenn Rifkin, *Radical Marketing: From Harvard to Harley, Lessons From Ten That Broke the Rules and Made It Big*, (New York: HarperBusiness, 1999), page 182.
7. Mark Fredrickson, interviewed by Jeffrey L. Rodengen, digital recording, 22 June 2004, Write Stuff Enterprises, LLC.
8. *Radical Marketing: From Harvard to Harley, Lessons From Ten That Broke the Rules and Made It Big*, page 188.
9. Tom Heiser, interviewed by Jeffrey L. Rodengen, digital recording, 22 June 2004, Write Stuff Enterprises, LLC.
10. Gil Press, interviewed by Jeffrey L. Rodengen, digital recording, 7 June 2007, Write Stuff Enterprises, LLC.
11. "EMC Plans to Build Massachusetts Plant and Expand in Ireland," *New York Times*, 25 August 1997, page D9.
12. EMC 1995 Annual Report.
13. Ibid.
14. "EMC Opens Brazil Subsidiary As First Direct Sales Presence In Latin America," EMC press release, 25 February 1997.
15. Ibid.
16. Ibid.
17. "The Long Haul," *PC Week*, 15 July 1996.
18. EMC 1997 Annual Report.

19. Ibid.
20. "EMC Corporation (A): From Inception Through 1998: The Rise to Market Leadership," Babson College case study, 2001, page 9.
21. "Storage Takes Center Stage," *InformationWeek*, 14 October 1996, page 38.
22. "Business Bulletin," *Wall Street Journal*, 8 February 1996, page A1.
23. "EMC Trumpets Its Dominance, and Wall Street Listens," *Boston Globe*, 3 February 1998, page D6.
24. "Network Storage: Overtaking the Host CPU on the Digital Highway," EMC internal report, 1996, page 3.
25. "EMC Corporation (B): 1999 and Beyond: Charting the Future," Babson College case study, 1999, page 10.
26. Ibid., page 9.
27. EMC 1999 Annual Report.
28. "EMC Corporation (B): 1999 and Beyond: Charting the Future," page 7.
29. Ibid.
30. EMC 1997 Annual Report.
31. "EMC Ranked 16th on the *BusinessWeek* 50 List of Top Corporate Performers," EMC press release, 18 March 1997.
32. Barbara Robidoux, interviewed by Jeffrey L. Rodengen, digital recording, 8 June 2007, Write Stuff Enterprises, LLC.
33. *Radical Marketing: From Harvard to Harley, Lessons From Ten That Broke the Rules and Made It Big*, pages 193–194.
34. "Twelve Industry Leaders to Develop World's First Fibre Channel Management Standard," FiberAlliance press release, 2 February 1999.
35. Ibid.

36. "Managing Storage: Trends, Challenges, and Options (2007–2008)," EMC research paper, page 6.
37. "North Carolina Schools: EMC Supports Math and Science Education," EMC Web site, http://www.emc.com/about/emc_philanthropy/ncarolina_schools/.

**Chapter Five Sidebar: Creating Storage Solutions**

1. Sam Hill and Glenn Rifkin, *Radical Marketing: From Harvard to Harley, Lessons From Ten That Broke the Rules and Made It Big*, (New York: HarperBusiness, 1999), page 193.
2. "EMC Corporation (A): From Inception Through 1998: The Rise to Market Leadership," Babson College case study, 2001, page 9.
3. "Give 'Em What They Want," *IndustryWeek*, 4 November 1996.

**Chapter Six**

1. "Another New King on the Cutting Edge; EMC Corp.'s $67b Market Value Overtakes Gillette's $64b and Speaks Volumes on Shifting Landscape of Economy, Wall St.," *Boston Globe*, 6 April 1999, page C1.
2. "Size and Growth Statistics," Online Computer Library Center Web site, http://www.oclc.org/research/projects/archive/wcp/stats/size.htm/.
3. "EMC Corporation (B): 1999 and Beyond: Charting the Future," Babson College case study, 1999, page 2.
4. Ibid., page 3.

5. EMC 1998 Annual Report.
6. EMC 1998 Annual Report.
7. "EMC Corporation (B): 1999 and Beyond: Charting the Future," page 3.
8. Steve Savard, interviewed by Eileen McKeever, digital recording, 15 June 2004, EMC Corporation.
9. Brian Powers, interviewed by Jeffrey L. Rodengen, digital recording, 21 September 2007, Write Stuff Enterprises, LLC.
10. Bob Basiliere, interviewed by Jeffrey L. Rodengen, digital recording, 26 April 2005, Write Stuff Enterprises, LLC.
11. Ibid.
12. Ibid.
13. "EMC leaps past IBM in data storage race," *Worcester Telegram & Gazette*, 17 January 1999, page E1.
14. EMC 1998 Annual Report.
15. EMC 2000 Annual Report.
16. EMC 1998 Annual Report.
17. "EMC Corporation (B): 1999 and Beyond: Charting the Future," page 10.
18. Ibid.
19. EMC 1998 Annual Report.
20. "EMC leaps past IBM in data storage race," *Worcester Telegram & Gazette*, page E1.
21. Irina Simmons, interviewed by Jeffrey L. Rodengen, digital recording, 7 April 2007, Write Stuff Enterprises, LLC.
22. EMC Corporation Interoffice Memo, 4 February 1998, EMC Corporate & Investor Relations.
23. "EMC Corp. Continues Its Streak," *Worcester Telegram & Gazette*, 21 April 1999, page E1.
24. "Growing by Gigabytes; EMC Scrambles in Search for New Employees," *Worcester Telegram & Gazette*, 15 October 2000, page A1.

25. "Sizing Up EMC's Buy; More Than Storage, Data General's 'Bright People' and Other Technology Enrich the Deal," *Worcester Telegram & Gazette*, 15 August 1999, page E1.
26. Jim Rothnie, interviewed by Jeffrey L. Rodengen, digital recording, 13 September 2007, Write Stuff Enterprises, LLC.
27. Bryan Fontaine, interviewed by Jeffrey L. Rodengen, digital recording, 23 June 2004, Write Stuff Enterprises, LLC.
28. Erin Motameni, interviewed by Jeffrey L. Rodengen, digital recording, 23 June 2004, Write Stuff Enterprises, LLC.
29. Rothnie interview.
30. Polly Pearson, interviewed by Jeffrey L. Rodengen, digital recording, 22 June 2004, Write Stuff Enterprises, LLC.
31. "Another New King on the Cutting Edge; EMC Corp.'s $67b Market Value Overtakes Gillette's $64b and Speaks Volumes on Shifting Landscape of Economy, Wall St.," page C1.
32. "Soapbox: EMC Corp. Computes Big Gains," *CBS MarketWatch*, 19 January 2000.
33. EMC 1999 Annual Report.
34. "Stock Watch: EMC Up After Salomon Says Top Pick for 2000," *AFX European Focus*, 4 January 2000.
35. "Street Signs: EMC Corporation—CEO Interview," CNBC Dow Jones, 7 February 2000.
36. "The Right Man for the Job," *InformationWeek*, 25 March 2002, pages 46–50.
37. "Rebuilding a High-Tech Giant," *Boston Globe*, 22 January 2004.
38. "EMC Chief Has Twice Led Turnarounds," *USA Today*, 26 September 2005, page 2B.

39. Ibid.
40. "EMC Chief Has Twice Led Turnarounds."
41. "EMC Sees Data Storage Products Overtaking Servers," *BusinessWorld Philippines*, 9 May 2000.

**Chapter Six Sidebar:
Remembering Jeff Goldberg**

1. Richard Egan, interviewed by Jeffrey L. Rodengen, digital recording, 22 June 2004, Write Stuff Enterprises, LLC.

**Chapter Six Sidebar:
Different Needs, One Source**

1. Sam Hill and Glenn Rifkin, *Radical Marketing: From Harvard to Harley, Lessons From Ten That Broke the Rules and Made It Big*, (New York: HarperBusiness, 1999), page 191.
2. EMC 1999 Annual Report.
3. Ibid.
4. EMC 1997 Annual Report.
5. Ibid.
6 "Symmetrix Sales Up Over 500 Percent to Telecommunications Industry," Business Wire, 8 September 1994.
7. EMC 1999 Annual Report.
8. "EMC leaps past IBM in data storage race," *Worcester Telegram & Gazette*, 17 January 1999, page E1.
9. EMC 1999 Annual Report.
10. Ibid.

**Chapter Six Sidebar:
Disk Technology
in the Nobel Spotlight**

1. "The Nobel Prize in Physics 2007: Information for the Public," The Royal Swedish Academy of Sciences, Nobel Foundation Web site, http://nobelprize.org/ nobel_prizes/physics/ laureates2007/info.pdf/.
2. Ibid.
3. Ibid.
4. "Hard Disk Pioneers Win 2007 Physics Nobel," Reuters, 9 October 2007.

**Chapter Eight**

1. "What's Eating EMC?" *Forbes*, 26 November 2001.
2. "Data Driven EMC Corp. Continues to Survive High-Tech's Stock Woe," *Post-Standard*, 18 December 2000, page 11.
3. "Amid Small-Company Layoffs, EMC to Hire 5,000," *Boston Business Journal*, Vol. 20, No. 53, 2 February 2001, page 1.
4. "EMC Says Job Cuts Aren't a Reflection of Any Downturn," *Wall Street Journal*, 12 February 2001, page B8.
5. "EMC Trims Forecast on Tech Slowdown," *Wall Street Journal*, 23 February 2001, page B56; "EMC Corp. Insiders Sell Before Latest High-Tech Rout," *Boston Business Journal*, Vol. 21, No. 5, 9 March 2001, page 5.
6. "Leading Change: An Interview with the CEO of EMC," *McKinsey Quarterly*, August 2005, page 39.
7. EMC 2000 Annual Report, page 21.
8. Joseph Tucci, interviewed by Jeffrey L. Rodengen, digital recording, 23 June 2004, Write Stuff Enterprises, LLC.
9. Ibid.
10. "Leading Change: An Interview with the CEO of EMC," page 40.
11. Ibid.
12. Mark Quigley, interviewed by Jeffrey L. Rodengen, digital recording, 8 June 2007, Write Stuff Enterprises, LLC.

13. "Leading Change: An Interview With the CEO of EMC," page 41.
14. "Leading Change: An Interview With the CEO of EMC," page 42.
15. Ibid., pages 42–43.
16. Ibid., page 41.
17. Michael Gallant, interviewed by Jeffrey L. Rodengen, digital recording, 25 April 2005, Write Stuff Enterprises, LLC.
18. Quigley interview.
19. "Joe Tucci: 'I Want to Be An Example for My Teams,'" *Le Figaro*, 30 June 2003, page 20.
20. "25 Turning Points in EMC History," *EMC.now*, August 2004, page 5.
21. EMC 2002 Annual Report.
22. "Joe Tucci: 'I Want to Be An Example for My Teams,'" page 20.
23. William Teuber, Jr., interviewed by Jeffrey L. Rodengen, digital recording, 23 June 2004, Write Stuff Enterprises, LLC.
24. "Leading Change: An Interview with the CEO of EMC," page 43.
25. "Private Sector; He Knows This Bumpy Hill Well," *New York Times*, 16 December 2001, page C3.
26. Tucci interview.
27. Tony Takazawa, interviewed by Jeffrey L. Rodengen, digital recording, 22 June 2004, Write Stuff Enterprises, LLC.
28. Chuck Hollis, interviewed by Jeffrey L. Rodengen, digital recording, 25 April 2005, Write Stuff Enterprises, LLC.
29. EMC 2002 Annual Report.
30. "Gartner Says Worldwide Storage Management Software Market Recorded its First Ever Revenue Decline in 2002," Gartner Inc. press release, 15 April 2003.
31. "Leading Change: An Interview With the CEO of EMC," page 41; Tucci interview.

32. "Leading Change: An Interview With the CEO of EMC," page 41.

33. Tucci interview.

34. "Joe Tucci: 'I Want to Be An Example for My Teams,'" page 20.

35. "Leading Change: An Interview With the CEO of EMC," page 43.

**Chapter Nine**

1. Joseph Tucci, interviewed by Jeffrey L. Rodengen, digital recording, 23 June 2004, Write Stuff Enterprises, LLC.

2. EMC 2003 Annual Report.

3. Jeff Goldberg, interviewed by Jeffrey L. Rodengen, digital recording, 22 June 2004, Write Stuff Enterprises, LLC.

4. "Faster, Compatible Storage," *InformationWeek*, 10 February 2003, page 55.

5. "EMC Piggybacks 'Matrix' to Tout Own Product Line," *MetroWest Daily News*, 15 May 2003.

6. "EMC Bets the Farm," *Worcester Telegram & Gazette*, 4 February 2003, page E1.

7. Ibid.

8. David Gingell, interviewed by Jeffrey L. Rodengen, digital recording, 8 October 2007, Write Stuff Enterprises, LLC.

9. Erin Motameni, interviewed by Jeffrey L. Rodengen, digital recording, 23 June 2004, Write Stuff Enterprises, LLC.

10. Paul Dacier, interviewed by Jeffrey L. Rodengen, digital recording, 23 June 2004, Write Stuff Enterprises, LLC.

11. Becky DiSorbo, interviewed by Jeffrey L. Rodengen, digital recording, 13 August 2007, Write Stuff Enterprises, LLC.

12. Mary Bracoloni, interviewed by Jeffrey L. Rodengen, digital recording, 26 April 2005, Write Stuff Enterprises, LLC.

13. "EMC Corp.," *Wall Street Journal*, 29 April 2003, page C13.

14. "New Tactics," *InformationWeek*, 5 May 2003, pages 18–20.

15. "Dell, EMC Extend Storage Partnership," *AFX European Focus*, 10 June 2003.

16. "EMC and IBM Work to Extend Interoperability and Support For Customers," Business Wire, 6 October 2003.

17. "US-based EMC's first China solution center in Beijing— report," *AFX European Focus*, 10 September 2003.

18. "EMC Corporation Plans Third Centre," *Hindu*, 20 February 2004; "EMC Corp. Plans to Double Storage System Sales in Russia," Interfax Information Services, 4 February 2004.

19. Motameni interview.

20. Ibid.

21. Sanjay Mirchandani, interviewed by Jeffrey L. Rodengen, digital recording, 30 October 2007, Write Stuff Enterprises, LLC.

22. "Built to Lead: EMC Celebrates 25 Years of Innovation and Achievement," Business Wire, 22 July 2004.

23. "The Difference is You: A Salute to Employees From Joe Tucci," *EMC.now*, August 2004, page 1.

24. Kathie Lyons, interviewed by Monya Keane, digital recording, 25 June 2004, EMC Corporation.

25. William Teuber, Jr., interviewed by Jeffrey L. Rodengen, digital recording, 23 June 2004, Write Stuff Enterprises, LLC.

26. "Remarks by Dick Egan for EMC's 25th Anniversary," speech, 22 July 2004.

27. Ibid.

**Chapter Nine Sidebar: The Art of Acquisition**

1. Frank Hauck, interviewed by Jeffrey L. Rodengen, digital recording, 7 June 2007, Write Stuff Enterprises, LLC.

2. Ibid.

3. Stacey Yeoman, interviewed by Jeffrey L. Rodengen, digital recording, 7 June 2007, Write Stuff Enterprises, LLC.

4. Ibid.

**Chapter Nine Sidebar: Lessons Learned During the Dot-Com Bust**

1. "Makeover King," *Barron's*, 16 August 2004, page 15.

2. "Leading Change: An Interview with the CEO of EMC," *McKinsey Quarterly*, August 2005, page 39.

3. Tucci interview.

4. Ibid.

5. EMC 2000 Annual Report; EMC 2004 Annual Report.

6. "Leading Change: An Interview with the CEO of EMC," page 43.

7. "Joe Tucci: 'I Want to Be An Example for My Teams,'" *Le Figaro*, 30 June 2003, page 20.

8. "Leading Change: An Interview with the CEO of EMC," page 43.

**Chapter Nine Sidebar: EMC's Starring Role**

1. "EMC Supports History-making Sporting Events, Entertainment Blockbusters," *EMC.now*, Vol. 2, Issue 9, September 2000, page 3.

2. Ibid.

3. Ibid.

4. Ibid.

### Chapter Ten

1. Joseph Tucci, interviewed by Jeffrey L. Rodengen, digital recording, 23 June 2004, Write Stuff Enterprises, LLC.
2. "EMC profit declines due to product missteps," *Boston Globe*, 15 July 2006, page B6.
3. "EMC to Get Smarts: Storage Giant Snaps Up Storage Management Innovator," *Network World*, 21 December 2004.
4. Howard Elias, interviewed by Jeffrey L. Rodengen, digital recording, 21 September 2007, Write Stuff Enterprises, LLC.
5. "Overcoming Great Walls," *EMC.now*, Second Quarter 2007, page 6.
6. Sanjay Mirchandani, interviewed by Jeffrey L. Rodengen, digital recording, 30 October 2007, Write Stuff Enterprises, LLC.
7. "EMC Corporation to Double R and D Team by Year-end," *India Business Insight*, 24 February 2005.
8. Ibid.
9. "EMC Announces Plans to Double Investment in China," EMC press release, 1 November 2007.
10. Charles Fan, interviewed by Jeffrey L. Rodengen, digital recording, 14 June 2007, Write Stuff Enterprises, LLC.
11. Ibid.
12. "Overcoming Great Walls," page 8.
13. Mirchandani interview.
14. Rona Newmark, interviewed by Jeffrey L. Rodengen, digital recording, 8 June 2007, Write Stuff Enterprises, LLC.
15. Mirchandani interview.
16. "From EMC Russia With Love," *EMC.now*, Third Quarter 2007, page 11.
17. Ibid., page 13.
18. Ibid., page 12.
19. "Overcoming Great Walls," page 8.
20. Ibid.
21. "Dogged by Skepticism," *Boston Globe*, 4 July 2006, page D1.
22. Art Coviello, interviewed by Jeffrey L. Rodengen, digital recording, 30 October 2007, Write Stuff Enterprises, LLC.
23. "Five Things You Don't Know About EMC," *Network World*, 5 July 2007.
24. Coviello interview.
25. Ibid.
26. "The Style Is Right," *EMC.now*, Second Quarter 2007, page 14.
27. Elias interview.
28. "Virtualization: It's About Doing More with Less," *Boston Globe*, 15 August 2007, page C1.
29. "A Software Maker Goes Up Against Microsoft," *New York Times*, 24 February 2007, page C1.
30. "EMC Plans Public Offering for 10% of Software Division," *New York Times*, 8 February 2007.
31. "Five Days: Moves to Protect Children, and Bottom Lines," *New York Times*, 18 August 2007.
32. Ibid.
33. "Stock Rocket," *Boston Globe*, 25 October 2007, page C1.
34. Mark Jewell, "EMC 4Q Profit Jumps 35 Percent, but Shares Fall Flat as Majority-Owned VMware Disappoints," Associated Press, 29 January 2008.
35. "EMC Academic Alliance Program Overview," EMC Web site, http://education.emc.com/main/guest/academy/overview.htm/.
36. "Math + Science = Innovation, But U.S. Lags in the Equation,"
*Boston Globe*, 27 November 2005, page D1.
37. "Information Heritage: How EMC Is Preserving National Treasures," EMC Web site, http://www.emc.com/about/emc_philanthropy/information_heritage/.
38. "Preserving Humanity's Information Heritage," *ON*, Spring 2007, page 17; "Information Heritage," EMC Web site, http://www.emc.com/about/emc_philanthropy/information_heritage/.
39. Ken Steinhardt, interviewed by Jeffrey L. Rodengen, digital recording, 7 June 2007, Write Stuff Enterprises, LLC.
40. "Information 2.0," *ON*, Spring 2007, page 7.
41. "New Study Forecasts Explosive Growth Of The Digital Universe; Spotlights Worldwide Phenomenon Of 'Digital Shadow,'" EMC Web site, http://www.emc.com/about/news/press/2008/20080311-01.htm/.
42. Ibid.
43. Dan Campbell, interviewed by Jeff Rodengen, digital recording, 17 March 2008, Write Stuff Enterprises, LLC.
44. Mark Fredrickson, interviewed by Jeffrey L. Rodengen, digital recording, 22 June 2004, Write Stuff Enterprises, LLC.
45. Steve Duplessie, interviewed by Jeffrey L. Rodengen, digital recording, 5 December 2005, Write Stuff Enterprises, LLC.

### Chapter Ten Sidebar: Strength in Numbers

1. "Preaching From the Ballmer Pulpit," *New York Times*, 28 January 2007.

2. "EMC and Oracle," EMC Web site, http://www.emc.com/ partnersalliances/ partner_pages/oracle.jsp/.

3. Charles Fan, interviewed by Jeffrey L. Rodengen, digital recording, 14 June 2007, Write Stuff Enterprises, LLC.

4. Ibid.

5. Steve Leonard, interviewed by Jeffrey L. Rodengen, digital recording, 13 August 2007, Write Stuff Enterprises, LLC.

6. "EMC Select," EMC Web site, http://www.emc.com/partnersa lliances/programs/select.jsp/.

7. "EMC Velocity Partner Program," EMC Web site, http://www.emc.com/ partnersalliances/programs/ velocity.jsp/.

8. "EMC Velocity Technology and ISV Program," EMC Web site, http://www.emc.com/ partnersalliances/programs/ velocity/isv/index.jsp/.

**Chapter Ten Sidebar:**
**Following the Boom**

1. "China Surpasses U.S. in Internet Use," *Forbes*, 3 April, 2006.

2. "Overcoming Great Walls," *EMC.now*, Second Quarter 2007, page 6.

3. "High Tech in China: Is It a Threat to Silicon Valley?" *BusinessWeek*, 28 October 2002.

4. "EMC Announces Plans to Double Investment in China," EMC press release, 1 November 2007, http://www.emc.com/ news/emc_releases/ showRelease.jsp?id=5422/.

5. "India: Internet Usage Stats and Telecommunications Market Report," Internet World Stats Web site, http:// www.internetworldstats.com/ asia/in.htm/.

6. "EMC Doubles Investment in India," EMC press release, 20 June 2006, http:// www.emc.com/news/ emc_releases/ showRelease.jsp?id=4499/.

7. "The Rise of India," *BusinessWeek*, 8 December 2003.

8. Charles Fan, interviewed by Jeffrey L. Rodengen, digital recording, 14 June 2007, Write Stuff Enterprises, LLC.

9. "Overcoming Great Walls," page 6.

10. "The Next Silicon Valley: Siberia," CNNMoney Web site, 26 March 2007, http://money.cnn.com/ rssclick/magazines/fortune/ fortune_archive/2007/04/02/ 8403482/index.htm/.

11. Ibid.

12. Steve Leonard, interviewed by Jeffrey L. Rodengen, digital recording, 13 August 2007, Write Stuff Enterprises, LLC.

# INDEX

*Page numbers in italics indicate photographs.*